The Wonder of It All

When Literature and Literacy Intersect

Nancy J. Johnson and Cyndi Giorgis

HEINEMANN ✚ Portsmouth, NH

Heinemann

A division of Reed Elsevier Inc.
361 Hanover Street
Portsmouth, NH 03801–3912
www.heinemann.com

Offices and agents throughout the world

The authors and publisher wish to thank those who have generously given permission to reprint borrowed material:

"Are You a Book Person?" by J. Patrick Lewis. Copyright © 2005 by J. Patrick Lewis. Reprinted by permission of Curtis Brown, Ltd.

"A Writing Kind of Night" from *A Writing Kind of Day: Poems for Young Poets* by Ralph Fletcher (Wordsong, an imprint of Boyds Mills Press, 2005). Text copyright © 2005 by Ralph Fletcher. Reprinted with the permission of Boyds Mills Press, Inc.

Library of Congress Cataloging-in-Publication Data
Johnson, Nancy J. (Nancy Jane)
 The wonder of it all : when literature and literacy intersect / Nancy J. Johnson and Cyndi Giorgis.
  p. cm.
 Includes bibliographical references and index.
 ISBN-13: 978-0-325-00973-5
 ISBN-10: 0-325-00973-2
 1. Reading (Elementary)—United States. 2. Children's literature—Study and teaching (Elementary)—United States. 3. Children—Books and reading—United States. I. Giorgis, Cyndi. II. Title.

LB1573.J565 2007
372.64—dc22   2007018477

EDITOR: James Strickland
PRODUCTION: Vicki Kasabian
INTERIOR AND COVER DESIGNS: Jenny Jensen Greenleaf
TYPESETTER: Publishers' Design and Production Services, Inc.
MANUFACTURING: Jamie Carter

Printed in the United States of America on acid-free paper
11 10 09 08 07 EB 1 2 3 4 5

A Dedication in Two Voices*

Kate Norem

We salute your
Third year as a teacher.

We appreciate
The invitation into your classroom

Where we heard:
Skippyjon Jones,

Pictures of Hollis Woods,

Sometimes I'm Bombaloo

Read aloud with gusto.

Where we read:
What to Write About
Choosing a Good Book
Retired Words
Anchor charts of learning.

Where we saw:
Poetry taped to desktops

Nonfiction exploration

Visual response projects

Kids learning everywhere!

We dedicate this book to you—
You've become our
Mentor, collaborator, friend.

Side by side

Megan Sloan
We salute your

Twenty-third year as a teacher.

We appreciate
The invitation into your classroom

Where we heard:

Mrs. Frisby and the Rats of NIMH,

Wild About Books,

and *Poppy*
Read aloud with gusto.

Where we read:
What Good Writers Do
Books We Recommend
Interesting Words
Anchor charts of learning.

Where we saw:

Poetry hung on windows

Inquiry on the desert

Reader's notebook sketches
Kids learning everywhere!

We dedicate this book to you—
You've become our
Mentor, collaborator, friend.

We've discovered

The wonder of it all.

Inspired by Paul Fleischman's Joyful Noise: Poems for Two Voices *(1988)*

Contents

Acknowledgments

Whose book this is I hardly know,
Considering the debt I owe . . .

—J. PATRICK LEWIS

J. Patrick Lewis' poetry collection *Please Bury Me in the Library* (2005) ends with a poem titled "Acknowledgements," an homage to Robert Frost. How appropriate for us to tip our hats to children's literature as we begin this book. We use this page to pay our debt to the many persons whose words, experiences, support, and wisdom provided a solid foundation for the ideas in this book. None of us learns in a vacuum—none of us writes that way, either. Our room of wonder is shared by many people. We're indebted to the following individuals from the world of children's literature, in classrooms, and from our own lives, and we offer them our accolades:

Authors and illustrators who opened their homes, interrupted their schedules, inspired our teaching, and invited us to learn about their creative process, especially Bryan Collier, Marla Frazee, Lois Lowry, Linda Sue Park, Brian Selznick, David Small, Sarah Stewart, David Wiesner, and Deborah Wiles.

Children's book editors Dinah Stevenson at Clarion Books and Allyn Johnston at Harcourt Books, and directors of marketing Lisa DiSarro at Houghton Mifflin Books for Children, Ellen Greene at Harcourt Books, Angus Killick at Hyperion Books for Children, Mimi Kayden at HarperCollins Children's Books, Jeanne T. McDermott at Farrar, Straus and Giroux Books for Young Readers, and Marjorie Naughton at Clarion Books.

Classroom teachers and their students who span the globe: Marianne Richardson from Georgia; Christine Jordan and Marie LeJeune from Nevada; Georgia Connor Schultzman from New York; Sarah Dunkin and Lisa Williams from Oregon; Barry Hoonan, Anne Klein, Kate Norem, and Megan Sloan from Washington; and Cheryl Perkins from Shanghai, China.

Professional colleagues: Lois Bridges, who believed in our ideas from the very beginning; Regie Routman, whose suggestions moved us forward; Jim Strickland, whose wit and enthusiasm validated our ideas and gently nudged us toward completion; and Laura Tillotson at *Book Links*, who engaged in lively conversations and shared our vision to intersect literature and literacy.

People in our daily lives, including our spouses, Fred and Jim; our parents and families; and the countless friends, students, colleagues, neighbors, even postal workers who unwittingly encouraged our progress with their "Is the book done yet?" queries.

And a special shout-out to DFL, who kept us alive more times than we can count!

To read is to borrow. To create from one's reading
is paying off one's debts.

—GEORG CHRISTOPH LICHTENBERG,
German scientist, 1742–99

Introduction

As a Student

Each day after lunch, Mr. Guymon read aloud two chapters from *Where the Red Fern Grows*, by Wilson Rawls—no more, no less. We sat quietly and listened as Billy and his precious coonhound pups romped relentlessly through the Ozarks, trying to tree the elusive raccoon. Once the second chapter concluded, we knew it was time to take out our math books so the lesson could begin immediately. Even though I enjoyed listening to the chapters, I longed to discuss them. When Old Dan and Little Ann died in the story, all of my classmates cradled their heads on their desks, afraid that others would see them cry. While we had a great experience in listening to a story read aloud, it didn't bring us together as a class—we didn't have the opportunity or the courage to share our thoughts and emotions about this beloved book. I wondered, "Why is he asking those dumb questions about the names of the dogs?" That's not what I cared about. What I cared about was the hole in my heart.

—Cyndi Giorgis, remembering fifth grade

As a Teacher

My first year of teaching felt like the loneliest job in the world. Everyone taught with her door shut tight. We organized our lessons into two-inch squares in light green planning books, fitting content areas into discreet spaces. We even made masking tape markings on the linoleum floor to line up desks into neat rows. Teaching and learning were controlled (and so was vocabulary!). I remember wondering, "What if they discover what I don't know? What can I choose for their Friday writing topic? What if they leave fifth grade and haven't learned anything?" I wondered if I would ever know enough, if I'd ever feel comfortable, if I could ever explain the schwa. Somehow I developed a belief that the emphasis was on teaching and the onus was on me. I referred to room 20 as "my classroom" and I kept my anxiety, my uncertainty, and my lack of knowledge (and control) to myself. It felt lonely and weighty. Teaching became burdensome. Where was the joy that accompanied my childhood afternoons playing school in our basement? Where was the freedom I felt when I read my favorite book to Zippo, my stuffed monkey? Where was my students' desire to keep reading that compelled me to risk getting caught with a book after bedtime?

—NANCY J. JOHNSON, remembering first-year teaching

As an Author

I try not to wonder—or worry—about anything but the story that is waiting to be told. "Can I do it?" creeps into my mind. "Will anyone want to read it?" also lurks about the edges. I'll admit, too, to wondering, "Is this appropriate for children?" from time to time, but when I am writing well, all those questions vanish. They only ask for my attention if I am procrastinating or stuck or being lazy. When I'm writing well and consistently (which involves a fair amount of discipline and respect), we have a trust between us and the story reveals itself to me. I try hard to be faithful.

—DEBORAH WILES, author of *Love, Ruby Lavender, Each Little Bird That Sings,* and *The Aurora County All-Stars*

Literature has always held a significant presence in our lives. It is reflected in memories of being read aloud to, in the anxiety we felt during early years of teaching, and in the questions we wonder as readers and writers. The one constant in our lives is story. When Cyndi's family moved to a new town during the summer after her fifth-grade year, she immediately sought out the public library and found it to be a welcoming place. She devoured every Nancy Drew mystery and then worked her way through novels, beginning with Alcott. Even though anxiety accompanied Nancy during her first few years of teaching, she made time daily to read aloud because it just felt right. Later on she recognized how this practice enhanced the lives of her students and her relationship with them, and also created community in the classroom. Author Deborah Wiles contends that her entire life is portrayed through stories. They weave their way into everything she writes and, even though her stories are fictional, there are threads in those stories that come from her own life. We agree with Wiles, who says that through telling (and reading) stories we create and define our lives, we understand ourselves and one another, and we find a place to call home.

The Wonder of It All: When Literature and Literacy Intersect is fueled by the inquiry "What if literature was a partner in the teaching and learning process?" While we acknowledge that literature has a presence in many classrooms, we often wonder if it is treated more as a tool rather than as collaborator, mentor, adviser, and respected member of the classroom to guide, inform, and inspire us.

During a recent conference of the National Council of Teachers of English, Shelley Harwayne exclaimed that it's time to take back our literacy classrooms. This call to action is especially pertinent, especially now. That premise of taking back our classrooms, of making the best teaching decisions we can make for our particular students, resonates throughout this book. This exploration into elementary and middle school classrooms where the daily presence of children's literature (both implicitly and explicitly) serves to inspire, demonstrate, and teach children and teachers as they participate as readers, writers, speakers, and thinkers is based on the following assumptions and beliefs:

Assumptions (About You!)

- There's a place for literature as a teaching partner in your classroom.

- You have some experience with reading aloud—perhaps you participate as a reader at home or in your classroom; perhaps you've listened to a book or story or poem read to you; perhaps you teach next door to someone who reads aloud daily and are curious about why he devotes so much time to it.

- You know that readers respond to literature for various purposes (to talk about a book they love, to relive last night's game, to concoct a new recipe) and in varied ways (raising questions, making connections, laughing or crying).

- You're not convinced that learning to read must be controlled through specific materials, taught from scripted lessons, or motivated by extrinsic rewards.

- You're intrigued by the possibility of literature as a partner in building community, creating readers, and inspiring writing.

- Someone has recommended (or required) you to read this book—or perhaps you have purchased it—because she (or you) believe there's something within these pages to ponder or talk about.

⊡ You share some of our wonderings about literature and literacy and are eager to consider possibilities for your teaching.

Beliefs (That Shape This Book's Contents)

⊡ We believe learning occurs most naturally when teaching is in response to the needs, interests, and experiences of learners.

⊡ We trust literature as a valuable member of the classroom.

⊡ We know there exists a dynamic partnership between literature, teachers, and learners.

⊡ We respect the read-aloud as both anchor and inspiration.

⊡ We honor time, value reflection, and respect response.

⊡ We believe that curiosity and wonder propel change and spark possibility.

You'll notice there are consistent threads that are woven into the design of each chapter—one is our belief in wonder and curiosity to keep us actively involved as teachers. The other is our confidence in the partnership of literature, teacher, and learner as collaborative members of the classroom. Each chapter will consider ways that literature's presence affects the daily rhythm of the classroom—to build community, nurture response, create readers, inspire writing, promote inquiry, and even cultivate wonder. Additional chapter components you'll discover include the following:

⊡ **Literary Letters:** Chapters 2 through 7 open with letters that present a written exchange between student and teacher in response to a book, offering evidence of the presence of literature in readers' lives and serving to introduce the focus of each chapter.

⊡ **Conversation with . . . :** This section features insights of authors, illustrators, and editors to extend and deepen you and your students' understanding about literature and about the creative process.

⊡ **Side by Side by Side . . . :** This section provides specific strategies to illustrate the partnership between literature, teacher, and learner.

As we profile numerous teachers in this book, our intention is to draw from their expertise while we bring together these voices to affirm and extend teaching possibilities. You'll meet a diverse group of teachers (and a school librarian) at all grade levels, in public and private schools around the world. You'll also spend time looking closely into two classrooms where the presence of literature is honored, natural, and invitational. Our intention in highlighting Megan Sloan, who teaches in a multiage primary-grade classroom, and Kate Norem, a fifth-grade teacher, is to reveal how veteran and new-to-the-profession teachers make intentional, inspired decisions. We also hope to demonstrate how the presence of literature in teaching and learning is not relegated to grade level or teacher experience but rather to how it accompanies us in the wonder of it all.

The Presence of Literature in Literacy Learning

In Sharon Creech's *Love That Dog* (2001b), readers experience the writerly woes, discoveries, and eventual joys of young Jack, who must keep a journal to respond to the poetry Miss Stretchberry reads aloud to her class. In this slim novel told entirely through Jack's journal entries, we spend a year inside a classroom with children's literature at its heart. While we never directly meet Jack's teacher or even hear her voice, we can infer how she partners with poetry to teach. By year's end, Jack not only perceives himself as a reader and writer but produces writing worthy of publication and discovers an author whose work he loves. From Jack's first journal entry ("boys don't write poetry. Girls do" [1]) to one written in early June ("Thank you for coming to see us Mr. Walter Dean Myers. Inside this envelope is a poem using some of your words. I wrote it. It was *inspired by* you *Mr. Walter Dean Myers*" [85]), this text reveals the dynamic partnership between literature, teacher, and learner—a partnership that grew over the course of one school year not by chance, but naturally through the insight and intentional decisions of a classroom teacher who included literature as a valued member of her class.

Through Jack's journal we also learn about Miss Stretchberry. We recognize her belief that poetry belongs to everyone. We sense she values how different poems and different poets hold appeal for different children. We notice she doesn't limit her selections to rhyme and haiku. Miss Stretchberry expects and accepts honest response and she makes a place for poetry throughout the year, not just during poetry month. She believes learning takes time. Miss Stretchberry allows curriculum to emerge from her students and the literature; we doubt if her yearlong planning in August included "Invite Walter Dean Myers to our class in May." She holds kids responsible and she also holds their hand. Most notably, Miss Stretchberry doesn't teach alone. She teaches in the company of literature by partnering with authors as diverse as William Carlos Williams, Valerie Worth, and Walter Dean Myers.

While *Love That Dog* is marketed as fiction, what happens in Jack's classroom is hardly fictional. We've spent time in many classrooms where literature was not only present but an active participant all day, every day. A visit to Portable A at

I like those
small poems
we read today.

. . .

When they're small
like that
you can read
a whole bunch
in a short time
and then in your head
are all the pictures
of all the small things
from all the small poems.

. . .

And especially I liked the dog
in the dog poem
because that's just how
my yellow dog
used to lie down,

. . .

and how he'd sometimes
chomp at a fly
and then sleep
in his loose skin,
just like that poet,
Miss Valerie Worth,
says,
in her small
dog poem.

—SHARON CREECH,
Love That Dog

Geneva Elementary School reflects this presence. Here the fifth graders in Kate Norem's class line the walls with oversized bookmarks representing every book she reads aloud during the course of the school year. The "Our Gallery" bulletin board includes writing inspired by their favorite poets, book reviews of recommended literature, even a "Meet R. L. Stine" report introducing a much-loved author. On top of every student desk appear two or three choice reading books, with titles as diverse as *Officer Buckle and Gloria*, by Peggy Rathmann (1995), *10,000 Days of Thunder: A History of the Vietnam War*, by Philip Caputo (2005), and *Warriors: Fire and Ice*, by Erin Hunter (2004). Student conversations are punctuated with vocabulary gleaned from literature. Even their social studies focus on exploration is accompanied by a towering stack of books that include Russell Freedman's *Adventures of Marco Polo* (2006), Peter Sís' *Follow the Dream: The Story of Christopher Columbus* (1991), and Sydelle Kramer's *Who Was Ferdinand Magellan?* (2004).

Like the fictional Miss Stretchberry and the true-to-life teachers you'll meet in this book, we believe that all children can become confident and competent readers, writers, and learners, regardless of their age, ability, or experience. We also know that classroom teachers play a significant role in making this happen, especially when they invite children's literature to serve as a partner to support both learners and teachers in this process. This leads us to wonder:

⊞ What are the benefits of partnering with literature?

⊞ How can teachers foster a partnership with literature?

⊞ How do teachers develop this partnership with authors and illustrators?

What Are the Benefits of Partnering with Literature?

Teachers who partner with literature are never alone. Whether we discover mentors like Miss Stretchberry who persevere during students' initial negative responses to poetry, or Mr. Noel in Susie Morgenstern's *A Book of Coupons* (2001), who shares *David Copperfield* with his fifth graders ("My gift to you is the story, the characters, the words, the ideas, the style, the emotions. Once you have read the book, all these things will be yours for life. I'll start by reading it to you" [17]), or even Charlotte, who remains "a true friend and a good writer" in *Charlotte's Web* (White 1952, 184), every character we meet, every genre we introduce, every idea, trait, or format we demonstrate can be accompanied by literature.

Teachers who partner with literature turn to it not only for curriculum support but also for life lessons. Early one spring, the morning rituals in Kate's class began productively but soon took a turn. It was one of those days when kids were edgy and impatient. Small-group discussions of the morning literary quote became silly. Students interrupted each other. In the middle of a math facts exploration, with the noise level rising, it was clear the students were distracted and distracting. Kate's patience had worn thin. As the volume increased, so did her frustration. She asked Kelly to dash to the school library and borrow a copy of Judith Viorst's *Alexander and the Terrible, Horrible, No Good, Very Bad Day* (1973). By the time Kelly returned, the fifth graders were gathered on the carpet, ready for the read-aloud. "I'm having a bad day," Kate announced. A number of kids nodded in agreement. With no further discussion, Kate read this classic picture book about the trials and tribulations that befell poor Alexander over the course of one full day. "Whew, that made me feel better," sympathized Kate. "I don't think my day is nearly as bad as his. You know what I love about books? I was able to think of a book that connected to my own life, read it, and realize I'm not the only one who feels that way."

Chelsea agreed, "It's like the story of the Little Red Hen. Last night I was making cookies and nobody helped, but everybody wanted to eat them!" The brief discussion that ensued diffused the morning tension and created an opportunity to reset the day's learning goals.

We've all read books that reminded us of people and situations in our lives and we've discovered literature that elicited an emotional response, opened up new ideas, created new insights, and even challenged our beliefs. Every time this happens, literature breathes life and possibility into what we know. When literature is present in our classrooms, students experience the same extension of their world. This can occur through the read-aloud, when students discuss stories and poetry, when they linger over facts and fantasies, even when they discover how stories, like life, don't always have tidy endings. In this way, literature grounds us as well as cultivates our wonderings.

Meeting the needs of learners

It's difficult to meet the needs of our students if we don't know who they are. We can examine test scores, read previous teachers' comments, and peruse cumulative files, but these paint impersonal portraits. To know our students well, we pay attention to what they tell us. For example, nothing in Sharon Creech's *Love That Dog* (2001b) reveals Jack's age or labels him as gifted or remedial. We come to know him through his words and ideas, his misunderstandings and miscues. Jack's response journal teaches us who he is, what he cares about, what he struggles with, and what he's ready to learn. He discovers a lot about writing through the course of the school year—from how ideas can grow from personal experience to how a computer's "spell-checking thing" is like a "little helper brain" (67). Jack also discovers plenty about reading. At times it doesn't make sense ("I don't understand the poem about the red wheelbarrow" [3]), and other times it evokes a strong, personal response ("That was the best best BEST poem you read yesterday" [42]).

We've all had students in our classrooms who reminded us of Jack. Reading about him offers insight into his thinking and behavior and also provides a literary observation of how a teacher responds. As with all literature, what we understand and find interesting in *Love That Dog* differs from what captivates our students. The same is true when we read Jack Gantos' novels about Joey Pigza or Beverly Cleary's gregarious character Ramona or Barbara Park's intrepid Junie B. Jones or even Ann Cameron's storytelling Julian. Children's literature with realistic characters opens up a window into children's complexities, absurdities, worries, and wisdom. By reading it, we glean insight into individual children who live not only in books but also in our classrooms (see Figure 1.1). As well, children's literature allows us to discover plenty about teachers and teaching, sometimes making us chuckle, other times making us cringe. Reading about Mr. Fogleman's excessive passion for his favorite children's book in Gordon Korman's

---

Joey Pigza Swallowed the Key, by Jack Gantos. New York: Farrar, Straus and Giroux, 1998.

Judy Moody Was in a Mood. Not a Good Mood. A Bad Mood, by Megan McDonald. Illus. Peter H. Reynolds. Cambridge, MA: Candlewick, 2002.

Junie B., First Grader (at Last!), by Barbara Park. Illus. Denise Brunkus. New York: Random House, 2002.

Lilly's Purple Plastic Purse, by Kevin Henkes. New York: Greenwillow, 1996.

Matilda, by Roald Dahl. New York: Puffin, 1998.

My Name Is Jorge: On Both Sides of the River, by Jane Medina. Illus. Fabricio Vanden Broeck. Honesdale, PA: Wordsong/Boyds Mills, 1999.

My Name Is Yoon, by Helen Recorvits. Illus. Gabi Swiatkowska. New York: Frances Foster/Farrar, Straus and Giroux, 2003.

Ruby the Copycat, by Peggy Rathmann. New York: Scholastic, 1993.

Sahara Special, by Esmé Raji Codell. New York: Hyperion, 2004.

The Skin I'm In, by Sharon Flake. New York: Jump at the Sun/Hyperion, 1998.

There's a Boy in the Girl's Bathroom, by Louis Sachar. New York: Knopf, 1987.

The View from Saturday, by E. L. Konigsburg. New York: Atheneum, 1996.

FIG 1.1 *Books with Student Characters Who Offer Insights for Teachers*

Counting on Grace, by Elizabeth Winthrop. New York: Wendy Lamb/Random House, 2006.

A Fine, Fine School, by Sharon Creech. Illus. Harry Bliss. New York: Joanna Cotler/HarperCollins, 2001.

Flying Solo, by Ralph Fletcher. New York: Clarion, 1998.

Hooray for Diffendoofer Day! by Dr. Seuss and Jack Prelutsky. Illus. Lane Smith. New York: Knopf, 1998.

Jack Drake, Teacher's Pet, by Andrew Clements. Illus. Delores Avendano. New York: Simon and Schuster, 2001.

Miss Nelson Is Missing, by James Marshall. Illus. Harry G. Allard. Boston: Houghton, 1977.

Nothing but the Truth, by Avi. New York: Orchard, 1991.

Sister Anne's Hands, by Marybeth Lorbiecki. Illus. K. Wendy Popp. New York: Dial, 1998.

The Secret School, by Avi. San Diego: Harcourt, 2001.

The Teacher's Funeral: A Comedy in Three Parts, by Richard Peck. New York: Dial, 2004.

Testing Miss Malarkey, by Judy Finchler. Illus. Kevin O'Malley. New York: Walker, 2003.

Thank You, Mr. Falker, by Patricia Polacco. New York: Philomel, 1998.

FIG 1.2 *Books with Teachers Who Offer Insights into Teaching*

No More Dead Dogs or the sly transformation of Miss Nelson into Miss Viola Swamp in James Marshall's Miss Nelson books serves as a mirror that maybe, just maybe, invites us to rethink how we teach (see Figure 1.2).

How Can Teachers Foster a Partnership with Literature?

When we include literature as an active member of our classroom, we infuse new life into learning through a literary voice that extends the possibilities we explore together and independently. Because we know that none of us can experience everything on our own, it seems natural to turn to literature as our partner. Teaching children how to think, feel, and discover, no matter the curricular area, is possible when we integrate literature with resources such as social studies textbooks and science kits. Many teachers read aloud books like *Nettie's Trip South*, by Ann Turner (1987), and *Aunt Harriet's Underground Railroad in the Sky*, by Faith Ringgold (1992), to complement the limited historical information about slavery available in a textbook. Some design a nonfiction literature circle unit with books like *Starry Messenger*, by Peter Sís (1996), *Maria's Comet*, by Deborah Hopkinson (1999), *The Magic School Bus: Lost in the Solar System*, by Joanna Cole

(1990), and *Reaching for the Moon*, by Buzz Aldrin (2005), to build background knowledge and develop interest prior to beginning a science inquiry on the solar system.

Partnering literature with content area learning can infuse life and depth into the curriculum. This is as true for literacy as it is for other disciplines. Professional books have long touted the benefits of literature as model and mentor in the writing classroom. When Lucy McCormick Calkins wrote *The Art of Teaching Writing* (1994), she shared experiences with children and literature that convinced teachers to integrate books, authors, and illustrators into writing instruction:

> If we are going to design writing workshops in which there are places not only for editing conferences and response groups but also for miracles, we need to bring powerful literature into those classrooms and to do everything possible to invite children to live and write inside that literature. It begins . . . with believing that the books we read aloud will change everything in the classroom community. And they do. (252)

Perhaps Miss Stretchberry read *The Art of Teaching Writing* or Shelley Harwayne's *Lasting Impressions: Weaving Literature into the Writing Workshop* (1992). Perhaps she modeled her teaching practices after educators like Joanne Hindley and Katie Wood Ray. And maybe she trusted her own instincts as a reader and writer. Wherever and however she learned to invite literature into her writing classroom made a difference in Jack's life, as it does in the lives of the teachers and students you'll meet in this book.

Spending time in Megan Sloan's multiage primary classroom affords us an opportunity to see how one teacher partners with literature throughout the day, particularly as a collaborative presence during writing workshop. Whether Megan reads aloud Patricia Polacco's *My Ol' Man* (1995) or Ellen Stoll Walsh's *Pip's Magic* (1994), she asks her students to pay attention to each author's lead sentences and linger over the language. When she pulls *All the Places to Love*, by Patricia MacLachlan (1994), off the shelf and reads aloud phrases such as, "where trout flashed like jewels in the sunlight" and "where cattails stood like guards," Megan introduces the way authors create rich images using similes. She knows her developing writers will borrow from authors whose work echoes in their ears, so she isn't surprised when Emelia's poem about a spring garden includes the line "tulips stood like guards." It's been months since Megan read *All the Places to Love*, but MacLachlan's language remained and eventually inspired an original poem, with some borrowed imagery. These children know they aren't writing alone, even if they can't recall their inspiration.

Getting started

If partnering with literature is new to you, you're probably wondering, "Where do I start?" As clichéd as it sounds, you start with what you know and believe. Then you ask, "Is what I know and believe reflected by how and what I teach?" and "How can literature collaborate with me to make these beliefs visible and honored?" For example, in the introduction, we state, "We respect the read-aloud as both anchor and inspiration." It's not surprising, then, that we both read aloud to our students the very first year we taught. Had we been asked why, we might have said, "Because my fifth-grade teacher did," or "Because it calms the kids down after lunch," or "There's this time between cleanup and dismissal and I don't know what else to do." All would have been perfectly legitimate reasons . . . at the time. But none echoes our beliefs about literacy and learning.

The children in Megan's and Kate's classes know their teachers believe in the value of reading aloud because they make time for it every single day. Sometimes the books align with a focus lesson about reading strategies or build background information about the desert. Other times books are chosen because they add humor, suggest compassion, or promote curiosity. Teachers slow down this time to develop a full sense of what a book can offer. As Mem Fox suggests in *Reading Magic: Why Reading Aloud to Our Children Will Change Their Lives Forever*, the read-aloud is about much more than curriculum:

> When we take the time to read aloud to the children in our lives, we bond closely with them in a secret society associated with the books we've shared. The fire of literacy is created by the emotional sparks between a child, a book, and the person reading. It isn't achieved by the book alone, nor by the child alone, nor by the adult who's reading aloud—it's the relationship winding between all three, bringing them together in easy harmony. (2001, 10)

Over the years, teaching improves with revision. We've both revised not only how and what we read aloud but also why. You'll notice we refer to reading aloud in every chapter in this book, because it offers many benefits and it's the most natural way we can make known literature's valued membership in our class. Now when we read aloud we read everything, including the dedication page, the note from the author or illustrator, and whatever information we can glean about the artist's medium from the small print on the back of the title page. While the story's plot or book's content presents plenty to discuss and appreciate, often the addition of the author's note serves to deepen our understanding and appreciation of the writer's inspiration or the illustrator's decisions. The few minutes it takes to include this in our read-aloud goes a long way toward illuminating the creative process and offering insights beyond any of our experiences.

We also suggest starting with a willingness to examine the knowledge and expertise of others. For example, when we read a professional book or attend a conference, we remain open to the possibility that we may want to revisit what we believe about literacy and learning. That reexamination doesn't negate what we believe or how we teach; rather, it may affirm what we know and believe. It may also offer book titles, suggest implementation, and elicit wonderings that we hadn't considered on our own. The same is true when we respect our students as our partners. Just like Jack's words in *Love That Dog*, what our students say or do can force us to reexamine what we know and believe and adjust our teaching accordingly. In addition, our beliefs and teaching decisions are informed by the authors and illustrators who write for children. We value them as coteachers, advisers, mentors, and friends. We listen to their advice, learn from their experiences, and appreciate their ideas.

How Do Teachers Develop This Partnership with Authors and Illustrators?

Throughout our school experiences, there were times during language arts, gym class, or science lab when the teacher instructed us to choose a partner. When presented with this directive, we almost always chose someone that we knew. Our selection criterion might have been that the person was our friend, the person might know the answers, or the person was willing to dissect the frog. Whatever the reason, we made a conscious choice based upon what we knew about that individual and how comfortable we felt working with her. In contrast, when our partners were assigned, sometimes the partnership worked out well, while other times it became a source for whining.

In developing a partnership with literature, we apply the same criteria we used when selecting a partner in school—we start with what we know. We often choose books that are old favorites and have worked well in the past. But it's also important to expand and incorporate new partners into the curriculum. Reading literary reviews, asking colleagues or friends for suggestions, and even listening to students as they reveal their favorite authors and illustrators will introduce us to new options. However, nothing informs us more about our literature partners than reading literature extensively and intensively and conducting inquiries about authors and illustrators.

Regie Routman states, "If we want our students to be excited about literacy . . . they need to have teachers who are literacy learners themselves" (2003, 1).

Teachers who are readers easily demonstrate enthusiasm for reading. Routman also recommends that teachers share their reading lives with students by talking about what they have just read, what they are in the process of reading, or what is on their list to read next. In addition to what they are reading—children's books, professional resources, journals, poetry, adult novels—teachers reveal their selection process, divulge their initial or ongoing response, and determine whether to recommend the book to a friend, colleague, or student.

One question teachers and librarians always raise is "When is there time to read?" We advise students in our children's literature courses to always carry a book with them. There are stolen moments to read a few pages or even an entire chapter while waiting in a doctor's office, eating lunch, riding the bus, or before turning out the lights at bedtime. Joining a book club forces us to read and prepare for a discussion. Spending a half hour before or after school discussing a book with colleagues doesn't take much time from the day and reaps the rewards of building collegiality and hearing others' responses to a story. And of course, summer is when many of us can catch up on our reading, taking books along on vacation or sitting down with an intriguing title after working in the garden. The bottom line is this: if it's important, we make time to read. When teachers are readers they derive pleasure from reading.

There is plenty of evidence that authors and illustrators are also informed and inspired by what they read. A check of author websites and speeches given by Newbery award winners reflects their reliance on and appreciation for reading in their writing lives. When Katherine Paterson was asked about the authors she read as a child, she responded, "I loved Kate Seredy, Robert Lawson, Dickens, Louisa May Alcott, 'Heidi'—What can I say? I read a lot" (www.terabithia.com). In his dedication to *Anonymously Yours*, Richard Peck discloses: "I read because one life isn't enough, and in the page of a book I can be anybody; I read because every journey begins at the library, and it's time for me to start packing" (www .carolhurst.com/authors/rpeck.html). One of Avi's secrets to good writing includes "Read, read, read. Reading is the key to good writing. The more you read, the better the writer you can be. You can NEVER read too much" (www .avi-writer.com).

When our teaching is accompanied by stories and poems, our ability to create active, curious, joyful readers also increases. A sense of excitement permeates each school day as students eagerly await the literature they will encounter, the discussions they will engage in, and the opportunities they will have to share the books they are reading. Each chapter in *The Wonder of It All: When Literature and Literacy Intersect* expands on this idea of a partnership with literature and authors. And just like Jack's familiarity with Walter Dean Myers in *Love That Dog*, we hope that our readers will experience a partnership with us in their literary and curricular pursuits.

Professional Literature Cited

Calkins, Lucy McCormick. 1994. *The Art of Teaching Writing*. Portsmouth, NH: Heinemann.

Fox, Mem. 2001. *Reading Magic: Why Reading Aloud to Our Children Will Change Their Lives Forever*. Illus. Judy Horacek. San Diego: Harvest/Harcourt.

Harwayne, Shelley. 1992. *Lasting Impressions: Weaving Literature into the Writing Workshop*. Portsmouth, NH: Heinemann.

Routman, Regie. 2003. *Reading Essentials: The Specifics You Need to Teach Reading Well*. Portsmouth, NH: Heinemann.

In this conversation, Marla Frazee and her editor Allyn Johnston reveal their partnership and process in creating the picture books *Roller Coaster* and *Walk On: A Guide for Babies of All Ages*, written and illustrated by Frazee, as well as *Harriet, You'll Drive Me Wild*, written by Mem Fox and illustrated by Frazee.

Describe your partnership as author-illustrator and editor.

FRAZEE: As an illustrator, there are different ways that I am guided through the process of making a picture book. What is most valuable is an editor who helps me think about the type of story I am telling through pictures. The focus is on what the picture story is saying as opposed to the style or the medium I am using. This is important to me and it's not easy to find an editor who can work with an illustrator on that level. The books that Allyn edited are ones where she looked at the art in a way that was about more than the narrative.

JOHNSTON: As an editor, I take the form of the picture book very seriously. I think of it as a piece of theatre that takes place within a thirty-two-page structure. Every part is important—what's happening on the title page, on the end pages, and on the back of the book. It's about taking the reader to another world. One of the reasons why working with Marla is so satisfying is that she thinks about all those pieces as seriously as I do. The picture book is a different type of format; the text and the art are blended together in a way that both of them bring different things. We want the text to say the same thing that is in Marla's illustrations, but we also want the pictures to offer something surprising. When Marla gives me something, I have to live with it for a while. I'm known to carry my work around with me. I'll be sitting at the coffeehouse and looking at the latest version of what we are working on and it's like looking at faint stars. If you look at it directly you don't see it, but if you look out of the corner of your eye, there it is. I look at picture books over and over again and notice different things. I feel my role as editor is to ask, "What's the emotional center?" Then we keep paring it down so that when Marla is done, what shines through is as pure as it can be.

Is this process different when you illustrate books written by other authors?

FRAZEE: I began illustrating other authors' manuscripts before I started writing my own. Part of the exercise I go through as an illustrator is to read the text and turn it around and upside down to try and figure out a way of telling a picture that isn't directly the same as the words being told. When I started to write my own stories, it was about the words and the pictures not saying the exact same thing. Because Allyn and I have worked together on several books, she can read the draft of a story and know there is something I will bring through my illustrations. With *Walk On*, Allyn knew even without seeing the illustrations that the pictures would play off the text.

How do you know when something is working?

FRAZEE: At a certain point, I lose my ability to judge. Sometimes I know something is working and I think, "Oh my gosh. I've really got something here." Other times, I have no idea and I just have to wait and see. I need to hear what Allyn thinks. It's like dumping a bunch of stuff into a pot and knowing it's going to come out again differently or it's going to concentrate down to something that makes more sense. I'm willing to get rid of what's not working.

At what point do you stop editing the text?

JOHNSTON: It depends on the person. Sometimes Marla will change a line and I have to think about whether or not I am going to fight to get it back. For Marla's new book, we worked for a long time on the text. She'll write, write, write, but until she actually starts drawing to see how it's going to look on a page, she won't really know if the text is working.

What have you discovered about young readers?

FRAZEE: One of the things crucial about picture books is that children don't need to be taught how to read pictures. They know how to do it better than grown-ups. I have to honor that process of how rigorous they are about reading the pictures. Children are going to notice everything, and it's going to matter to them in a way that won't matter to adults because adults are reading the words and are using the words as their way of getting through the story. But a child's path is a visual one, especially after someone has read them a story and they go back and look at the illustrations. It occurred to me as I illustrated my first book that I needed to bridge the gap between what the words were saying with the pictures. Some of the gaps were vast and they actually required a sequential footbridge of pictures to get from here to there. Some were little hopping points where the weight of the story didn't rest on the pictures.

What can teachers learn about the editing process?

FRAZEE: When I am describing the editor partnership, I tell kids that an editor is like your teacher. They are trying to get you to do your very best work and so sometimes they might say, "This isn't the best you can do." So you have to go back and try and figure out what that means. What is satisfying is when Allyn looks at my work and says, "Oh my gosh, this is working now," and I think, "Whew, that's great." At some point, I lose my judgment and I need an objective eye. What I love about the books Allyn edits is this deep emotional resonance. She will keep asking me questions like, "What is it you are trying to say here?" That's the whole point of a picture book—the emotion carries from page to page and every page needs to resonate in some emotional way, whether it is joyful, fearful, or funny. It has to be doing something. That's often hard to discern on the first go-around when there are only sketches. It takes a lot of time. You just can't rush it.

Harriet, You'll Drive Me Wild! by Mem Fox. Illus. Marla Frazee. San Diego: Harcourt, 2000.

Roller Coaster, by Marla Frazee. San Diego: Harcourt, 2003.

Walk On: A Guide for Babies of All Ages, by Marla Frazee. San Diego: Harcourt, 2006.

Side by Side by Side
Literature/Teacher/Learner: Literary Letters

Book

Creech, Sharon. 2002. *Ruby Holler*. New York: Joanna Cotler/HarperCollins.

> When thirteen-year-old "trouble twins" Florida and Dallas leave their miserable lives at the Boxton Creek Home for Children, chances are they'll return in a flash. But this time is different. They're taken in by an eccentric older couple with adventure on their minds, and the young orphans fall into the rural warmth of Tiller, Sairy, and a place called Ruby Holler . . . but not without near disaster and tall tale–ish mystery.

Related professional literature

Guiding Readers and Writers, Grades 3–6, by Irene C. Fountas and Gay Su Pinnell. Portsmouth, NH: Heinemann, 2001.

Teaching Response

Kate Norem chooses *Ruby Holler* as the first novel she reads aloud to her fifth graders. The story's archetypical characters, the weaving of mystery and adventure, and the unique and likable protagonists elicit plenty of response. A few weeks into the read-aloud, Kate introduces literary letters and uses her own response to this novel to demonstrate the process. Interested in promoting independent reading choices and seeking to interact with her students about what they're reading, Kate adapts the strategy of writing literary letters, a yearlong response-based project, from *Guiding Readers and Writers, Grades 3–6*. These letters will be kept in students' reading notebooks and collected on predetermined days for Kate's response.

Kate uses a focus lesson to demonstrate how to think about and write a literary letter. Beginning with a blank sheet of chart paper, Kate mentions where she'll put the date and how she'll use "Dear Class" as the salutation. As she begins writing, she talks through her decisions:

> I need to remember to underline the book title. . . . Even though I've read this book before, I'm noticing new things that I think are important to include. . . .

Since books often remind me of something from my own life, I'm going to mention how Ruby Holler reminds me of the foster kids who lived with my dad. (See Figure 1.3.)

Since the students are familiar with *Ruby Holler* and because there have been conversations about how good readers make connections, Kate's literary letter holds interest for them. Its informal tone reflects her unique understanding of this book. She rereads her letter aloud "to make sure it makes sense." Then Kate distributes students' reading notebooks with a bright green insert marking the section where literary letters will appear. This green page, adapted from *Guiding Readers and Writers*, contains suggestions of what students can include in their letters.

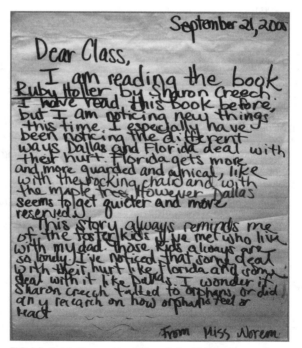

FIG 1.3 *Kate's Literary Letter About* Ruby Holler

In the days that follow, focus lessons clarify the purpose and process of writing literary letters. Kate's introductory literary letter remains visible in the classroom for reference.

Student Response

Literary letters from Kate's fifth graders, including her responses, appear at the beginning of the remaining chapters in this book, offering evidence of the presence of literature in readers' lives and honoring ways that literary response links reading, writing, inquiry, and wonder. We've consciously chosen to retain the language, spelling, and punctuation in these letters to honor the informal nature of this correspondence.

September 28

Dear miss norem
I love the tale of despereaux. I like it becuause the
cerictors are very cool. I also love it because the topic
grabs me and reels me in. It looks like Despereaux is a
woeror on the front of the book because he has a needle.
If I was a mouse I wouldn't really want to fall in love with
a Prinses. I herd som thing about rat's. I think the rat's
are the bad guy's. I em estimating the rat's and the mice
are going to have a big big battle. And Despereaux is going
to be a worreyor.
   I think this book is andventureis and alittle funny. I
wonder how many family members he has. This book is my
favorite book. My friend read this book and he really liked
it. Same for me, well so fare. I bileav if I die I would want
to be a mouse that could talk. I'm almoset to the Part were
the rat's come.

From,
Dylan B.

October 4

Dear Dylan,
The Tale of Despereaux certainly is a great book! Many people
must agree because it won the Newbery Medal. Why do you think
it won the Newbery?
   One thing I think is interesting about The Tale of Despereaux is
that the author speaks to the reader by saying things like, "So,
dear reader . . ." Do you like that or dislike it? I know many
people who have really thought it made the book better and
many people who didn't like it at all!
   I think it was very clever of you to use the cover to get clues
to the book. Despereaux definitely does look like a warrior on
the cover! Did you notice that his sword is a needle?
   Dylan, thank you for your letter! I have been so impressed by
all of your hard work this year. I look forward to learning more
about you and your thinking this year as we write to each other!

Love,
Miss Norem

The Presence of Literature to Build Community

If you poked your head into our offices, it would be hard to miss the books—they're stacked high into piles, sorted onto shelves by our own systems, even leaning haphazardly from bulging boxes and plastic tubs. Books decorate and define our work space—we can't imagine it any other way. For us, our teaching community begins with the literature we cart around campus (sometimes literally!) and bring into whatever classrooms we've been assigned each term. But it hasn't always been this way.

When we taught first grade, fifth grade, and ninth grade, we had our own classrooms, a space we could design, decorate, and even redecorate to fit the needs of our students and the work we were doing. Because we believed the environment mattered, we invested many hours creating a welcoming place for learning and learners. Now when we prepare for our first class of the term, we don't have the luxury (or the burden) of our own classroom, so we invest our energy differently. And maybe that's a good thing. Our community in a college classroom depends more on the people and the content than it does on physical space. We pull literature off our shelves, wondering whether to read aloud from *Wild About Books*, by Judy Sierra (2004), or poetry from *Please Bury Me in the Library*, by J. Patrick Lewis (2005), on the first day. We grapple with tantalizing choices for the extended read-aloud—should we try out a new novel, perhaps Deborah Wiles' *The Aurora County All-Stars* (2007), or read an old favorite, such as Kate DiCamillo's response-rich *Because of Winn-Dixie* (2000)? Or, might this be the perfect term to read *The Breadwinner*, by Deborah Ellis (2001), certain it will provoke conversation about issues of justice and acts of courage?

We know we are not alone in making these decisions. As summer wanes, planning for a new year occupies and transforms all teachers' thoughts and preparation. Like you, the teachers in this book devote great care to building their classroom community, and they consciously choose literature as a companion in this effort. They believe in the presence of literature. Its relationship within the classroom involves more than seeking out books to serve as the inspiration for early-in-the-year writing or to tap into children's reading interests. Literature also partners to set the tone, establish common ground, even focus on expectations

Are You a Book Person?

A good book is a kind
Of person with a mind
Of her own,
Who lives alone,
Standing on a shelf
By herself.
She has a spine,
A heart, a soul,
And a goal—
To capture, to amuse,
To light a fire
(You're the fuse),
Or else, joyfully,
Just to be.
From beginning
To end,
Need a friend?

—J. PATRICK LEWIS

and behaviors that promote engaged learners. Creating and maintaining community becomes a focus throughout the year as we include literature to ignite the curriculum and as we come to know our students' interests and needs.

As we prepare to match faces and personalities with names on class lists, we find value in designing ways of coming to know who is in our classroom—the individual students who each bring a wealth of experiences, interests, and feelings to the work we will do. Contemplating not only the presence of children in our classrooms but also the presence of literature leads us to wonder:

- How can literature play a role in creating and defining our classroom community?

- What benefits exist when we partner literature with community building?

- What can authors and illustrators teach us about creating community?

How Can Literature Play a Role in Creating and Defining Our Classroom Community?

Whether community is defined as an environment of respect and trust, as the foundation to support leadership and learning, as the creation of a classroom family, or even by the individuals who will contribute to the establishment of the group, the attention to community as worthwhile grows out of a belief that learners shape curriculum as they integrate who they are with what is being learned. In classrooms where literature is always present, it is not uncommon to discover books, authors, and illustrators also shaping the curriculum and serving as collaborators throughout the day, beginning on the first day of school.

If you are an avid reader, you already know the power and possibility that literature affords. You probably don't need to be convinced of the presence of literature to offer a glimpse into people and places, to illuminate themes and topics, even to remind us of our own lives while providing experiences unlike anything we'll ever know. Literature in all genres and formats—stories and poems, fiction and nonfiction, books, magazines, and newspapers—belongs in our classrooms because of its inherent benefits.

As we glimpse the specific effects of literature in our teaching lives, we can't help but think about the role of literature in our reading lives. The wisdom and experience of others who promote the power of reading include a provocative response to the question "Why literature?" from Charlotte Huck (1987, 69–71), longtime advocate for children's literature. Huck's response bolsters our recommendation for the presence of literature in our classrooms.

> **Why Literature?**
>
> Because literature has the power . . .
>
> - ⊡ to make us more human; to help us see the world from inside the skin of persons very different from ourselves; to live more lives than the one we have; to try on various roles
>
> - ⊡ to develop compassion and insight into the behavior of ourselves and others (through characters so real that the reader lives and suffers and rejoices with them)
>
> - ⊡ to show us the past in a way that helps us understand the present
>
> - ⊡ to move us in ways that facts, statistics, and history texts can never do (or rarely do)
>
> - ⊡ to develop the imagination; to help us entertain ideas we never could have had; to interpret and translate our experiences, to shape our world, and to enlarge our imaginations
>
> - ⊡ to take us out of ourselves and return us to ourselves as a changed self; to enlarge our thinking while educating our hearts

Every time we read Huck's list, we are reminded of specific books that align with each quality she presents. For example, when we read Beverly Cleary's *Ramona the Pest* (1968), we are immediately transported to kindergarten. We slip into Ramona's shoes, filled with anticipation and willing to curb our enthusiasm while we "wait for the present," only to realize there's no gift from the teacher, just a misunderstanding. Lois Lowry's *Number the Stars* (1989) allows us to experience some hold-your-breath moments of life in Denmark during the Nazi occupation and discover the risks everyday people took to save their friends. David Wiesner's *The Three Pigs* (2001) delights us as we revisit a familiar story through a humorous, skewed perspective, challenging us to reconsider a tale we thought we knew. Reading *Dooby Dooby Moo*, by Doreen Cronin (2006), allows us to pay tribute to a wild imagination, not unfamiliar to many children who find "let's pretend" as natural as breathing. And to think literature can do all of this—and more—as a member of our classroom!

Charlotte Huck's list of literature's powers inspires us to think of how literature's presence in our classrooms helps to establish and maintain community. Among the reasons we turn to literature with community building as our focus include its power to

- value individuality and honor uniqueness

- define us as a classroom

- establish beliefs, values, and expectations

- introduce our shared work as we learn together

- promote risk taking and build success

This chapter peeks into classrooms where a growing relationship with books results in these benefits, specifically exploring how building and maintaining community develops through the availability of literature, reading aloud, and written response inspired by the ideas of authors who write for children. What we propose here are not isolated getting-to-know-you activities. Instead, we ask you to consider how literature becomes a natural partner and friend from the very first day of school, woven into the introductions, conversations, and discoveries that teachers and students create throughout the year.

Making literature accessible through classroom libraries

Literature's presence in the classroom supports and promotes literacy. Classroom libraries directly relate to the design of the community by inviting in authors and illustrators whose work inspires students to respond as readers, writers, and learners. Books that are meaningful and personally interesting from a variety of genres, topics, and formats naturally promote greater amounts of reading, increase reading frequency, and demonstrate diverse experiences for inquiry and writing. Classroom libraries also encourage social interaction as students discuss and recommend books they have read.

When Christine Jordan began teaching fifth grade, she recognized the importance of book availability in her classroom. At first she controlled access by checking out books with cards, issuing fines, and making students pay for missing books. Christine noticed that students visited the library less and less. "I was sad that the new books stayed new," she said. "My second year of teaching, I let the kids just go for it. Did books walk away? Yes. Did they get grimy and slimy? Yes. Did they get read? *Yes!* I still have incomplete sets of Chronicles of Narnia and the Little House on the Prairie series, but I hope that the book they kept sparked some excitement about reading."

As Christine discovered, if limited access to literature detracts from enjoyment, it can result in students avoiding the classroom library altogether. Students need ownership as well as access to their classroom library. For this reason, it is important not to organize the library by leveling books. Labeling books by readability shortchanges the many purposes and values that literature offers. It also assumes that students are one-dimensional readers and limits their book selection. And it disregards the range and variety of books we want in our classroom, from picture books to novels, from fiction to nonfiction, and from student-published books to class creations.

In many classrooms, teachers encourage students to organize the library. Sometimes this is done by genres, authors, topics, or themes. Inexpensive plastic tubs can house books organized by kid-created categories (e.g., bug books, books with award stickers, books by Sharon Creech, friendship books). Tubs enable students to re-sort the books throughout the school year in ways that make sense to them. An additional benefit is listening in on students' conversations and recommendations as they develop a manageable system. For example, teacher Joanne Hindley relates the experience of her third and fourth graders during this September ritual as they sort books and organize their classroom library: "I hear children talking over each other in excited voices about books they recognize and have read before, authors they've heard of, and books that look interesting. By handling the books, children will really know something about what is available in those bookcases around the perimeter of the classroom. Choosing books will be a bit less intimidating for those who feel overwhelmed by the shelves and shelves of colorful spines looking out at them" (1996, 90). When students design the library, we make sure we ask them why they placed books with certain other books and how they generated the categories. This teaches us something about how students think about books and, in turn, how we might view the literature in the classroom with more thoughtfulness.

Reading aloud to create and define community

If we could choose one nonnegotiable teaching decision we make every single day, it's the read-aloud. There is no question, the benefits are numerous when the read-aloud is treated as a curricular choice and not as a time filler or an activity to calm students after recess. Learning about writing, developing active reading strategies, and deepening knowledge related to content areas can all radiate from literature. Numerous studies, books, and articles advocate sharing literature aloud with children for reasons that are academic, motivational, and pleasurable (Anderson et al. 1985; Fisher and Elleman 1984; Michener 1988; Giorgis and Johnson 1999, Trelease 2006; Serafini and Giorgis 2003). In addition, we make a case for the read-aloud as relational, in particular as it shapes and defines classroom community.

Because we believe that the presence of literature to support literacy can grow naturally from the read-aloud, don't be surprised to see a reading-aloud thread woven through every chapter of this book. But for now, we examine the read-aloud as the collaborator in building and maintaining community.

Many teachers read aloud children's literature as a daily ritual. What we read and why we choose certain books vary widely from classroom to classroom. And it should, especially when we think of literature as a unique member of our class. As you examine how you already include reading aloud, we hope you will find affirmation and new considerations to extend your thinking about how the read-aloud can become an anchor and an inspiration, not only for the literacy program but for your entire day.

The students who step into Portable A at Geneva Elementary School in early September are treated to lots of picture books read aloud. Their teacher, Kate Norem, selects these books to introduce who she is, what she cares about, and the authors and illustrators whose work she admires. While twenty-seven fifth graders gather on the carpet, Kate sits in a comfy chair she has resurrected from a garage sale and reupholstered with a blue-and-yellow slipcover, with a stack of picture books at her side. "This week I'm going to tell you a little about me through some of the books I love," she begins as she lifts Patricia MacLachlan's *All the Places to Love* (1994) from the pile. Kate reads expressively and at a pace that exhibits how she savors MacLachlan's language. She takes her time as she shows the illustrations and encourages attentive lingering, a strategy she will return to throughout the year. After she turns the last page, Kate pauses and then explains why she loves this book and how it reminds her of her own life. She invites student response and may follow with another book or wait until later that day to read aloud again. During the first week of school, Kate's students come to know their teacher from the picture books she shares aloud. They discover she loves to laugh and values wordplay and imagination (*Skippyjon Jones*, by Judy Schachner [2003]), she is an avid reader and grew up with a mother who is a school librarian (*The Library*, by Sarah Stewart [1995]), and she is a genuine human being with idiosyncrasies and behaviors that might remind her students of themselves (*Sometimes I'm Bombaloo*, by Rachel Vail [2002]). They learn that picture books hold a special place in Kate's life, even as an adult, and they are encouraged not to abandon this literary format just because they are in fifth grade.

Primary teacher Megan Sloan claims, "It's my job that students leave this classroom absolutely inspired to read and write," and she's resolute in the ways that reading aloud supports this belief. She pulls poetry books off the shelf at the beginning of the year, reading from *Autumnblings*, by Douglas Florian (2003), *Honey, I Love*, by Eloise Greenfield (1978), and *Good Books, Good Times*, by Lee Bennett Hopkins (1990), even before she distributes reading notebooks and sets up the writing workshop. Inspired from poetic language received in their ears, the children in Megan's class begin to look around their classroom, their playground, and their lives with a poet's discerning eye. She reads *Wild About Books*, by Judy Sierra (2004), to remind students of their favorite books and to lay the groundwork for informal book talks as ways students can introduce books they recommend. In September, Megan also reads aloud *Tight Times* (Hazen 1979), *Amazing Grace* (Hoffman 1991), *The Relatives Came* (Rylant 1985), and *I Have a Sister, My Sister Is Deaf* (Peterson 1977) to inspire conversation about children's lives, address their doubts and experiences, and acknowledge their feelings associated with learning. She reads *The Recess Queen*, by Alexis O'Neill (2002), or *Enemy Pie*, by Derek Munson (2000), to support her desire to "create a family" in the classroom, build trusting relationships, and think about strategies for getting along with each other. The literature Megan reads aloud the first month of school leads to conversations that indirectly introduce her students to her, something she believes is vital to her teaching. She states, "If I don't know them, I will never be able to teach to my full potential." Megan also selects stories that will make sense to her students, even to those whose listening comprehension far exceeds their reading comprehension. After all, meaning resides in the ear of the listener. When Megan reads aloud *Amber on the Mountain*, by Tony Johnston (1994), she affirms the complex mix of doubts and confidence shared by many of her first and second graders. It is not surprising to discover that her students empathize with Amber's struggle and celebrate her accomplishment as a reader, and when Megan reads from the last page and Whitney interrupts with "Way to go, Amber!" she knows the children understand.

Georgia Connor Schultzman contends that "building community through literature is a major element" in her seventh-grade language arts class. She loves to begin the year by reading aloud Cynthia Rylant's *The Heavenly Village* (2002). "This fabulous book offers a unique look at how people are connected through their choices and their actions. As the story unfolds, my students recognize how each character is, in some manner, related or joined to another. They also understand how profoundly the characters' actions are like the ripples surrounding a stone landing in water, creating one ripple and then another and another. As a class, we discuss how we influence our environments both directly and indirectly through actions and words—developing an awareness of the most basic element of the community: each member influences the whole." Georgia selects this book as her initial read-aloud to create a community of trust. She demonstrates her thinking during the first two chapters of the book, making it clear that other readers might see the story and characters differently. As she contributes personal comments to the discussion, Georgia allows students to recognize her willingness to take a risk by sharing aloud thoughts and ideas, even if they are tentative. She believes "*The Heavenly Village* works well because it is fairly short and the characters portray identifiable emotions easily grasped by the seventh graders. It is a novel that can be interpreted on many levels. Rylant wastes no time moving readers through a tapestry of interrelated lives." By the end of the book, Georgia's students have become more comfortable speaking to one another, sharing, and disagreeing with respect.

As we choose our first read-alouds of the year, some of the questions we consider are What do we want our first read-aloud to do? What do we hope will linger? Will we introduce a newly published book to avoid enthusiasm dampened by "We heard that last year!" or will we select a book we have read aloud previously? If we're reading aloud an old favorite, why have we made that decision? What responses do we anticipate—laughter, tears, questions? What kinds of connection making might the read-aloud promote? How might our choice captivate students who seem less enthralled with books? How might the read-aloud launch us into writing? Into content area inquiry? There's certainly no one purpose for choosing a specific book for reading aloud—especially at the beginning of the year—but reading a book aloud with no reason (even if it's just for fun) seems like a missed opportunity. As you contemplate what to read aloud during the first few weeks of school, consider focusing on one of the following purposes as they relate to building community, and then select literature accordingly:

⊡ Choose read-alouds to introduce yourself.

⊡ Choose read-alouds that make listeners think and feel.

⊡ Choose read-alouds that provoke interesting and rich conversation.

⊡ Choose read-alouds that inspire reading, writing, and learning.

⊡ Choose read-alouds that echo and affirm the joys and rigors of childhood, adolescence, and learning.

If you're curious about what other teachers read aloud to build community, and desirous of seeking new books or titles you maybe haven't thought about, take note of the suggestions several teachers have provided in the following section, along with their reasons for selecting a particular book or books. As you read through their recommendations for first-of-the-year read-alouds, you'll discover how different books serve different purposes. You'll also notice the wide variety of literature, including some brand-new publications and some tried-and-true books. There are as many benefits to beginning a new school year with a desire to develop relationships as there are books. Rather than become paralyzed by too many possibilities, we suggest you take the advice of sixth-grade teacher Barry Hoonan: "Begin with a book you're thrilled to share or one you feel you can rely on—a book that brings out the best of your thinking and living to examine and share with your students. The kids will follow. Nothing beats passion, and starting the year passionately sends a message that school is a place to live passionately."

Read-Alouds to Build Community at the Beginning of the Year

At the beginning of the year, I read *Wemberly Worried* by Kevin Henkes [2000] and we talk about our worries. I also read *The Blanket That Had to Go* by Nancy Evans Cooney [1984] about a girl who discovers that she can't take her blanket to school, so she cuts it smaller and smaller until it fits into her pocket. Then I give students a small piece of blue fabric, just the size of the blanket in the book. I tell them they can put it in their desk or pocket and rub it any time they need to, and they do! It lets me know when they are feeling a little apprehensive about some new skill we are learning. I read and re-read my all-time favorite "old" book *The Little Engine That Could* by Watty Piper [1930/1978] and we talk about all the new things we will learn this year. And, I read aloud *Ramona the Pest* by Beverly Cleary [1968] because the children still love hearing about this silly kindergartner. Some books are timeless.

—CHERYL PERKINS, first-grade teacher, Shanghai, China

When choosing my first read-aloud, I love to begin with something of high interest, such as *Each Little Bird That Sings* [2005] or *Love, Ruby Lavender* [2001], both by Deborah Wiles. Because literature plays such a profound role throughout the entire year, it is essential for me to share with my students the power and wonder of literature right away. Choosing books with strong male characters such as *The Jacket* by Andrew Clements [2002] is helpful in the beginning because it's often the boys who need to be hooked and to value our literature-rich environment. Books dealing with social justice, such as *So B. It* by Sarah Weeks [2004], *Becoming Naomi Leon* by Pam Muñoz Ryan [2004], or *Maniac Magee* by Jerry Spinelli [1990] have been great leadoffs in the year because of the discussions we have around community and issues of respect and responsibility.

—SARAH DUNKIN, fourth- and fifth-grade teacher
and literacy coach, Beaverton, Oregon

I begin the year by reading *The War with Grandpa* by Robert Kimmel Smith [1984] because the protagonist is a fifth grader whose teacher's name is Mrs. Klein (even spelled the same as mine). This book deals with several issues that are perfect for discussion—communication within a family, life changes, death—but it's humorous in places, too. Later in the year, I refer to this book to teach several writing minilessons—for example, we examine sentence fluency from one chapter where the entire page is one long sentence and from another chapter where each sentence is only one to three words long.

—ANNE KLEIN, fifth-grade teacher, Edmonds, Washington

There have been years when the comfort of a well-worn and well-known book seems just right. This past year I reached into my bag of "can't misses" and pulled out Barbara Park's *Mick Harte Was Here* [1995]. I know this book so well I can recite the opening two pages without looking. "Just let me say it was a bike accident, it was about as accidental as it gets. . . ." Eighty pages of roller-coasting emotions and less than two weeks later my students and I have bonded. We've talked about life matters—about family, troubles, death, confusion, God, even the all-consuming "If only I had . . ." pondering we all muddle through as we grow up and experience making mistakes. Isn't it nice to provide that initial experience through the safety net of excellent literature and discussions?

—BARRY HOONAN, sixth-grade teacher, Bainbridge Island, Washington

The very first book I read is *The Way to Start a Day* by Byrd Baylor [1978]. This sets the tone right away because we write quick responses to the book and then talk about how we intend to start our school year and our time together. It's only a short introduction, but it gets us talking right off the bat. I then read aloud *Pictures of Hollis Woods* by Patricia Reilly Giff [2002] for several reasons. My students are expected to read *When Zachary Beaver Came to Town* by Kimberly Willis Holt [1999] over the summer. I believe both of these books provide an opportunity to reflect on and wonder about themselves—a common theme for seventh grade. Students change so much physically, emotionally, and socially at this age. Based on their actions and their writing I see how they're constantly at odds with themselves and their peers as they try to understand who they are. I believe these novels give students a starting point to think about themselves and how they might respond in similar situations.

—MARIANNE RICHARDSON, seventh-grade English/language arts teacher, Newnan, Georgia

I always read aloud a selection that has to do with names from *The House on Mango Street* by Sandra Cisneros [1994]. We then follow with a name activity to build community by getting to know each other. The first couple of weeks I read excerpts from different young adult novels—both new releases and classic young adult literature—to spark students' reading interests. These titles and authors then go on the wall under a "Ms. LeJeune Recommends" banner. I also start the year with some picture book read-alouds, beginning with a sophisticated book like *Pink and Say* by Patricia Polacco [1994c], so that students realize right away that picture books have something to offer high school students, or with fun books like *A Bad Case of Stripes* by David Shannon [1998a], *Hunwick's Egg* by Mem Fox [2005], or anything by Mo Willems, just to give us something to laugh about.

—MARIE LEJEUNE, high school English teacher, Las Vegas, Nevada

Our year begins with reading aloud *The Library Dragon* by Carmen Agra Deedy [1994] to students at all grades. This book offers an excellent introduction to the library, a librarian, and caring for books. It also has "hot vocabulary" and idioms and puns. I love referring to myself as the Library Dragon throughout the year when I see kids mistreating books. Another great read-aloud for young children to promote discussion on library use is *What Happened to Marion's Books?* by Brook Berg [2003]. And then there's *Wild About Books* by Judy Sierra [2004], read to kids in all grades because it has a librarian as the star! It also introduces the different genres found in a library, which results in a library tour to discover where the genres are located, and serves as a great springboard to poetry and learning about Dr. Seuss.

—LISA WILLIAMS, elementary school librarian, Beaverton, Oregon

The presence of literature to value individuality and honor uniqueness

Written and oral responses to literature, especially at the beginning of the year, can explicitly teach the process of thinking and creating as readers and writers. As it does, students discover how literature offers connectedness to who they are, inspiration for their own creations, as well as implicit lessons that writers and illustrators teach as they reveal what's possible. When we read aloud literature with the express purpose of inspiring conversation and writing about our uniqueness, we strengthen the connections between books, ideas, and individuals. We also offer support as students move from process to product fairly quickly, resulting in gratification and the belief in their abilities to write something worthy of being read. When literature's presence motivates children to express themselves with clarity and honesty, we understand its value not only as a member of the classroom but also as a means that helps us create our community.

Inviting students to introduce themselves through books allows for an early-in-the-year focus on the relationships we have with literature. Barry Hoonan begins each school year asking his sixth graders to bring in their favorite materials they like to read on their own. Students meet in small groups or with a partner to discuss what they enjoy about reading and why they have chosen this specific literature. Barry calls this connection of readers and literature Declare Your Literacy, and he allocates time for discussions as well as honors the ways these informal conversations make a statement about literature and personal taste.

Over the years, we've seen many examples of student writing that have been adapted from patterns in literature. One common book for such writing is Margaret Wise Brown's *The Important Book* (1949). Reading aloud each page introduces Brown's pattern as she defines and describes everyday objects, from spoons to snow to shoes.

> The important thing about a shoe is that you put your foot in it.
> You walk in it,
> and you take it off at night,
> and it's warm when you take it off.
> But the important thing about a shoe is you put your foot in it.

As students hear these descriptions, they pick up on the pattern, realizing that each item is described with four qualities and of the four, one is the most important. That description is stated as the first sentence and is then repeated as the last. Using this pattern to introduce themselves, students can write a quick description of who they are and what they care about.

> The important thing about Max is that he likes to play baseball.
> He likes to read and draw.
> He collects baseball cards
> and thinks Ichiro is the best hitter ever.
> But the important thing about Max is he likes to play baseball.

Once students have drafted their "important things about me" poem, they can design a border or illustrate their own page to offer a visual introduction to accompany the words. These can be compiled in a class book or displayed on a bulletin board. Similarly, students can interview each other, learning about a classmate's interests, unique features, family, and favorite experiences and then borrow *The Important Book* pattern to write about their classmate.

When second- and third-grade teacher Leanne Nordstrom guides her students' first autobiographical writing of the year, she borrows a format from literature, such as a riddle, for the model. Riddles offer a short, focused frame to present individual traits and interests as well as to attract readers' involvement as they guess the writer from the clues. Before inviting students to write, Leanne immerses them in riddles with books like Lillian Morrison's *Guess Again: Riddle Poems* (2006), Susan Joyce's *ABC School Riddles* (2001), and *Elephants in the Bathtub and Other Silly Riddles* (2006) with its lift-the-flap pages that reveal the riddle answers. These lively brainteasers are engaging and fun—and they invite active reader participation. After reading aloud a number of riddles and discussing their components, Leanne reveals a process for riddle writing, first by demonstrating how she gathers ideas on a planning sheet (see Figure 2.1) and then how she selects from these ideas to write an autobiographical riddle.

Traits	**Things I Like to Do**
*kind	play the piano
funny	go on vacation with my family
sometimes shy	play with our dog
good friend	tease my husband
mysterious	*teach kids to read
musician	sing
quiet	*read mysteries
slim	*sleep in
outdoor lover	run
*friendly	go camping
curly-haired	*eat Cherry Garcia ice cream

Autobiography Riddle (Template)

_____ and _____,
I like to _____.
I also like to _____ and _____.
But, my favorite thing to do is _____.
Who am I?

Riddle About Me

Friendly and kind,
I like to eat Cherry Garcia ice cream.
I also like to sleep in and ready mysteries.
But, my favorite thing to do is teach.
Who am I?
(Mrs. Nordstrom)

FIG 2.1 *Autobiography Riddle Planning Sheet and Template*

Once Leanne's students create their lists of traits and favorite things they like to do, she asks them to star three or four items in each column. Then they partner with a classmate and share what they starred, explaining why those particular qualities matter to them. This informational conversation serves as a test run and an introduction. As the children talk about the starred items, they discover whether these really do represent who they are or if there might be something else on their list to substitute. Then they use the autobiography riddle template to draft their actual riddle, with a reminder to read it aloud to make sure the ideas sound good and make sense. Students handwrite their riddle on a clean page and draw a self-portrait on a six-by-six-inch piece of white paper. The riddles are glued to the upper half of a large sheet of construction paper and the portraits are secured about two inches below, with a flap attached over the top to keep the portrait hidden. As classmates read the riddles, they pause to make a guess after reading the last line, "Who am I?" and then lift the flap to reveal the author of the riddle.

A month or two later, Leanne returns to the riddle poems with a new opportunity—to incorporate a grade-level focus on oral language (interviewing) into the creation of a book of riddles about important people in the school. Using the same template, students work in teams to interview school personnel (e.g., principal, secretary, janitor, crossing guard, librarian), then write riddles, illustrate portraits, and publish *Riddles About Special People at Woodbury School*. This book will reside in the front office of the school, available to visitors who wish to learn more about the school community.

Literature's presence to spark response, especially for writing about uniqueness and individuality, not only suggests possible formats for writing but also helps shape topics. Last summer Kate was introduced to Wendy Ewalt's *The Best Part of Me: Children Talk About Their Bodies in Pictures and Words* (2002), a book she knew would provoke discussion with her fifth graders. She saw rich potential in this collection of prose and poetry written by fifteen third, fourth, and fifth graders who offer observations about their favorite body part ("I love my neck for all the things it can do. It connects to my lovely face and to my strong body"). Kate felt confident this book would ignite discussion about self-esteem and valuing unique personal qualities and inspire her students to take a close-up look at their own special qualities and then write about what they selected. Kate first read aloud selected excerpts from the book and showed the design of each page. Her students discussed how the individual selections were hand printed and accompanied by a black-and-white photograph, offering a written and visual voice from each contributor (see Figure 2.2). Kate immersed her students in the book—in the writers' ideas and in its presentational format—before any writing began. What resulted was the first polished piece of writing for the year, poetry

My Eyes

My eyes are dark brown just like my Mom's, Dads, and brothers. My eyes look like dirt, but without the worms. My glasses are the same color as my eyes. But the only difference is my glasses shimmer more and are a lighter brown. My eyes are the size that I like. I like my eyes and the color they are which I would not want to change.

FIG 2.2 *Garrett's "Best Part of Me" Piece*

and prose that mimicked the style found in *The Best Part of Me* and was published along with sepia-toned photographs as a "Best Part of Portable A" bulletin board located on the interior wall of the main school building.

What Benefits Exist When We Partner Literature with Community Building?

The creation of class books and bulletin boards is one way for individual students to construct products accessible to the class. When such collaborations are shared with an audience other than their classmates—for example, when students display their writing in the halls of the school or read their *Riddles About Special People* book to their kindergarten buddies—they create an identity outside the classroom. What happens inside the classroom, especially when literature plays a role, is more subtle, yet still definitive. It may come in the form of shared language that grows out of the class read-aloud, such as when Kate's students fell in love with the word *putrid* during the reading of Sharon Creech's *Ruby*

Holler (2002) and wove it into their conversations and writing, or how they identified their class through the picture book *Skippyjon Jones* (Schachner 2003), first heard in early September, then requested repeatedly throughout the year (including Jon's strong appeal in late October of "You *have* to read it to Kelly!" referring to a student who had recently transferred to Portable A from another school), and finally brought "on the road" to other classes later in the year in the form of readers' theatre. This class defined themselves by a picture book; Kate claimed it became their theme book, a book they all knew by heart (and in their hearts) by year's end, a book they will always associate with fifth grade.

Another way to build community with literature is to read aloud books with a specific focus on school. Some of our favorites include books about the first day of school (see Figure 2.3), books about the school and classroom as a community (see Figure 2.4), and poetry about school (see Figure 2.5).

The presence of literature to establish beliefs, values, and expectations

When Megan reads aloud Peggy Rathmann's Caldecott Medal–winning *Officer Buckle and Gloria* (1995) in September, she encourages her first and second graders to pay close attention, not just to the story but also to the illustrations, including the endpapers. As they do, they discover the book is filled with rules,

---

Countdown to Kindergarten, by Alison McGhee. Illus. Harry Bliss. San Diego: Harcourt, 2002.

First Day, Hooray! by Nancy Poydar. New York: Holiday House, 2000.

First Day Jitters, by Julie Danneberg. Illus. Judith Dufour Love. Watertown, MA: Charlesbridge, 2000.

Get Ready for Second Grade, Amber Brown, by Paula Danziger. Illus. Tony Ross. New York: Putnam, 2002.

Ham and Pickles: First Day of School, by Nicole Rubel. San Diego: Harcourt, 2006.

Junie B., First Grader (at Last!), by Barbara Park. Illus. Denise Brunkus. New York: Random House, 2001.

Miss Bindergarten Gets Ready for Kindergarten, by Joseph Slate. Illus. Ashley Wolff. New York: Dutton, 1996.

Miss Mingo and the First Day of School, by Jamie Harper. Cambridge, MA: Candlewick, 2006.

Mr. Ouchy's First Day, by B. G. Hennessy. Illus. Paul Meisel. New York: Putnam, 2006.

Vera's First Day of School, by Vera Rosenberry. New York: Holt, 2003.

FIG 2.3 *Books About the First Day of School*

The Best School Year Ever, by Barbara Robinson. New York: HarperCollins, 1994.

David Goes to School, by David Shannon. New York: Scholastic, 1999.

Dear Mr. Rosenwald, by Carole Boston Weatherford. Illus. R. Gregory Christie. New York: Scholastic, 2006.

Flying Solo, by Ralph Fletcher. New York: Yearling, 2000.

Mr. Lincoln's Way, by Patricia Polacco. New York: Philomel, 2001.

My Name Is Maria Isabel, by Alma Flor Ada. Illus. K. Dyble Thompson. New York: Simon and Schuster, 1993.

The Name Jar, by Yangsook Choi. New York: Knopf, 2001.

One Green Apple, by Eve Bunting. Illus. Ted Lewin. New York: Clarion, 2006.

The School Story, by Andrew Clements. Illus. Brian Selznick. New York: Simon and Schuster, 2001.

Sideways Stories from Wayside School, by Louis Sachar. Illus. Adam McCauley. New York: HarperCollins, 1985.

Star of the Week, by Barney Saltzberg. Cambridge, MA: Candlewick, 2006.

FIG 2.4 *Books About School and Classroom as Community*

I Thought I'd Take My Rat to School: Poems from September to June, selected by Dorothy M. Kennedy. Illus. Abby Carter. Boston: Little, Brown, 1993.

My Name Is Jorge: On Both Sides of the River, by Jane Medina. Illus. Fabricio Vanden Broeck. Honesdale, PA: Wordsong/Boyd Mills, 1999.

No More Homework! No More Tests! Kids' Favorite Funny School Poems, by Bruce Lasky. Illus. Stephen Carpenter. Minnetonka, MN: Meadowbrook, 1997.

Put Your Eyes Up Here: And Other School Poems, by Kalli Dakos. Illus. G. Brian Karas. New York: Simon and Schuster, 2003.

School Supplies: A Book of Poems, by Lee Bennett Hopkins. Illus. Renee Carpenter. New York: Simon and Schuster, 1996.

Schoolyard Rhymes, selected by Judy Sierra. Illus. Melissa Sweet. New York: Knopf, 2005.

There's a Zoo in Room 22, by Judy Sierra. Illus. Barney Saltzberg. San Diego: Voyage/Harcourt, 2000.

What a Day It Was at School! by Jack Prelutsky. Illus. Doug Cushman. New York: Greenwillow, 2006.

FIG 2.5 *Poetry About School*

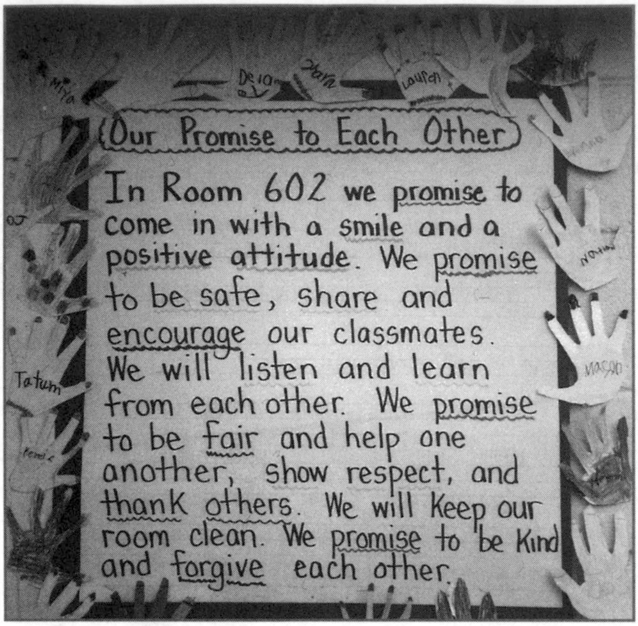

FIG 2.6 *Megan's Class Promise*

expectations, and safety tips. Capitalizing on this concept, Megan asks her students to think about the tips they would recommend in order for their classroom to run smoothly. She encourages them to think about how they want to be treated, how to conduct themselves in school and on the playground, even what they want from each other. One year she also read aloud Todd Parr's *Peace Book* (2004) as a springboard to discuss the kind of people the students wanted to be. The children mentioned being kind to one another and respecting differences, qualities that found their way into the collaborative writing that Megan called their class promise (see Figure 2.6). She was adamant: "I am not a rule maker, so we create[d] a promise to each other." This promise was posted on the classroom wall, framed by the students' own handprints and referred to throughout the year as a shared commitment to each other.

What Can Authors and Illustrators Teach Us About Creating Community?

While children's book authors and illustrators are vital and valued members of our classrooms, they also provide readers with an understanding of communities, both real and fictional, past or present. There is an old adage, "Books take you places," that certainly applies to children's literature. We will never be able to go back in time to medieval England, but after reading the rich descriptive passages in *Crispin: The Cross of Lead*, by Avi (2002), or Karen Cushman's *Catherine, Called Birdy* (1994), readers will become steeped in the story's events and disgusted by the living conditions. Or they can experience the adventure and hardships of life on the Oregon Trail through Jane Kurtz's slim chapter book *I'm Sorry, Almira Ann* (2001) or Ann Turner's poems in *Mississippi Mud: Three Prairie Journals* (1997). Author Mari Takabayashi takes readers across the ocean to discover more about Japanese life and customs in *I Live in Tokyo* (2004). And Bryan Collier explores the sights and sounds of Harlem through visual images, unique patterns, and vibrant colors in *Uptown* (2000). He shares his process in creating this picture book in the "Conversation with . . . author-illustrator Bryan Collier" section that appears at the end of this chapter. Authors and illustrators inform us about their communities through appealing text and varied illustrative styles.

Authors and illustrators are a necessary and essential part of our literate lives. They are the reason books exist. They provide us with stories and art that amaze and delight us as readers, and they influence the work we do in the classroom. Throughout our professional careers, we've been fortunate to meet a number of children's book authors and illustrators. We share with our students how we learned the inspiration for Beezus' name when we were graciously invited into Beverly Cleary's home to interview her for an article in *Book Links* magazine; how an animated dinner conversation with David Wiesner offered nuance and insight into his award-winning book, *Flotsam* (2006); and how we sat on the couch in Doreen Rappaport's apartment in Manhattan, learning firsthand how she conducts research for her books. We share these anecdotes with students because it creates an understanding for them that these individuals are real, interesting, passionate about what they do, and often have a great sense of humor. It also creates their strong presence in our classroom and solidifies authors and illustrators as members of our community.

As Joanne Hindley states in *In the Company of Children*, "I want the year my students and I spend together to be one that we will forever remember. Yes, I want them to remember literature discussions, and writing projects, and mathematical investigations, but what will make them memorable is that they are learned and shared in a community of people. It is in building this community that we will lay the foundation for a year of academic learning but also for learning about people and the way we live in the world together" (1996, 7). That building of community can be accomplished through literature that is our partner in teaching and learning.

J. Patrick Lewis' poem "Are You a Book Person?" in *Please Bury Me in the Library* (2005) seems a natural metaphor for the stance we take in creating classrooms where literature serves as an active member. But the physical presence of literature isn't enough. It needs the reader ("You're the fuse") to give it life and to enhance its role in our classrooms. Because we believe in literature's characteristics of heart and wisdom to impact learning, we also see how it can define each year's class. Most teachers seek to create an optimal learning environment, one that is friendly, inclusive, responsive to students' rich experiences, supportive of growth over time, and understanding of the risks and challenges inherent in learning. Including literature to shape this environment helps to establish the communities we value.

Professional Literature Cited

Anderson, Richard C., Elfrieda Hiebert, Judith Scott, and Ian A. G. Wilkinson. 1985. *Becoming a Nation of Readers*. Washington, DC: National Institute of Education.

Fisher, Carol J., and Barbara Elleman. 1984. "The Read Aloud Remedy." *Instructor* (January): 66–68.

Fox, Mem. 2001. *Reading Magic: Why Reading Aloud to Our Children Will Change Their Lives Forever*. Illus. Judy Horacek. San Diego: Harvest/Harcourt.

Giorgis, Cyndi, and Nancy J. Johnson. 1999. "Reading Aloud." *The Reading Teacher* 53 (1): 80–87.

Hindley, Joanne. 1996. *In the Company of Children*. York, ME: Stenhouse.

Huck, Charlotte S. 1987. "To Know the Place for the First Time." *The Best of the Bulletin* (1): 69–71.

Michener, Darlene, M. 1988. "Test Your Reading Aloud I.Q." *The Reading Teacher* (11): 118–22.

Serafini, Frank, and Cyndi Giorgis. 2003. *Reading Aloud and Beyond: Fostering the Intellectual Life with Older Readers*. Portsmouth, NH: Heinemann.

Trelease, Jim. 2006. *The Read-Aloud Handbook*. 6th ed. New York: Penguin.

Conversation with . . .
Author-illustrator Bryan Collier

Bryan Collier takes us on a walk through his Coretta Scott King Honor Award book, **Uptown**. We invite you to come along on this visual stroll through the community of Harlem.

You have stated that **Uptown**, *the first book you wrote and illustrated, is one of your favorites. Why did you decide to share your community of Harlem through a picture book format?*

Initially, I only wanted to illustrate a book. My editor, Laura Godwin at Holt, wanted me to write it first. I had never written a book. That was ten years ago and I had no idea about format or even how many pages were in a children's book. I never paid attention. I'm an artist—just paint it and turn it in. So, the writing part was the first stumbling block. Laura said, "Write about what you know." What does that mean, write about what you know? I had to ponder that for a while and say, "OK, what *do* I know? What do I know about my neighborhood?" So I took a walk. I looked at the architecture and the indoor and outdoor spaces in my neighborhood. When I saw the park, I thought, "I can paint that park." I eat at a lot of restaurants. I know about chicken and waffles, so I can paint that. What else did I know about my neighborhood? I know the first time I saw a brownstone I thought about how beautiful and wonderful it was. It looked like it [was] made of chocolate because it was brown. I noticed that wonderful, double meaning. So I made the brownstones out of chocolate bars in *Uptown*. We are talking about visuals, about sound and taste, and about the music of Harlem. Harlem of yesterday. Harlem of the present. I tried to bridge those two gaps. The book is like this little kid walking through Harlem. At the end, eventually he says, "Uptown is home and this is my neighborhood." *Uptown* was a little love note to my neighborhood.

Your editor encouraged you to tell a story through both text and illustration.

My whole approach to storytelling is like being lost in the forest and having to figure my way out. That's the exciting part; there is no map. But writers and readers have instincts and intuitions and they have to trust that inner voice. With standardized tests, kids look for X, Y, and Z and that's it. These tests do not ask children to feel and they are not asking teachers to feel either. I think the learning comes first, only when your heart submits to the text. Your spirit says, "Oh I feel that text." Then it comes alive. Reading should conjure up thousands and thousands of images. With so much focus on testing, children are not taught to do that.

In *Uptown*, I don't want readers to just see a little boy walking through Harlem. I want them to see the colors, to feel the rhythm happening, to look and read on a lyrical and whimsical level. There are other things happening—metaphors, subliminal ideas. That's why picture books are so powerful, but they haven't always been given their due. In picture books things are unspoken, but they happen. In *Uptown*, the boy wakes up, looks out the window, and sees the red awning. On the next page he is under the red awning in the same building having chicken and waffles. The brownstones are not mentioned in the text, but they appear visually for the first time on that page. One page introduces the next in many ways and that's intentional as visual stories are told.

Don't readers need the text as well as the illustrations?

With every good picture book, you should be able to take the words out and the visual story should stand alone. There is a parallel between text and the visuals and they should run side by side. Every time a kid reads the book, or anyone reads the book, they should bring something new to make each reading slightly different, slightly more alive. So twenty years from now you can come back to this book with twenty years' more experience and you should read it differently. Now, that's an alive book! It's grown and changed as you've changed. When you reminisce and conjure up the past, you make a bridge between your childhood and adulthood, and an amending takes places. No textbook can do that for you. That's something that you live and experience.

How did you learn to tell a story through a book with your art?

When I was in school and the teacher spoke, I would see the actual words float out of her mouth. I thought something was up with me, and I couldn't articulate. I would look around, and say, "Did you see that?" When I was read to in school, I would go zoooom. I was gone. Oftentimes, I would change the story in my mind as the teacher was reading it. If the kid was going on a sleigh ride, I'd make it a sleigh ride with hyperspeed. So I've always seen stories as pictures.

As you take readers on a walk through Harlem, it seems that you introduce them to this place or, if they are familiar with that community, remind them of what exists.

The Apollo Theater is the center of Harlem. My grandfather says jazz and Harlem are a perfect match, just like chicken and waffles. There are a lot of motifs happening in the illustrations that foreshadow something else coming down the road. *Uptown* is like a caterpillar and becomes a metamorphosis during the boy's walk through the neighborhood.

You were a painter before becoming an illustrator. How did you make that transition to telling a story through a book, rather than a story through one piece of art?

I took some graduate courses in filmmaking at Columbia. Also, my grandmother made quilts. So I bring both resources to my collage. With telling stories, you piece each page together and make it relate from one page to the next and the next. It doesn't have to be a linear flow. It can be something metaphorical, very subtle and lucid. My biggest goal is to try and think of what the reader is thinking when they read this text, and then surprise them.

Uptown, by Bryan Collier. New York: Holt, 2000.

Side by Side by Side
Literature/Teacher/Learner: Life Lessons

Book

Carlson, Nancy. 1994. *Life Is Fun*. New York: Viking.

> To be happy on earth, this book suggests following these simple instructions: Don't bring snakes inside the house; be nice to the nerdy kid next door—and to any space creatures you may meet; laugh a lot; and, most importantly, make big, big plans.

Related literature

Cookies: Bite-Size Life Lessons, by Amy Krouse Rosenthal. Illus. Jane Dyer. New York: HarperCollins, 2006.

How to Lose All Your Friends, by Nancy Carlson. New York: Viking, 1993.

What Pets Teach Us: Life's Lessons Learned from Our Best Friends. Minocqua, WI: Willow Creek, 2006.

Teaching Response

Kate Norem introduces *Life Is Fun* by gathering her fifth graders on the carpet and beginning to read: "To be happy on Earth, follow these simple instructions!" Occasionally she pauses and asks what her students notice about these lessons related to friendship. Dustin finds many are somewhat serious ("Remember to wash your ears"). Stuart suggests that some also seem funny and he wonders if the author meant to be funny or if it's the illustrations that make the serious advice seem humorous ("Be nice to yourself"). Kate continues reading aloud, allowing time for students to linger, notice, and read the illustrations as well as the words. A book like this one, simple in structure and content, could easily be dismissed for fifth graders. But Kate understands that Nancy Carlson's instructions offer some lessons about life that directly relate to what she values about building community, honoring individuality, and creating a place for fun and seriousness. She also chooses this book to inspire her students' own writing about life lessons.

During the second reading, Kate asks students to notice whether any of the tips start with *Don't*. They also pay close attention to the language of the lessons as well as clarify ways that the author-illustrator pokes some fun at people whose behavior ruins rather than builds friendships and also offers some tried-and-true instructions for life. Kate capitalizes on her students' ten-plus years of experience on earth by suggesting they will all contribute to a class book called *Life Lessons from Portable A*. Borrowing from the some-are-funny-and-some-are-serious format used by Nancy Carlson, students create a list of five to ten life lessons, things they've learned and would suggest as valuable tips for others, based on their own lives. Before they begin their lists, Kate thinks aloud a few ideas she *might* include on her list and requests some suggestions. Just as she recommends for her students' writing, some of her lessons are serious, some are silly, and none begins with *Don't*. Students then embark on their own list making, eventually rereading their life lessons and starring the two or three they will contribute to the class book.

Student Response

Figures 2.7 and 2.8 show two students' contributions to *Life Lessons from Portable A*.

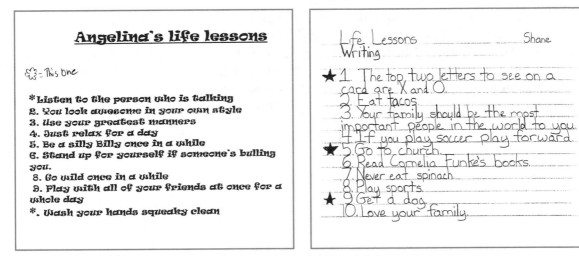

FIG 2.7 *Angelina's Life Lessons*   FIG 2.8 *Shane's Life Lessons*

Jan 31

Dear Miss Norem.
I just started the best book in the world! It is called The Direy of Anne Frank. The difference between This direy and Dear America books is that this was writton by a real girl. This book was writton by a young girl in world wore two. This book pulls me in by knowing that what she said really did happen. I love the way Anne Frank dosn't just right her feelings she describes them. There is a sentence in the book that I will remember whenever I look at a bird.

This sentence is This "I look out the window and see birds flying away and think it is unfair that they can fly away and be free." I love that sentence because it reminds me that they couldn't flyaway and how strong she realy was and how people couldn't even show who they where. I am glad things are diffrn't now and I am realy enjoying things now all for now!

Renée

January 31

Renée,
This book is so fabulous! I love it for the same reason you do! Everytime I read it I can't believe it was written by a real girl.

Anne definitely was brave. Sometimes I wonder what I would have done in her situation. Do you wander that? How do you think you would have responded? The Holocaust was such a horrible time in the world's history. When I was your age, I read TONS of books about this subject, so if you want more book recommendations for this subject, I have many. Also, we have a nonfiction book about Anne in our library.

Renée, I cannot wait to read more of your letters and write back to you. I am so interested in your thinking!

Love,
Miss Norem

The Presence of Literature to Nurture Response

Miss Binney . . . read aloud from *Mike Mulligan and His Steam Shovel*. . . . As Ramona listened a question came into her mind, a question that had often puzzled her about the books that were read to her. . . .

"Miss Binney, I want to know—how did Mike Mulligan go to the bathroom when he was digging the basement of the town hall?"

Miss Binney's smile seemed to last longer than smiles usually last. Ramona glanced uneasily around and saw that others were waiting with interest for the answer. Everyone wanted to know how Mike Mulligan went to the bathroom.

"Well—" said Miss Binney at last. "I don't really know, Ramona. The book doesn't tell us."

"I always wanted to know too," said Howie . . . and others murmured in agreement. . . .

Miss Binney faced the twenty-nine earnest members of the kindergarten, all of whom wanted to know how Mike Mulligan went to the bathroom.

"Boys and girls," she began, and spoke in her clear, distinct way. "The reason the book does not tell us how Mike Mulligan went to the bathroom is that it is not an important part of the story. The story is about digging the basement of the town hall, and that is what the book tells us."

Miss Binney spoke as if this explanation ended the matter, but the kindergarten was not convinced. Ramona knew and the rest of the class knew that knowing how to go to the bathroom was important. They were surprised that Miss Binney did not understand, because she had showed them the bathroom the very first thing. Ramona could see there were some things she was not going to learn in school.

—BEVERLY CLEARY, *Ramona the Pest*

Whenever we read Beverly Cleary's books, we're immediately immersed in children's lives, reminded of their sometimes unreasonable fears, their open curiosity and wonder, their hunger to understand, be accepted, and see the world as fair and honest and comforting. Ramona (as well as Beezus, Henry, and the rest of the kids on Klickitat Street) reminds us what kids think about, worry about, and care about. These characters portray childhood's universals and illuminate human needs as relatable, whether the readers are six or sixty, whether they live in rural Kansas or reside in temporary housing, or whether they're new to a neighborhood or even new to this country. As readers make connections to the heart of a story like *Ramona the Pest*, they are reminded of their own feelings of confusion, sometimes related to school, other times related to their family, their friends, even their world. Similarly, readers invested in Deborah Wiles' *Each Little Bird That Sings* (2005), Kevin Henkes' *Julius, Baby of the World* (1990), or even Linda Sue Park's *When My Name Was Keoko* (2002) respond first and foremost to "that reminds me of . . ." connections that draw them into the story. Active reading—reading that elicits response—is participatory. And it promotes comprehension.

Humans seek understanding. We do so when we wrestle with issues at all levels of complexity—we want to understand how to create peace or how to live with differences or why people exhibit hatred. Our response to anything, whether it's newspapers, television, or even each other, is our wide-awake mechanism to get involved. The same is true for readers. They respond by raising questions ("Why doesn't Miss Binney understand Ramona?"). They respond by making connections ("I remember when my teacher read *Mike Mulligan* too!"). They even respond with inference ("I can tell Ramona's feelings are hurt. I bet she won't raise her hand again."). Such responses offer clues into readers' comprehension. They also denote readers' engagement. Both reflect the kinds of rewards that keep people reading, not only to the end of the book but also for the rest of their lives.

Nearly every writer we know values (even hungers for) reader response. In *The Spying Heart*, Katherine Paterson claims, "the author has no right to tell a reader how to read her book. It is the privilege of the reader to discover what a book means for his or her particular life. The book either speaks for itself to the reader, or it fails to speak" (1989, 15). Paterson trusts her readers to understand and make connections; she also reveres response as a reader's "privilege." Paterson continues, "A book is a cooperative venture. The writer can write a story down, but the book will never be complete until a reader of whatever age takes that book and brings to it his [or her] own story" (37).

Katherine Paterson is by no means the only author who honors readers' responses. Karen Cushman's acceptance speech for the 1996 Newbery Medal winner *The Midwife's Apprentice* (1995) acknowledges the reciprocal relationships inherent in response: "Writing for me is feeding each other—writer and reader—fifty-four-year-old me and the young people who pick up my books. Me whispering in their ears and them talking back. They read and I am nourished, and my book becomes something richer and more profound than ever I hoped" (1997, 414). Children's book illustrators also value and respect their readers.

When illustrators Leo and Diane Dillon spoke at the 2005 NCTE Books for Children Luncheon, they said, "The act of illustrating is to clarify or explain. In a picture book you have thirty-two pages to build a world. Our challenge is to attract the reader. When we design the book jacket we do so carefully so that our readers will not go back to the cover and feel they were lied to."

Given this insight into and regard for response by those who write and illustrate the books that create readers, we can't help but wonder:

- What benefits does response have for children learning to read, write, and think?
- How can valuing the privilege of the reader to respond personally shape what we teach?
- What can we learn from authors and illustrators about response?

What Benefits Does Response Have for Children Learning to Read, Write, and Think?

Defining reader response

During graduate school, both of us were fortunate to learn from teachers whose philosophy was shaped by the scholarship and from reading Louise Rosenblatt's groundbreaking (and probably controversial) work *Literature as Exploration* (1938/1996), with its strong stance honoring the transaction between the reader and the text. While we run the risk of simplifying Rosenblatt's ideas, what continues to resonate is her expectation and trust in both the reader and the literature to elicit response and her belief in reading as an experience that is active, creative, and purposeful. Rosenblatt reminded teachers to acknowledge that "reading is always a particular event involving a particular reader at a particular time under particular circumstances" (1991, 445). She sought to explain the difference in stance that readers take when participating in literary and nonliterary reading. And she proposed language to accompany this commonsense philosophy about readers and texts, stating a continuum of stances from efferent (Latin for "to carry away") to aesthetic (Greek for "lived through"). As Rosenblatt reiterates, because there is usually no pure act of reading (entirely efferent or aesthetic), "it becomes important for readers (and writers) to keep their main purposes clear" (1991, 447).

While Rosenblatt denied claims by those who believed she encouraged an anything-goes response, she vehemently supported readers who responded personally, especially as their entry point in comprehending a text. Depending upon purpose, there are times when a personal response is not only adequate but effective, ideal, and enough. There are other times when it simply won't get the job done. Nancy remembers Rosenblatt explaining at a seminar a number of years ago the consequences of readers who don't adjust their response based on purpose. She admonished the recipe reader who makes cookies using an aesthetic stance. "Just imagine the results," Rosenblatt said, "if the reader gets lost in the beauty of words like *cinnamon* and *nutmeg* and *applesauce* instead of paying close attention to the amount required." Bakers create aesthetic pleasures for our taste buds, but they do so when they read recipes efferently!

Rosenblatt's philosophy, and her trust in readers and texts, offers important implications for our teaching:

> Confusion about the purpose of reading has in the past contributed to failure to teach effectively both efferent reading and aesthetic reading. Why not help youngsters learn to understand that there are two ways of reading? We do not want to give them theoretical explanations, nor do we need to. We communicate such understandings by what we do, by the atmosphere and the activities we associate with the two kinds of reading, and by the kinds of questions we ask and the kinds of tests we give. Children who know that the teacher usually quizzes them on factual aspects of a reading, even if it is called "a poem" or "a story," will adopt the efferent stance and will read to register the facts that will be required after the reading. They know that they will be successful and rewarded if they recall the color of the horse or where the bunny hid, rather than if they linger over the experiences and feelings encountered. (Actually, that kind of fragmented questioning doesn't much improve efferent reading, either!) (1991, 447)

Not only does Rosenblatt give us permission to teach readers to adjust their reading strategies based on purpose, but she holds us responsible to rethink the ways we set a purpose for reading (explicitly and implicitly) and how we create opportunities for students to read for authentic reasons (for fun as well as to solve problems). In the classroom this is often subtle and usually quite natural. Returning to Chapter 2 and sixth-grade teacher Barry Hoonan's read-aloud of *Mick Harte Was Here* (Park 1995), we are reminded that Barry chose that book with clear intention. He knew it would elicit discussions "about family, troubles, death, confusion, God, even the all-consuming 'If only I had . . .' pondering we all muddle through as we grow up and make mistakes." Such response—and the trust that developed as a result—did not occur by requiring students to answer multiple-choice questions or create a diorama. It emerged in a classroom guided by a wise teacher who trusted literature and readers to evoke an aesthetic response.

Benefits of response

The advantages for writers and readers when response is valued, encouraged, and respected include

- encouragement to think for themselves and to trust their own ideas

- opportunity for active, strategic reading and writing, with a focus on comprehension (e.g., making connections, raising questions, inferring, synthesizing)

- understanding that the creation of ideas is a process—by honoring first-draft, first-thought reactions and building on these to discover deeper, sometimes more complicated thinking

- realization that literate acts are often subjective

- engagement in the pleasures and rewards of reading, writing, and learning.

The benefits for teachers when student response is valued include

- windows into what students know, can do, and care about and how they think

- surprise and serendipity that allow new insight and extend our understanding, not only about students but also about literacy

- reminders of the complex and wondrous ways that meaning evolves.

Response to reading

If we revisit Ramona Quimby's classroom and attend closely to the kindergartners' responses to *Mike Mulligan and His Steam Shovel*, we notice what Rosenblatt values about reader response and we discover plenty to guide our teaching. By listening (and hearing), we learn not only about our students but also about their understanding (including their misunderstanding). For example, Ramona's question about Mike Mulligan's all-day digging without a bathroom break tells us she paid close attention to her teacher earlier in the day ("Ramona knew . . .

that knowing how to go to the bathroom was important. . . . She was surprised that Miss Binney did not understand, because she had showed them the bathroom the very first thing" [17]), and it demonstrates her ability to make connections and to infer. We can also make a case that her response demonstrates an ability to empathize. After all, going all day without a bathroom break sounds mighty uncomfortable—even to adults!

But, you might argue, this is fiction. What about real classrooms with real learners who respond in ways that don't match what we expect? How can we embrace these responses and use them to inform our teaching? A look into a few classrooms offers insight into the dynamics of response and the benefits it offers learners and teachers.

When Nancy chooses Suzanne Fisher Staples' *Shabanu: Daughter of the Wind* (1989) as required reading for her language arts methods students, she does so believing it will change them as readers and as a community. In this novel, the young daughter of a camel herder living in the Cholistan Desert of Pakistan must reconcile her independent spirit with cultural expectations. Not an easy understanding for any of us. On one level, Nancy chooses this novel because she knows it will prompt heated response and raise questions with no easy answers. On another level, she chooses it as the novel her students will read in community (both small and large groups) as they learn about the practical and theoretical pedagogy of literature circles. If you tracked how many times *Shabanu* has appeared on Nancy's required reading list for this class, you'd notice it's been there for more than ten years. She knows that every time she discusses this book with other readers, she'll discover aspects she never thought about before, and her understanding will be shaped by her students' lives and values as well as events and issues in the world. Nancy's perception of the characters' motivations will deepen, and she'll raise new questions about life in the desert, expectations of young women in a culture so unlike her own, even parents who are forced to make seemingly impossible decisions.

In March, Kate Norem read aloud Patricia Reilly Giff's *Pictures of Hollis Woods* (2002) to her fifth graders, a novel about artistically talented Hollis Woods who makes a habit of running away from foster homes. Kate chose this book not only because it prompted lively, engaged response the previous year but also because it's one of her favorite novels. During much of the read-aloud, Kate's students responded similarly to the previous year's class. They noticed Giff's visually rich language ("eyes the color of cinnamon," "fingers of fog drift over the water," "he folded himself down on the step"), they expressed concern for the characters ("What will happen if people find out about Josie?" "Is Steven dead?" "Why does Hollis always call herself a Mountain of Trouble?"), and they tried to unravel the plot ("Something's going to happen to Steven; I can just tell." "Will Hollis go back to the Reagans?").

This year, near the middle of the book, one student spoke up, responding on behalf of his discussion group: "We don't like this book. We don't see the point in it. There's not a lot of action, just visualizing. In *Ruby Holler* and *Love, Ruby Lavender*, I could write a lot, but in this book I can only draw."

Celina interjected, "I disagree. I like how this book stays with one character."

Brian explained, "I don't live with my parents right now and it's hard for me. I want to know why she's not with her parents. If I was Hollis I'd do lots and lots of research to find out where my parents are."

Jon suggested, "Maybe her parents died."

Phelicia responded, "I expected it to be more adventurous. I like it though."

And then Shane affirmed, "This book does make you draw." These students responded honestly, to the book and to each other. When students reveal their own lives, their tastes as readers, and their connections to other books and to personal experience, we are reminded of Katherine Paterson's wisdom. We learn about the individuals in our classroom and we come to view literature through a new lens.

Response to writing

Response doesn't just involve readers, it also plays a valuable role in our interactions with each other as writers, shaping knowledge about the process, acknowledging the writing-reading relationships, and building on these to revise, rethink, and reveal written products.

When Megan Sloan's first and second graders gather on the carpet during the end of writing workshop and listen to a few of their classmates read something they've written that day, they always have time to respond to each other's ideas. After hearing a classmate's story about her cat's crazy antics, the children comment, "That was funny when your cat drank from the toilet," and "My cat does that too!" Since the students in Megan's class often publish their work in individual and class books, they react in ways similar to how they respond to books read aloud. Megan might even add her own response: "Your story reminded me of my cat when I was your age. I'm wondering where you got the idea to write about that." She asks not only because she's keenly interested but also because she has a hunch this student's writing was inspired from a book she read. Megan knows this is an opportunity to teach the writers in her class how ideas for writing can be inspired from their response to literature and she doesn't want to miss out on this informal lesson.

In February, two of Kate's students gathered at the round table where they met for feedback on their writing. Cameron came with a handful of original poems, a breakthrough genre for him, since earlier in the year he was consumed with writing short chapters about action figures, adventure, and semiviolent situations. The work on his "novel" was put on hold by a whole-class genre study on poetry. Cameron had requested this response conference with his classmate. He proceeded by reading aloud a few short poems, ranging in length from four to six lines and all written with a basic ABAB rhyme pattern. While his response partner was respectful, he was also honest. Cameron's heavy-handed rhyme was distracting, it felt forced, and it got in the way of descriptive and interesting word choice. He suggested that Cameron might want to revise with a focus on powerful word choice and not worry so much about the rhyme. As Cameron took in this suggestion, he retorted, "Nobody ever told me that before. How come nobody ever told me poems don't have to rhyme?" Response—and readiness to hear it—resulted in Cameron's shift as a poet. Soon after, he wrote some unrhymed poems and found success as well as positive response from his classmates. Response to writing, like response to literature, can instruct as well as enlighten.

How Can Valuing the Privilege of the Reader to Respond Personally Shape What We Teach?

Literature is the most natural partner we have for inviting response into our classrooms. If we return to the read-aloud examples shared by classroom teachers in Chapter 2 and focus on the purposes for reading these selections at the beginning of the year, we notice how every book was chosen because it prompted some type of response from the teacher and held the promise of a response from his or her students. Barry Hoonan knows that Barbara Park's *Mick Harte Was Here* (1995) will touch an emotional chord with his sixth graders. He also knows they can readily identify with what happened to Mick because most of Barry's students have ridden a bicycle, and you can bet they've all heard lectures about wearing a bicycle helmet. Similarly, when Cheryl Perkins reads aloud *The Blanket That Had to Go* (Cooney 1984) and distributes small pieces of soft fabric to each of her new students, she expects many will respond not only to the story but to their own apprehension. She affirms and honors her young students' connections by creating a tactile response object to keep the story's theme in mind as they work through their own anxieties and learning challenges. Both Barry and Cheryl have read aloud these books before. They know the stories will elicit genuine response, plenty of discussion, and opportunities to connect to students' own lives. Just as Nancy repeatedly selects *Shabanu*, Barry and Cheryl will continue to choose books they know are response rich. But they will also try new books. They trust what they've learned about response to determine a new book's potential (from their own reading, their students' responses, and even the responses of colleagues, friends, and book reviewers).

If you're an avid reader, you probably already trust your own response to what you read, even if it differs from someone else's. But not all readers are confident in their responses, especially those who've been held hostage by questions such as "What did the author mean when . . .?" or after-reading activities with prescriptive expectations. While we both advocate *teaching* some strategies for response, our patience runs short with scripted programs that expect the same answers and don't trust either the readers or the literature to create unique responses.

Threading response to literature into children's work as readers, writers, and learners

Response is ever present in Megan's classroom. Charts decorate the walls reflecting her students' thinking about books she's read aloud. Kid-created poetry inspired from the poets Megan has introduced appears on tables, in class books, even taped to windows. The author's chair sharing that ends each writing workshop is filled with the sounds of children responding to their classmates' writing. Each read-aloud—whether from a novel, picture book, or poetry collection—echoes Megan's thinking about what she reads and encourages children's participation when she pauses every few pages and asks, "What are you thinking right now?" and "How does this story make you feel?" (see Figure 3.1). In addition, Megan's first and second graders each maintain a reader's notebook where they are expected to write and sketch responses to the books, stories, and poems they've chosen to read during the morning reading workshop.

Classrooms with literature and response threaded together throughout the day exhibit the artful relationship that develops between learners, teachers, and literature. Whenever we linger in classrooms with response at the heart, we discover the presence of literature. We also find it impossible to sit still, captivated by the invitations to participate, learn, create, and discover. There is something infectious about genuine response when it's rich with the voices of literature and learners. How we achieve this response is a direct (and sometimes an indirect) result of choosing response-rich literature, designing interactive read-alouds, and nurturing response to literature as a process and a product.

FIG 3.1 *Students Respond to Texts*

Choosing response-rich literature

The collaboration of literature and reader holds the promise of response. We've heard it said that a book is like a blueprint of a house: It creates a general shape and offers a plan, but it is one-dimensional and lifeless. When a builder takes that blueprint and creates something from it, that's when the magic happens. The same is true for a book: it sits motionless on a shelf, needing a reader to give it life.

Choosing books with the potential for response is one of the most pleasurable aspects of our teaching. The more we know our students, the easier it becomes to select books that speak to their interests and experiences and to trust there will be plenty of "That reminds me of . . ." responses. But knowing your students isn't the only guide you have in choosing books with potential for response. As Rosenblatt suggested, reading can serve as a guide. For example, if we want to encourage young readers to make smart guesses, we might read Deborah Guarino's *Is Your Mama a Llama?* (1989), making sure we linger over Steven Kellogg's illustrations for clues. If we want to inspire careful observation, we might read Peggy Christian's *If You Find a Rock* (2000). If we want to link the real-life childhood of a migrant child to governmental debates, we might read selections from Francisco Jiminez's *The Circuit* (1999).

While all literature holds the potential for response, some books seem richer with possibility. We often refer to these books as "literature with meat on its bones" because of their full, lively potential. Whether we know our students or not, when we choose books for read-alouds, for literature circles, or even for inquiry studies, we read with an eye and an ear toward response, seeking some common qualities to guide us (see Figure 3.2).

Above all, we consider the literature we bring into our classroom in the same way we think about the people who play key roles in our lives. We want variety, quality, heart, and wisdom. We want to be surrounded by different ages, experiences, and interests. We want to learn from others, and we also want to feel affirmed. When author Mem Fox explains what she values from a "terrific book," we notice many qualities similar to what we anticipate from response-rich literature:

> A terrific book matters to us as human beings. It's not terrific for adults or children if it leaves readers unmoved. It *is* terrific if we've had to shift around the furniture in our heads as we've listened, if it has affected us profoundly, one way or another—to laughter or tears, horror or delight, disgust or dismay, fascination or fright. If a book makes children laugh, cry, squeal, shiver, or wriggle and jiggle in some way, it takes up residence in their hearts and stays there. (2001, 125)

Books that prompt response exhibit the following:

Qualities that arouse a reader's interest and emotions

Can readers relate to the characters or issues? Do they care about what happens? Will they hope for a sequel and/or feel some loss at the end of the book? Does the presentation of topic, theme, or issue elicit curiosity and a desire to know more? Are the language and vocabulary lively, interesting, and provocative?

Compelling content

Does the literature offer any elements of action, suspense, or mystery? Does the content prompt curiosity and wonder? Is the dialogue intriguing and does it illuminate the characters, time period, or culture with a fair portrayal? Is there humor or controversial characters and situations or even unexpected events to prompt discussion?

Intriguing format

Does the author offer a unique way to tell a story or present the information? Is the book written as poetry, in letters, as diary entries? Does the format encourage participation? Are there interactive elements, such as pop-ups or flaps that lift?

Realistic characters

Are characters portrayed as round and multidimensional? Do they remind readers of anyone they know? Are there some good-guy and bad-guy characters? Do the characters grow and change?

Strong, colorful illustrations or images that support and extend the story

What medium or style did the illustrator use and why? What do the illustrations or photographs do to present and extend meaning? Does the written description create images in the reader's mind, and if so, what do these images do to help readers understand the story? How do the book's illustrations and/or language give life to the story or information?

FIG 3.2 *Qualities of Response-Rich Literature*   Adapted from *Getting Started with Literature Circles* (Schlick Noe and Johnson 1999, 36)

Nurturing response to literature as process

It is literally impossible to separate response from the processes of thinking, creating, feeling, and discovery. Response not only fosters readers' and writers' thinking but also highlights the value of process as well as product. Because of these natural links, teasing out lessons or activities just to teach response can be challenging. Instead we suggest the following strategies or tools to integrate response naturally into reading and writing processes:

- interactive read-alouds

- response through talk and conversation

- dramatization and role play

- written and sketched response during reading

- author's chair responses

Interactive Read-Alouds

We both spent many years in classrooms where the read-aloud *always* occurred after lunch and before math, and where we were expected to listen with our eyes on the teacher, our feet planted firmly on the floor, and our hands clasped on top of our desks. "No doodling!" and "Pay attention now" echoed in our ears, the only commentary our teachers added to what they were reading. Other than in kindergarten, time to talk about the book and to respond personally either didn't occur or wasn't encouraged. We hope you have discovered (and will continue to discover) ways the read-aloud can become your most trustworthy collaborator in nurturing reader response, especially as you focus on purpose and demonstration.

We think of the read-aloud as the optimal anchor and inspiration for what we teach, mostly through the time set aside before and after the reading for response. Encouraging response doesn't require a list of preplanned questions. In fact, we've found the best encouragement for response to be "So . . .?" followed by silence. We also know wise teachers who take time early in the year to teach a variety of open-ended prompts that students then internalize while they respond to read-alouds, their independent reading choices, and during literature circle discussions.

When Marianne Richardson taught third grade she decided to rethink the role of the read-aloud in her class. She revised not just when she read but the purpose for this whole-class activity. Borrowing from Alice (in *Alice in Wonderland*), who asked: "What's the use of a book without pictures and conversation?" Marianne gave each student a spiral notebook dedicated specifically to the picture book read-alouds. The first day of school she read Byrd Baylor's *The Way to Start a Day* (1978) and asked the children to write and sketch their suggestion for how to start their brand-new school year. She followed the next day by reading *Albert*, by Donna Jo Napoli (2001). Then she read Jim LaMarche's *The Raft* (2000), Anais Vaugelade's *The War* (2001), and Mem Fox's *Wilfrid Gordon McDonald Partridge* (1985). One picture book per day, with time for students to think in writing and in images. Marianne participated, too, as a responsive reader. She demonstrated strategies such as raising questions ("I wonder . . .") and made connections to her own life, to other books, even to what was going on in the world ("That reminds me of the book . . ." and "That reminds me of what's happening in our community when . . .").

As Marianne demonstrated a new strategy and when she noticed a student responding in a new way, she added it to an evolving chart of strategy ideas and open-ended prompts posted on the classroom wall. Because she made time immediately after reading to talk about the words and the illustrations, her students developed an interest in art media as well as story ideas. By the end of the year, the third graders' list of response possibilities was ample and their ability to support and explain their responses to text and illustrations reflected extended comprehension and literary appreciation. And while Marianne never planned for this, the students' read-aloud notebooks became authentic portfolios of their responses over time, offering a glimpse into their individual interactions with selected literature, a reflection of what they were discovering about picture books, and a picture of their developing ability to respond to literature (see Figure 3.3).

When Kate reads aloud, her fifth graders know the time is sacred and won't be rushed. Before she opens the book, Kate allows a minute or two for students to quietly peruse their response notebooks. Then two or three students mention something from the previous day's reading that caught their attention or that seemed puzzling. To aid classmates who missed the previous read-aloud, Kate asks, "Who wants to tell us what we read about yesterday—not all the details, just a quick summary?" As she reads, students sketch, jot down "golden lines," raise questions, or simply sit and listen. Kate understands and respects the different ways students participate as active listeners and she values how this involvement is usually not the result of clasped hands and straight backs. Immediately after she concludes the read-aloud for that day, she says, "Take a minute and write down what you're thinking." Early in the year she might add, "I'll put a few prompts on the board if you need these to get started. Some will look familiar since they're the same ones we used for yesterday's literature circles." Then she writes the following starters on the board: I wish . . . ; I was surprised by . . . ; That reminds me of. . . . Silence ensues as students quick-write or quick-sketch, capturing their immediate response onto the page. As the year progresses, students compile an extensive repertoire of response ideas gleaned from the informal demonstrations Kate offers through her think-alouds, the focus lessons on reading response strategies, open-ended prompts used in literature circle response, and their classmates' responses. They also gain an appreciation for the messiness of immediate response and develop an understanding about how thinking is sometimes a tentative process leading to discoveries and understanding, rather than a fine-tuned product (see Figure 3.4).

Kate allows between three to five minutes for personal, individual response before she interrupts with "Go ahead and lean in with your group to talk." During the next few minutes students share what they're thinking, raise questions, and generally talk with their table group members about what's on their mind at

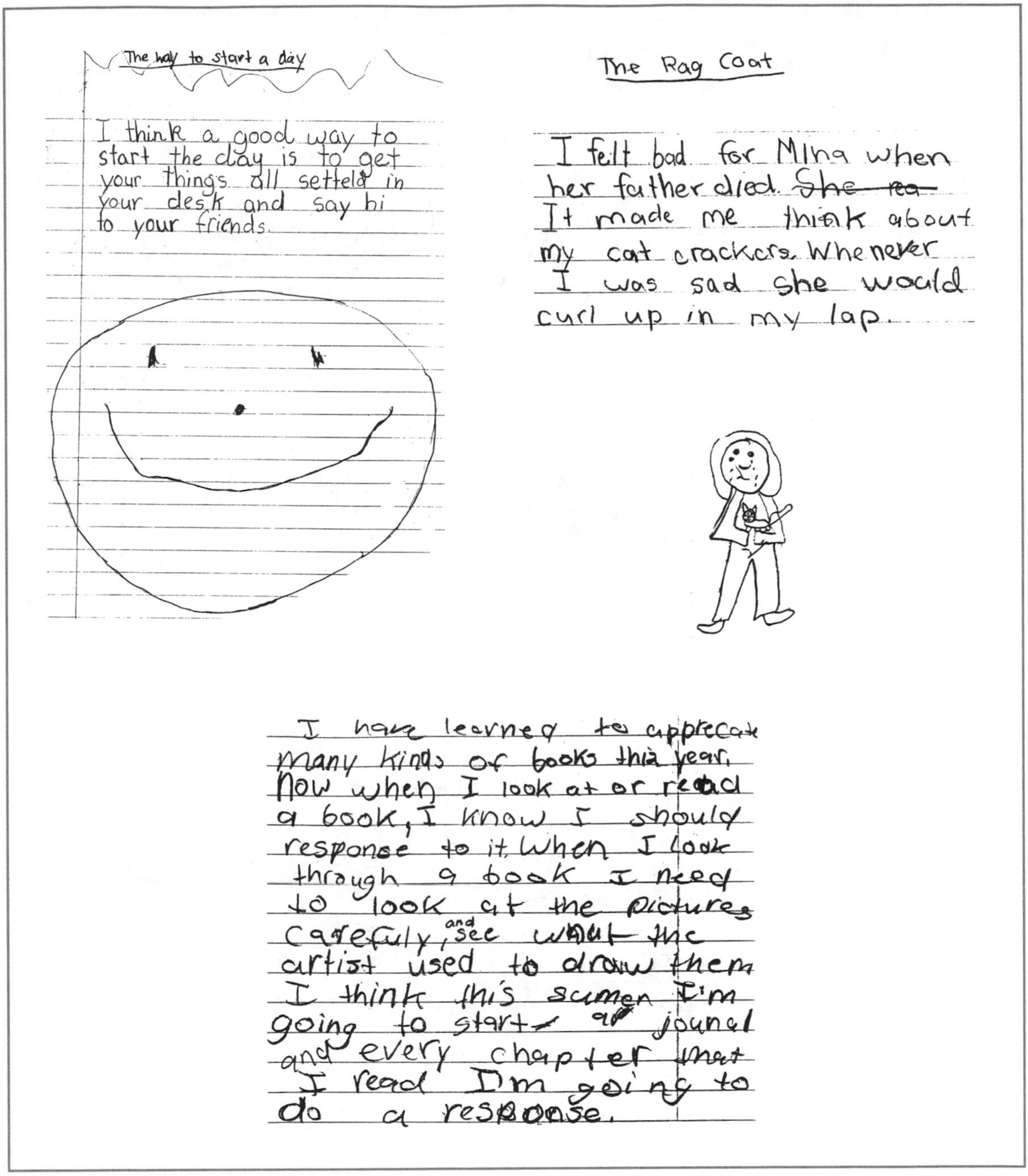

The way to start a day

I think a good way to start the day is to get your things all settled in your desk and say hi to your friends.

The Rag Coat

I felt bad for Mina when her father died. ~~She rea~~ It made me think about my cat crackers. Whenever I was sad she would curl up in my lap.

I have learned to appreciate many kinds of books this year. Now when I look at or read a book, I know I should response to it. When I look through a book I need to look at the pictures carefully, and see what the artist used to draw them. I think this summer I'm going to start a journal and every chapter that I read I'm going to do a response.

FIG 3.3 *Lydia's Read-Aloud Response Entries (First Day, Midyear, and Last Day)*

Love,
Ruby
Lavender
AWESOME
BOOK
prettier
omg

I'm glad ruby is so happy now. there is Not ONE soul she hates now!

I love this Book !!!!!!! !!!!

*Why did Ivys chick take longer to hatch?

* Ya, miss Ula is home!

* Melba is nice! What chagned her atituid!?

* Great ending!

FIG 3.4 *Terra's Response to* Love, Ruby Lavender

that point in the read-aloud. When Kate refocuses the class, she opens the floor for whole-group sharing. One student volunteers, "Our group wondered . . . ," then someone else states, "We disagreed with each other about . . . ," and soon we hear, "Did anybody else notice . . . ?" as students collaboratively make visible their thinking. Kate then guides students to one more written response that signals the conclusion of the read-aloud. She asks students to quickly jot down something they contributed today or something they learned. Her goal isn't to end the discussion time with finite answers. The goal is to develop student response-ability as active, invested listeners who extend and deepen their understanding through individual and shared response.

Like Marianne, Kate gives her students some freedom to discover and experiment with their responses. These freedoms reside within an intentionally designed structure that supports student participation. Instead of constraining or assigning response, the structure allows for time, choice, support, and expectation to think, discover, and create.

Some common features to the interactive read-aloud time include

- time to respond independently and individually (This can occur through silent thinking or through writing or sketching.)

- time to share responses with others

- opportunities to listen to others' responses, including other students and the teacher

It has been four years since Marianne implemented the daily picture book read-alouds. Now she teaches seventh-grade language arts. Many of her students were in the third-grade class when she introduced interactive read-alouds. When we asked about her current teaching, Marianne claimed, "I'm very excited this year. I am teaching students who experienced my dedication to the read-aloud and the response journal. The difference in their approach to the opening of school this year is palpable. They wanted to know immediately if I was going to read aloud and if we were going to respond. They didn't forget, and they were emphatic about returning to reading aloud and response, even though they haven't done it since third grade."

Response Through Talk and Conversation

A writing or sketching response notebook offers a container for individual students' myriad connections, questions, feelings, and visualizations. It captures and reveals in some concrete ways the thinking associated with response. But writing and sketching are not the only effective ways to promote immediate, honest response to the read-aloud. Interacting through talk is both easy and natural, but surprisingly it is the most neglected way to begin developing response strategies.

Talk is often the tool we turn to initially when we respond to a book or movie. Within minutes after Nancy finished reading *Pictures of Hollis Woods* (Giff

2002), she called Cyndi to tell her about it. When eleven-year-old Dylan completed *Saving Shiloh* (1997), the third book in Phyllis Reynold's Naylor's Shiloh trilogy, he sighed deeply and said, "I never want to read a book again. It's so sad, leaving a book." Soon after Megan finished reading aloud Avi's *Poppy* (1999), first grader Robbie responded, "It can't be over. Can you read it again?"

The next time you read a book or poem or story aloud to your students, consider honoring talk as the response form of choice. "Turn to someone close by and talk about what you're thinking" will always result in response, especially if we choose literature worth talking about and when we give students the time to sift and sort out their ideas informally.

Creating time for whole-class responses to the read-aloud encourages a stance of discovery as you and your students track and discuss how different responses enhance and deepen understanding and how they develop over time. When third-grade teacher Adam Miller reads aloud Pam Muñoz Ryan's *Riding Freedom* (1989), his students fill up a large piece of chart paper with their wonderings about the California gold rush, stagecoaches, the story's characters, even which parts of the story were fact and which parts were fiction. Following each day's read-aloud, students talk with a partner about what's on their minds and then collaborate to raise a question. They write the questions on sticky notes, and as response partners attach the notes to chart paper, they explain their wonderings to the rest of the class. Sometimes other students can answer the questions, but most often, the wonderings grow and grow and grow. Before the next read-aloud, Adam reads a few of the questions from the day before to set a purpose for listening. At the end of the book, the class rereads all stickies and then transfers them to a new chart with sections: Questions We Answered, Questions We Still Have, Questions That Don't Matter to Us Anymore.

As we hope the previous examination of the interactive read-aloud shows, allocating time for informal talk in response at any stage in the reading is richly valued. Turning to one or two classmates for a quick chat about a book is natural and pressure free. There is also something incredibly beneficial about these conversations. Time to think aloud, time to test out a prediction, and time to sort and sift ideas motivated by an honest desire to discover and uncover meaning gives rise to the kind of thinking students can and will bring to their independent reading. Informal book chats as well as more organized literary conversations such as literature circles or book clubs (see Chapter 4) provide such opportunities.

We'd be naïve to claim you don't need to do anything to promote literary conversation other than to choose response-rich books, yet sometime that's all it takes. Other times, and for students who don't yet trust their own responses, you might need to introduce some tools to encourage or guide students' conversations.

These don't need to be complex. In fact, the more open-ended the prompt, the better. When Sarah Dunkin reads aloud, she invites literary talk by asking her fourth and fifth graders, "What's bubbling up for you?" This quick question brings to mind the image of thought bubbles with the implication that thinking will evolve, bubble, and brew from all of her students. And it does—if not immediately, then in the development of ideas being tossed around among other readers. Sarah reintroduces this same question for students' informal written and sketched responses as well. "What's bubbling up for you?" implies and invites response, no matter the age, experience, or ability of the reader.

Following are a few other discussion tools we've used with our own students at all grade levels.

Sticky notes to flag thinking The invention of sticky notes has eased all of our lives, especially those of us who like to mark texts without defacing them with pen, pencil, or highlighter. We know that active readers keep a running conversation going in their heads. Because they raise questions, make connections, wonder, and even notice intriguing words or phrases, there's a lot to attend to while they read. Readers tend to keep going, but later they struggle to remember what they thought and what parts of the book elicited different wonderings. Teaching students to flag their thinking not only reminds them to slow down a bit and to interact with what's being read but also creates an easy means of marking the exact place where thinking occurs. This shows how and where readers and texts work together.

When we introduce using sticky notes to flag thinking, we do so in a focus lesson, suggesting that readers become conscious of just one or two reading strategies at a time. For example, Nancy distributes two sticky notes to her students for their first chunk of reading in *Shabanu* (Staples 1989), referring to these as the Q2s. One sticky will mark a place in the reading where a *question* is raised; the other will mark a *quote* (a passage or even a word) that for some reason catches the reader's attention. At the beginning of the year, Kate invites her students to use sticky notes to mark their thinking, starting first with connections, writing T/S (text to self), T/T (text to text), and T/W (text to world) on the small paper flags in order to notice what kind of connection they are making (see Figure 3.5). In follow-up focus lessons, she introduces other markings, such as using a question mark where the text raises a question, GL to note a golden line, and P for a prediction. By the end of the year, they've also added T (thought), F (feeling), O (opinion), and ! (aha) to their repertoire.

Sometimes Megan distributes sticky notes to encourage students to mark the "hot spots" in their books; other times she suggests her young students use these flags to mark where there was a change in their thinking. As you probably

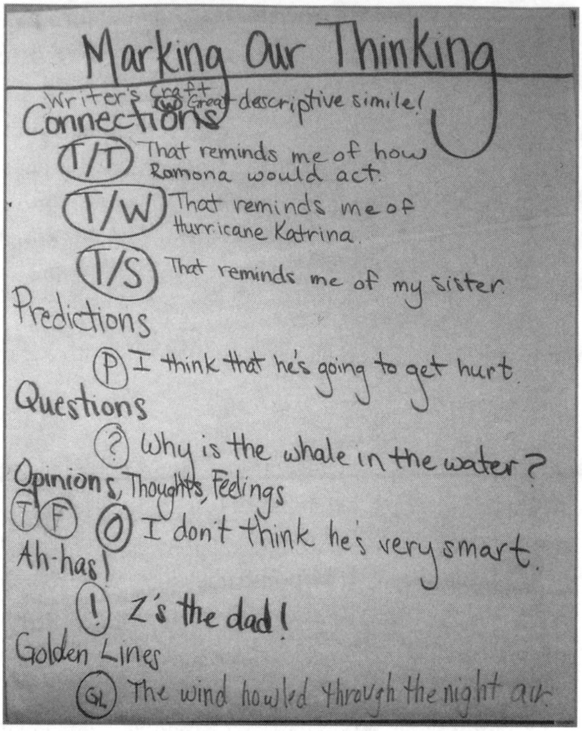

FIG 3.5 *Kate's "Marking Our Thinking" Wall Chart*

realize, there is no ideal or most recommended item to focus readers' attention, nor must you use sticky notes for this work. Thinking can be flagged with torn-paper bookmarks, with paper clips, or even by jotting down page numbers and notations onto a page in a reading journal. The purpose is to create a tool that offers readers ready access to their thinking, providing them with something specific to talk about with other readers in the process of responding to and comprehending what they are reading.

Anchor charts of open-ended prompts When our minds go blank, or when we need an extra nudge to get us going, we turn to open-ended prompts. Young readers, especially those who haven't yet developed a repertoire of response strategies, rely on prompts such as "I think . . . ," "I feel . . . ," and "I wonder . . ." as useful starting places to move their responses beyond "I liked it." Megan introduces a prompt such as "That reminds me of . . ." when she's reading aloud *Stuart Little* (White 1945) to demonstrate her own connections to the book. After she reads a bit further, she invites students to respond to the same prompt. Then she adds "That reminds me of . . ." to the anchor chart of open-ended prompts attached to the classroom wall near a chart of tips for choosing just-right books.

We recommend creating anchor charts along with your students, allowing the lists to evolve with each strategy you introduce (Miller 2002). Premade charts may look attractive, but they can be overwhelming. Adding one or two prompts at a time, rather than presenting students with a list of ten prompts all at once, encourages readers to get a feel for each one through practice.

Golden lines to attend to author's craft Because we ascribe to Rosenblatt's belief in both the reader and the text to create meaning, we suggest teaching readers how to attend to the language, the format, the ideas, and even the phrasing and word choice an author uses. One year Kate invited Nancy to introduce ways of choosing golden lines in preparation for her fifth graders' literature circle discussions. Following a conversation about why readers pay attention to the language in their books, Nancy distributed a half-page handout with some ideas to keep in mind when selecting a golden line to mark for discussion (see Figure 3.6). As Nancy introduced each possibility, students mentioned examples from the read-aloud and from their independent reading books. Students kept this handout in their reading notebooks as a reference for when they read their literature circle books, noting a word, phrase, or passage that evoked one or two of the reactions on the list. They wrote the passage (including page number) in their response notebooks and were encouraged to talk about these during their literature circle discussion later that week. As the year went on, students integrated this attention to author craft as a way to focus on their own writing.

Select a passage, phrase, or sentence that

- ⊕ is very descriptive (helps you see, smell, feel, taste, hear something in the book/story)
- ⊕ sounds poetic
- ⊕ connects with your life
- ⊕ connects with another book (or movie or TV show)
- ⊕ makes you wonder
- ⊕ makes you laugh
- ⊕ makes you sad or upset
- ⊕ makes you stop and think
- ⊕ is your favorite part

Don't forget to include the page number at the end of your selected passage (put it in parentheses).

FIG 3.6 *Some Suggestions for Choosing Golden Lines*

Dramatization and Role Playing

One of the most neglected and undervalued in-school responses to literature is drama, yet dramatic response occurs naturally whenever children role-play books they love. How many characters from the Harry Potter books appear at your door on Halloween? How often do young children reenact adventures from Curious George or Junie B. Jones books on the playground? To children, drama isn't a subject in school; it's a playful, natural way to try out another life.

Barry Hoonan often invites his sixth graders to participate in informal role playing of dramatic key scenes or situations faced by characters as he supports students' inference and teaches layered understanding. When he reads aloud the dance scene from the novel *Crash*, by Jerry Spinelli (1996), Barry might engage students in what he calls revolving role playing. He pauses the read-aloud during this scene where the characters are faced with a conflict or important dilemma. To better understand the conflicting feelings of each character, Barry asks for student volunteers to pick up the story from where he stopped reading, dramatizing what might happen next or replaying what just happened. Then he pauses to ask the character what he was thinking and feeling during that scene. After students talk about their role, Barry has them switch roles, encouraging them to understand another character's situation.

Another dramatic strategy Barry incorporates to teach inference is the talk show (which can also be interpreted as character interviewing, or what he calls hotseating). In this exercise, readers are asked to become a character and answer questions that are posed by the audience or the host. Readers must infer in order to pull together what they know of the story and what they believe would be a truthful response for the character. The talk show format also helps readers gain new insights into cultural and gender perspectives. One year, after Barry's students read *The Skin I'm In* (Flake 2000), they wrote diary entries from the perspective of one of the characters in the book. This served as a rehearsal to prepare students to discover important issues and raise questions integral to their selected character's personality and situation. Following the writing, students were invited to attend the talk show, prepared to respond in character to any question raised. Barry has discovered that "carrying both the writing and interviewing over a two-day period gives the readers in [his] class enough time to make many new connections. The questions they raise and responses they create help students examine motivations and inner thoughts of the characters in the book."

Written and Sketched Response During Reading

Just as talk and conversation allow readers a chance to discover and present their thinking about what they are reading, so does written and sketched response. In Chapter 1 we introduced how literary letters can create an authentic purpose and audience for responding to reading. Examples of these letters also bridge the chapters in this book. We've done this not only to highlight how this strategy honors readers, literature, and teachers but also to showcase how much can be learned (and taught) through this response form. But literary letters are not the only means of soliciting written response. There are a number of ways students can write and/or sketch as a process of thinking on paper.

Sketched responses While many of us have no trouble turning to words to reveal our thoughts about what we read, there are others who find image making a more comfortable and effective way to envision a text. Inviting readers to sketch what they're thinking doesn't necessarily require them to draw well or to draw at all. For example, when Nancy read aloud Chapter 13 in Lois Lowry's *Gossamer* (2006), she distributed crayons and oil pastels to her students, encouraged them to listen to the entire chapter, and directed them to select one or two colors to capture the mood or tone of what was happening and then use those colors to create shapes and designs that evoked the feeling of the chapter. The purpose wasn't a visual representation of what was happening in the chapter, but rather a capturing of the chapter's essence. As students talked about their responses in small groups, they became more aware of the changing shape of the story and their concern for the growing conflict.

Reading workshop notebooks, literature circle journals, and reading journals Response notebooks or journals hold the potential of being useful, but they are too easily overused. When our students are expected to keep science journals, math journals, literature circle journals, and writing journals, we need to reexamine their effectiveness. We also need to remain vigilant about purpose and reward. That said, we both advocate using journals as places for students to explore, to create, to think, and to discover. We know writers who can't imagine *not* keeping a journal as a repository for their ideas. We also know readers who willingly pause and ponder on paper, lingering over a line or phrase from something they've read that they want to save and savor. When we ask our students to keep a journal in response to their reading, we do so believing there are benefits that reach beyond providing teachers with assessment information, and there are audiences in addition to us.

Megan's students keep their reading journals nearby during reading workshop as a place where they can respond to their independent reading choices. When Megan shows students her own reading journal, she explicitly teaches how to set up a response journal and why people keep one. She writes in her journal in front of the children, modeling responses to books her students know and have heard or books she's certain are available in the classroom library. She also shows them where she responds to what she's reading outside of school. Students have the option to decorate their reading journal covers using crayons, markers, and stamps to personalize their work.

It's not uncommon for Megan to conclude each day's reading workshop by gathering everyone on the carpet to share what books or genres they chose to read that day or to listen to two or three children read something from their journals and show what they've sketched. Some days Megan asks the children to share about their process, answering a question like "What did you learn about yourself as a reader today?" More often than not, this sharing time encourages the children to think about ways they, too, might respond to the books they're reading. It also serves as a form of book talk as children introduce and recommend literature to each other through their responses.

Writing in response to literature circle books allows students to do some thinking in preparation for their discussion or following their discussion to capture new insights. Sarah Dunkin's fourth and fifth graders maintain a literature journal where they respond to both the read-aloud and their literature circle books together. When she chooses her read-aloud to align with the focus of the literature circle, this journal becomes the place for students to alternate responses to both books. For example, during an author study of Karen Hesse, Sarah read aloud *Out of the Dust* (1997) while each literature circle group read a different novel by this author—*Just Juice* (1998), *A Time of Angels* (1995), *Letters from Rifka* (1992), or *Phoenix Rising* (1994). Students alternated their responses to both books. Sarah encouraged personal response as well as connection making, not only to their own lives but also between the books (text-to-text connections). She also suggested that readers remain open to any discoveries they made about the author's craft. Kirsten's response reflected this thinking: "In Karen Hesse's books she writes a lot about people who are struggling through a situation and in the end they always get something good out of it. I think there is a lot of loss in her books, like in *Out of the Dust* she loses her mother, and in *Just Juice* they might lose their house." McCord wondered, "Almost all the books have characters with innie in their name like: Dinnie, Zinnie, Mary Lou Finnie. Why is that?" To promote further comparison, toward the end of the read-aloud and literature circle focus, Sarah distributed a Venn diagram and encouraged students to compare and contrast the read-aloud with the Hesse novel their group was reading and discussing. She then invited a representative from each group to participate in a fishbowl discussion in front of the class to talk about the students' discoveries.

If purpose helps guide response to literature, so does audience. Reading response notebooks or journals are most effective when the audience matters. This might mean the most important audience is the reader herself. It might also mean the audience includes classmates, who listen to ideas from the response journal to learn about other books, to deepen their understanding about a book or topic, or even to discover how another reader shapes his own understanding about what was read. Whether the audience is the teacher who writes a brief response in the journal's margins or classmates who respond by listening and discussing, when students know there will be an opportunity to share their thinking about literature, they tend to write or sketch their responses honestly, with insight and wonder, just as eleven-year-old Elizabeth did in her written response to *Maniac Magee* (Spinelli 1990):

> You know how I said that Maniac couldn't stay with the janitor forever? I regret what I said. He could very well live with the janitor, he could go to school, come back, and do homework. Or he could find out if he had other relatives that he could live with.
>
> I just realized something. This book is a little like *Witness* [2001] because it has four different stories. The first one was about him living on his own and with his aunt and uncle. The second story is of him and Amanda Beale's family. Then the third story is of him and Grayson, and the fourth is of him going back to Amanda Beale's family. . . .
>
> This was a great representation of how people live. We argue over lots of little, petty things, like how we dress and stuff, but it just makes you realize how unnecessary that is. What happened in New York and Washington D.C. was very serious, but if your hair is poofy, it's no biggey. You may think your life is bad now. Well, would you like to switch places with Maniac?

Author's Chair Responses

Many teachers conclude the writing workshop with an opportunity for student writers to share what they're working on. In classrooms where students respond to literature often, their response to each other's writing grows from this collaboration between reader and writer. Megan gathers her students on the carpet to offer them a chance to read their writing aloud, discovering what an audience has to say about their ideas or format or even process. While Kate doesn't have an official author's chair, her students also value response to their writing from classmates. In Portable A, writing responses occur throughout the writing workshop. Students can request a conference with a response partner, or they can wait for a chance to read their writing to the whole class. During this time, the writer perches on the stool Kate uses for the read-aloud, presenting their work aloud with the express purpose of receiving response. Sometimes they come with a specific question in mind. Other times they only want feedback, aware their classmates will offer praise as well as raise questions. Knowing there is the possibility for an audience to respond at any stage in the writing process goes a long way for some writers, especially those who become inspired and energized by feedback.

Nurturing response to literature as product

Response to literature that results in the creation of a "published" product can be taught through whole-class projects (such as the riddle book and *The Best Part of Me* activities explained in Chapter 2). It can also be nurtured in the ways we involve students with any work—oral, written, artistic—that is read and viewed by the public. Published work holds the expectation of being prepared with care and concern regarding presentation (i.e., neatness and attention to spelling, grammar, and penmanship) and with respect for how it looks and how it reads. While we do not advocate literary products for everything our students read (just as we would never create a product for everything we write), we recognize the benefits and pleasures that result when readers create something to culminate a reading experience. Following are some possible literature response products.

Read-Aloud Bookmarks

On the first day of school, Kate reads aloud Sharon Creech's *A Fine, Fine School* (2001a). She also chooses this book because it focuses on school as community. *A Fine, Fine School*, and every book Kate reads aloud throughout the year, is preserved by the creation of an oversized bookmark, designed by a student to capture the class' visual and written response. Kate explains how these bookmarks show that they've read these books together. She asks for one volunteer to represent the book with an image of something that seemed significant or important, a phrase or passage to capture the author's words, and the book title, author, and illustrator (if there is one). These colorful four-by-eleven-inch tag board bookmarks are attached to a piece of yarn that runs along the upper walls of the classroom, serving as a visual record of all the books this community of learners read and discussed together during their fifth-grade year (see Figure 3.7).

Extension Projects

Response projects designed to extend readers' understanding following the completion of a book not only culminate the reading experience they also invite readers to return to the book to seek specifics, clarify, confirm, and understand what was read in order to provide an accurate and honest presentation of the literature. We often encourage artistic interpretation, both visual and performance, as a means of honoring all forms of expression for students who might struggle with more traditional response forms.

FIG 3.7 *Read-Aloud Bookmarks from Kate's Class*

One way to think about extension projects, and maybe to introduce them to your students, is to liken them to the process an illustrator goes through when creating a visual interpretation of someone else's words. For example, when illustrator Bryan Collier received the written text to Doreen Rappaport's *John's Secret Dreams* (2004), his first question was "How can I connect to this text?" He read Doreen's text multiple times, but he had to find his own way to interpret and create a visual meaning. Collier (2005) calls this individual response "the creation of magic" and he views illustrating as a collaboration with an author. "For me it's a dance. Doreen does her thing and I need to step back and then join in!"

Worthwhile extension projects should grow naturally out of the literature, whether it is read aloud, read independently, or even read alongside others. Kate concludes the reading aloud of novels with some type of project that encourages students to reexamine the story and demonstrate something they understand about a character, a literary device, or the plot. After reading aloud Avi's *The True Confessions of Charlotte Doyle* (1990), students wrote letters they imagined characters would write to each other after the events that occurred at the end of the novel. At the conclusion of *Pedro's Journal* (Conrad 1991), each student represented a different chapter from the book by designing a visual image of that chapter onto a template of an ocean wave. Kate then taped the waves side by side along the hallway walls, offering an artistic ocean of responses. The fifth graders also created "understone fund" artifacts and then buried them in the piles of leaves at the edge of their school playground as a connection to the characters in Sharon Creech's *Ruby Holler* (2002), and they designed colored pencils to honor Hollis' artistic ability after listening to *Pictures of Hollis Woods* (Giff 2002). For each extension project, Kate prepares a one-page handout explaining the process for thinking through the response, including space for drafting ideas, noting page numbers, and explaining intentions (see Figure 3.8).

Extension projects are always shared with an audience, sometimes within the class (students read letters from *Charlotte Doyle* to classmates, and they offered a brief oral explanation to describe what they created as an understone fund treas-

---

Several times during *Ruby Holler* our class has discussed the possibility that the understone funds *could* have contained special memories rather than money. Of course, we discovered that Tiller, Sairy, Florida, and Dallas's understone funds did contain money. But what if they didn't? Think about what special memories each character might have kept preserved under the stones. You may need to look back over your read-aloud responses to remember what the characters treasured or you may know right away what you think they found sacred.

Your job is to choose one of the characters and then create something to represent his or her treasured memory. You can use any of our classroom art supplies to create this representation. When you finish, write a paragraph explaining why you chose your creation and what it represents.

You'll present your understone treasure in class next Wednesday. Then we'll put all of the treasures in a box and bury them under a stone at the edge of the school playground.

Have fun—be as creative as possible!

Use the space below to plan what you will create:

FIG 3.8 *Understone Funds Response Project*

ure) and other times with readers in the school (a display of *Hollis Woods* colored pencils and *Pedro's Journey* ocean waves graced a hallway leading to the school library).

Extension projects designed to culminate a literature circle or in response to a favorite independent reading book serve the same purpose as Kate's read-aloud literary projects. They ask readers to pause and create something that represents not only the book they read but also the reader's unique response to it. Including color and design, rhythm and music, voice and action as ways to extend meaning promotes an invigorated interpretation that can happen only after the literature has been read and experienced. A valuable resource for extension projects (including planning forms and evaluation guides) can be found at www.litcircles.org/Extension/extension.html.

What Can We Learn from Authors and Illustrators About Response?

One of the reasons we respect writers and illustrators of children's literature is because they know what a demanding (as well as appreciative) audience children can be. For the most part, children's literature is written by adults who *choose* young readers as their audience, not by default and not because they didn't make the cut in the adult book world, but because they revere children as wildly unpredictable, highly judgmental, and wonderfully grateful readers. These are writers who know their readers will criticize them on a factual error, a less-than-plausible character, or a weak ending and illustrators who understand their readers expect the same accuracy and honesty from them.

Listening to authors and illustrators at bookstore readings and conferences and reading their websites and blogs provide a glimpse into their regard for audience and their expectation for response as they write, illustrate, and then turn their creations over to readers. Some voices that ring in our ears include those of Caldecott Medal–winning illustrators Leo and Diane Dillon, who negotiate their responsibility to text and reader as they create images to accompany an author's words: "[While] we have to be true to the text . . . to us a successful illustration is one a child can read numerous times and still discover something" (2005). As well, at last year's International Reading Association Convention, we heard Newbery Medal winner Linda Sue Park credit reader expectation as her "favorite writing tool" when she said, "What I want most from response is that when kids finish my book, they will reach for another book (not necessarily mine)."

We can also learn about the dynamic role of response in the creation of an illustrated book, especially since most authors and illustrators do not directly collaborate. A number of years ago, George Ella Lyon wrote the text to *Book* (1999), a picture book that welcomes a reader to pick up a book and discover its possibilities. She likened a book to a house, a treasure chest, a tree, and a farm: "A BOOK is a FARM, its fields sown with words. Reader, you are its weather: your tears, your eyes shining. The writer, working these words, cried and laughed, too. Now you meet as the gate of the book swings wide." Lyon knows that any book, including the ones she writes, needs the companionship of a reader to give it life and create its magic. One of *Book*'s initial readers was its eventual illustrator, Peter Catalanotto, who received a copy of Lyon's text from the publisher. It was probably typed onto a single sheet of paper in plain, black font. He read it and responded by creating visual images to accompany Lyon's metaphors. Catalanotto's rich watercolor illustrations, appearing as double-page spreads, add color and life to the words in *Book*. Picture book artists are keen responders as they create *an* interpretation with color, shape, line, and design. Readers have this same potential for response, whether through images, movement, or even silent contemplation.

Conversations with authors, whether informally following a book reading, during a question-and-answer period, or even through email, also reveal the reciprocal give-and-take that evolves between writers and readers, a give-and-take that we call response. When Nancy's undergraduates sent Suzanne Fisher Staples their visual arts extension projects to *Shabanu* (1989), she responded in an email:

> The imagery students find in my work is always astonishing to me. It isn't so much that I haven't purposefully included the imagery they suggest (though in truth it was not purposeful) but that it is so *true*. Had I been more conscious of what I was doing while writing, I might have seen this imagery without having it pointed out by your students. This is an amazing thing to me—it demonstrates the magic in the writing-reading connection, the mystery inherent in the process of writing, and the ever-amazing subconscious coming to light. So I thank you and your students for revealing this to me all over again!

Authors and illustrators remind us that response is what their work is all about. At the 2004 International Reading Association Convention, Mo Willems explained the responsibility he feels for his work: "We are the catalyst for readers' responses." This is confirmed whenever we bring William Wise's *Zany Zoo* (2006), David Shannon's *No David!* (1998b), or Mo Willems' Pigeon books into a classroom. Hearty laughter always erupts along with kid-created Pigeon illustrations and replica books starring Pigeon. Hilarity is response, as is writing, illustrating, and talk. We understand the significant role that authors and illustrators play in nurturing response when Sarah Dunkin's students write, "What do I think of *Maniac Magee* so far? . . . Well . . . I LOVE IT!!!" and "I'm so glad Maniac went back with the Beales because everyone likes him and cares for him there. Thank you, Ms. Dunkin for picking this book. —Your thankful student, Hanna." And we share Sarah's appreciation for the author-reader relationship as she exclaims when reading her students' response journals, "This is why I will never take real books out of the hands of kids."

Professional Literature Cited

Collier, Bryan. 2005. Speech. Children's Literature Assembly Breakfast, National Council of Teachers of English Convention, November, San Antonio, TX.

Cushman, Karen. 1997. "Newbery Acceptance Speech." *The Horn Book Magazine* (June/July): 414.

Dillon, Leo, and Diane Dillon. 2005. Speech. Books for Children Luncheon, National Council of Teachers of English Convention, November, San Antonio, TX.

Fox, Mem. 2001. *Reading Magic: Why Reading Aloud to Children Will Change Their Lives Forever*. Ill. Judy Horacek. San Diego: Harcourt.

Miller, Debbie. 2002. *Reading with Meaning: Teaching Comprehension in the Primary Grades*. York, ME: Stenhouse.

Park, Linda Sue. 2005. Presentation. International Reading Association Convention, May, Chicago.

Paterson, Katherine. 1989. *The Spying Heart: More Thoughts on Reading and Writing for Children*. New York: Dutton.

———. 1995. *A Sense of Wonder: On Reading and Writing Books for Children*. New York: Plume/Penguin.

Rosenblatt, Louise. 1991. "Literature—S.O.S.!" *Language Arts* (68): 444–48.

———. 1996. *Literature as Exploration*. 5th ed. New York: Modern Language Association.

Schlick Noe, Katherine L., and Nancy J. Johnson. 1999. *Getting Started with Literature Circles*. Norwood, MA: Christopher-Gordon.

Conversation with . . .
Author Sarah Stewart and illustrator David Small

Sarah Stewart and David Small are both author and illustrator and wife and husband. In this conversation they provide insight into the inspiration and artistic process of creating **The Friend**.

At a conference several years ago, you told the story that eventually became **The Friend.** *How long did it take you to write this book?*

STEWART: I've worked on it off and on for a dozen years. Because I'm a writer, I write every day. When I hit upon something, a poem or a story that I think has merit, I put it away. And I mean I really put it away. The great Greek poet Homer said write your poem and then put it away for ten years. When you come back to it, you'll be able to see it clearly. So I put my writing away for ten days or two weeks or a month. That's what I did with this story because it was so close to me and initially too sentimental. When I finally wrote it as a poem, it was written in first person. Two winters ago, I gave the little girl a name and separated myself from her. That made a huge difference. Another dramatic change had to do with David when he said, "I wish I knew Bea better. I wish I could see what she lived." So I rewrote one scene, taking readers up to Bea's room to gain a better sense of who she was. In that way, I honored David's request to get to know Bea better. This made the end of the book more powerful.

Where did the character's name, Annabelle Beatrice Clementine Dodd, come from?

STEWART: I have a big name, Sarah St. John Stewart Small. I also sign my name S[4] when I'm writing friends a note. S to the fourth power. So I gave Annabelle Beatrice Clementine Dodd a big name. It's also A. B. C. D., which I know some child is going to get.

Since **The Friend** *is such a personal story, was it more difficult to illustrate than Sarah's other stories, such* **The Journey** *or* **The Gardener?**

SMALL: It was incredibly difficult because I've lived with Sarah. I've known her for thirty years and we've obviously talked about our childhoods. I knew the back story on this one. It wasn't like *The Gardener*. It wasn't like *The Journey*. It wasn't like *The Library* where I could simply make something up. In this case it was a real situation. I knew the child. I knew about the family's troubles and saw it as a very dark book. Then Sarah gave it to me in light verse form.

STEWART: But it's from the child's point of view. The light verse is the child. The child sees the light.

SMALL: I think it was exactly the right form for the text to take. I had to transition from what I saw as these two women imprisoned in this sort of fancy cell to my vision of the story. This child was living all alone in a big house with the parents basically absent. And there was this woman who I initially saw as just an employee, but who became so much more.

You used a number of wordless double-page spreads where the reader doesn't see Bea's face.

SMALL: On these spreads, she's obviously concentrating on something, but readers only see her back. There's something about that view. I'm not sure how to put it into words. It draws you to the character and makes you look at her body language more than her facial expressions.

You have to "read" her, don't you?

STEWART: I know that my poem says she is an extraordinary, remarkable woman. But I think you're right. The language of the illustrations adds to her power. I think that Bea turned away from us is her sense of self revealed. The certainty, the pride, the assuredness of her role. She was much more than just the head of my grandparents' and parents' household, and it shows. She had her own life. Turning away from us says that.

Do you ever work from photographs, especially since this story is based on a real person?

SMALL: I did use a model for this book. When I was thinking about how to illustrate it, I saw a woman in a restaurant in our village. I kept my eye on her all during lunch and realized that she was exactly the character I wanted. I approached and told her that Sarah had written this story about a woman who used to work for her family. I asked this woman to be my model, assuring her that she wasn't going to have to pose. All I needed were photographs from all angles with different expressions on her face. She said she thought she could come up with something. Within a week, she had gone to the local mall and had copies made of about fifty photographs of herself, some of them most unflattering. She was wonderful. So I used the images from some of those photographs.

Were there any artifacts from Sarah's life that were incorporated into the illustrations, such as her typewriter?

STEWART: David created the way everything looked in the story except at the end. The artist has the right to make the world and David made up that world. But I did grow up in a big house on the ocean.

SMALL: I've seen that house. In my memory it was surrounded by big plants with a tunnel running under the road to the ocean. So the ocean drive was between the house and the beach. But that was too complicated to illustrate. So I made steps to the beach instead.

STEWART: I think each painting is a symbol of something. In every painting David caught some philosophical or psychological moment and expanded on it. I have watched him illustrate thirty or more books and in each case he has to conquer the manuscript and make it his own. In the case of *The Friend*, I don't think he's ever done it better.

David, at what point do you show Sarah the work in progress? Do you ever ask for her opinion?

SMALL: *The Friend* was done with more privacy than any of Sarah's other books I illustrated. When I needed feedback, I didn't ask her because it was such a personal story. I felt I was messing with her life. If I had run back to Sarah every day asking her was this right, I never would have agreed to illustrate the book.

Sarah, when did you see the illustrations for the first time?

STEWART: David had the entire dummy sketched and tacked up on the wall. One day he ran up the stairs and said, "I have something to show you." He was very excited. Generally, we don't interrupt each other as we work. When I saw the work on the wall, I was stunned. The art appeared just like it is in the book. Jumping off the wall.

SMALL: The characters were no longer just an idea and I knew the story would work as literature. At that point, it wouldn't matter to Sarah whether it was her life or the life of somebody she had never met. If it would matter to Sarah the reader, I knew that it would work for other readers.

STEWART: The reader is my best friend.

You both have such respect for each other's work. Sarah, can you imagine anyone else illustrating your books?

STEWART: It will never happen. If David doesn't like the story, then the publishers don't use him and that's all right with me. It makes me work harder. It has to be him. Every manuscript feels like a battle and the battle is real. Neither of us takes this lightly. With my own writing, the struggle is largely to do something better than anyone could possibly do. Many of my manuscripts sit on the shelf. I don't mind.

The Friend, by Sarah Stewart. Illus. David Small. Farrar, Straus and Giroux, 2004.

The Gardener, by Sarah Stewart. Illus. David Small. Farrar, Straus and Giroux, 1997.

The Journey, by Sarah Stewart. Illus. David Small. Farrar, Straus and Giroux, 2001.

The Library, by Sarah Stewart. Illus. David Small. Farrar, Straus and Giroux, 1995.

Side by Side by Side
Literature/Teacher/Learner: Responding to Literature

Book

Stewart, Sarah. 1997. *The Gardener*. Illus. David Small. New York: Farrar, Straus and Giroux.

When Lydia Grace is sent to live with her grouchy uncle in the city during the Depression, she packs a suitcase with necessities that include a packet of seeds from her family's farm and lots of stationery. Ever the optimist, Lydia sends letters home that reveal plans to surprise her hardworking uncle by planting a rooftop garden. This reflects wisdom learned from her grandmother: "I've tried to remember everything you taught me about beauty."

Related literature

Flower Garden, by Eve Bunting. Illus. Kathryn Hewitt. San Diego: Harcourt, 1994.

Miss Rumphius, by Barbara Cooney. New York: Viking, 1982.

Planting a Rainbow, by Lois Ehlert. San Diego: Harcourt, 1988.

Teaching Response

Megan Sloan gathers her first and second graders on the carpet to continue their author-and-illustrator study of Sarah Stewart and David Small. Over the past week she has read aloud *The Library* and *The Friend* and shared some specifics about the author's inspiration for these books. Today she will introduce *The Gardener*, a story told through a young girl's letters that Megan knows will intrigue her students. Megan reads the book in its entirety, then "rereads" it as a picture read to encourage the children to notice the ways David Small's artwork enhances and extends Lydia Grace's letters.

Then Megan asks, "So, what do you think? How do you feel about this book?" to invite oral response and spark conversation. Since a number of students have already turned to their writer's notebooks to craft poetry and create sketches following the discussion of *The Library* and *The Friend*, Megan feels confident in the author's and illustrator's relevance to their lives. Today she plans to demonstrate written response through shared writing to connect ideas inspired from *The Gardener*. She begins by thinking aloud about how Lydia's decision to plant a garden to make her uncle smile reminded her of the school's tulip garden that the children weeded for Earth Day. Then she recalls some of Eve Bunting's beautiful language in her picture book *Flower Garden* and borrows from these ideas to jot down a word, a line, or a phrase onto chart paper. Encouraged by this beginning, Megan's students contribute other ideas, which she scribes onto the paper. Before sending the children back to their desks, Megan reads through their list of ideas and mentions that she'll have watercolors and a box of cut and torn paper available to encourage responses to *The Gardener* with words or images or both.

Student Response

Figures 3.9 and 3.10 show two students' responses to *The Gardener*.

Garden of Gems

Garden of gems,
Under a roof of
Brown and green
Dangling leaves.
Yellow tulips
Standing
Like guards,
Protecting the blooming
Red and purple tulips
From aphids.
Wind whistling,
Blowing,
Singing a lovely song.
Garden of gems,
Garden of gems,
Garden of gems.

My Mom's Garden

My mom's garden
is surrounded with
flowers.
They look
like lollipops,
popping up,
one by one,
every year,
Pop, pop, pop,
beautiful
colors..
I walk in
my mom's
garden
surrounded
by
lollipops.

FIG 3.9 *Emelia's Poem, "Garden of Gems"*

FIG 3.10 *Siobhan's Poem, "My Mom's Garden"*

February 8

Dear Miss Norem,
I think I will read more Fanatsy now. I just started <u>Bridge to Terabithia</u>. So far I'm at chapter 3. It's <u>really</u> good. I think Jesse secretly likes Lesslie. I think that because while she ran home she thought "*beautiful*." I also think that the girls should be able to run with the boys if she wants to. I'm also glad that lesslie and Jess are friends. I also had a Text-Text connection with <u>Number The Stars</u>. They both had to do something to get the little sister to not play with her.

I'm still read <u>So You Want To Be President</u>. I was wondering how croquet was pronounced. I'm going to look it up in the dictionary.

Love,
Breydan

P.S. Do you think I should write in cursive for now on?

2·9

Dear Breydan,
I am so glad you are enjoying <u>Bridge to Terabithia</u>. I couldn't help but notice that you called it a fantasy book. Are you sure it is actually fantasy? The previews for the new movie version certainly appear to be fantasy, but I think the book is actually realistic fiction. Let me know what you think as you continue reading!

I read <u>Bridge to Terabithia</u> when I was your age and then again as an adult. Both times I read it I just loved it. I think one of the reasons I loved it is because it is a story of friendship. Good books about friendship <u>always</u> suck me right in. In fact, I am reading an adult book about friendship right now called <u>Broken for You</u>. Can you think of any other books you have read about friendship?

Brey, thank you so much for writing such a thoughtful letter. I love, love, love talking about books with you. You are an amazing reader!

Love,
Miss Norem

P.S. I think you should choose about the cursive!

The Presence of Literature to Create Readers

It's the first week of school, and this year Miss Malarkey said our class would be doing the *Everybody Reads in America* program.

She thinks that reading is about the finest thing a person can do and she promises to find each of us a book we'll love before the end of the year.

. . . But, there's one problem.

I hate reading. . . .

Miss Malarkey keeps giving me books. She says she'll find a book for me if it kills her. I don't want her to die, so I told her I'd keep trying. When I tried to read one of them after I played video games, I fell asleep. . . .

On June 10, our school had a big assembly for the reading program. We're getting close to the goal of reading 1,000 books. I tried to like reading. I really did. I tried sports books, science books, joke books, fantasy, explorer, and detective books. . . .

When I got to Miss Malarkey's room, she had this crazy smile on her face. . . . Then she yelled. . . . Have I Got a Book for You!

—JUDY FINCHLER, *Miss Malarkey Leaves No Reader Behind*

M iss Malarkey believes that everyone can and should be a reader. In Judy Finchler's *Miss Malarkey Leaves No Reader Behind*, some students' incentive is to read one thousand books so that Principal Wiggins will dye his hair purple and sleep on the school's roof. Other students become enamored with reading when they discover books about interesting topics. And, of course, there are those students harboring a competitive spirit whose goal is to read more books than anyone else. Regardless of the motivation to read (or not to read), Miss Malarkey learns about each student's interests and suggests books he might enjoy. She even manages to find the "greatest book ever made" for the story's video game–loving protagonist.

Miss Malarkey's goal is to encourage children to become hooked on books and to find the pleasure of reading both in and out of school, a goal we assume you share. "When we read, we really have no choice—we must develop literacy. . . . Through literature, students will grow intellectually and be exposed to a wider variety of books, which can stimulate more free reading" (Krashen 2004, 15). The presence of literature in the classroom enables teachers to support children in building language competence, acquiring reading strategies, contributing to intellectual growth, and becoming lifelong readers. This premise leads us to wonder:

- What does it mean to create readers?

- How can literature create effective and affective readers?

- How do children's book authors and illustrators become our teaching partners?

The definition of what it means to teach reading varies among teachers, librarians, administrators, parents, and politicians. Some believe the primary focus of reading instruction should be on the teaching of skills. Others acknowledge that while children need skills to support them as readers, they must also engage in significant and meaningful experiences with literature to nurture their reading growth. Frank Smith (1988) points out that sometimes we confuse cause and effect by assuming that children must first master language skills and then apply these to reading and writing. Regie Routman (1996) contends that skills and strategies should be taught within the literacy context rather than through the fragmentation produced by drills and worksheets. Reading for meaning and reading about things that matter support language development and promote learning to read (Krashen 2004). Our experience as readers and teachers has shown this to be true.

With literature as both partner and resource, skilled teachers can adapt methods, strategies, and purposes for reading to best meet the needs of their students. When literature serves as a collaborative partner, it becomes more than a tool for instruction in skills, vocabulary, and comprehension. Literature in all genres and formats gives readers something worth reading, something to stretch their imaginations, and something to extend their experiences. We can't imagine teaching reading and creating readers without it.

What Does It Mean to Create Readers?

On her website (www.patriciapolacco.com), Patricia Polacco relates the embarrassment she suffered and the bullying she endured as a child learning to read. Polacco reveals "feeling dumb . . . and so sad [she] didn't want to go to school anymore" because she was "dyslexic, disnumeric, and disgraphic." When her fifth-grade teacher, Mr. Falker, noticed her struggles and referred her to a reading specialist, Polacco's life changed. She fondly remembers "the first day that words on a page had meaning" to her. "Mr. Falker reached into the most lonely darkness and pulled me into bright sunlight and sat me on a shooting star. I shall never forget him." So she wrote the autobiographical picture book, *Thank You, Mr. Falker* (1998), to honor the "teacher that took time to see a child that was drowning and needed help."

Chances are we have all encountered students like Patricia Polacco who have struggled as readers. For these students, reading is far from enjoyable as they wrestle to make sense of print, seldom experiencing a sense of accomplishment by independently reading an entire picture book or novel. Fortunately, there are numerous strategies and techniques to involve all students in reading experiences that will encourage, motivate, build their self-confidence, and boost their self-esteem. One of the best strategies is to help children realize they aren't alone. Sharing stories about authors like Polacco who labored early as readers but eventually found success and enjoyment in books reveals hope. So does introducing students to literary characters who are challenged by reading but eventually find success (see Figure 4.1).

Teaching reading and creating readers must be about more than scripted programs and basal readers. And it can be. A glimpse into classrooms with knowledgeable teachers and access to literature reveals children learning to read for various purposes *all day long*. Teaching reading and creating readers doesn't

---

Amber on the Mountain, by Tony Johnston. Illus. Robert Duncan. New York: Dial, 1994.

The Bee Tree, by Patricia Polacco. New York: Philomel, 1993.

But Excuse Me That Is My Book, by Lauren Child. New York: Dial, 2006.

Edward and the Pirates, by David McPhail. New York: Little, Brown, 1997.

More Than Anything Else, by Marie Bradby. Illus. Chris Soentpiet. New York: Scholastic, 1995.

Mr. George Baker, by Amy Hest. Illus. Jon J. Muth. Cambridge, MA: Candlewick, 2004.

The Red Book, by Barbara Lehman. Boston: Houghton Mifflin, 2004.

A Story for Bear, by Dennis Haseley. Illus. Jim LaMarche. San Diego: Silver Whistle/Harcourt, 2004.

Tomás and the Library Lady, by Pat Mora. Illus. Raul Colón. New York: Knopf, 1997.

The Wednesday Surprise, by Eve Bunting. Illus. Donald Carrick. New York: Clarion, 1989.

Winston the Book Wolf, by Marni McGee. Illus. Ian Beck. New York: Walker, 2006.

Wolf! by Betsy Bloom. Illus. Pascal Biet. New York: Scholastic, 1999.

FIG 4.1 *Picture Books About a Character's Path to Reading*

happen overnight, and it doesn't happen with a one-size-fits-all curriculum. Intrinsic lessons about reading can be learned through demonstration and shared experiences—the read-aloud, participation in shared reading—while explicit lessons make the most sense during guided reading, focus lessons, and one-on-one conferences. But it's the time and opportunity to *apply* skills and strategies that make the difference. To become proficient, competent, and confident readers—those who not only know how to read but choose to read—students need to participate as readers with purpose and pleasure. Therefore no reading curriculum seems complete without time for actual reading, perhaps independently, with a partner, or within a group such as during readers' theatre work or in literature circles.

How Can Literature Create Effective and Affective Readers?

Richard Peck, author of numerous award-winning books for children, claims, "the literature of our childhood becomes our lifelong luggage," and he advises authors, teachers, and parents to remember that "a book for the young must live in their world, not ours" (n.d.). Provocative words indeed. Curious to discover how (or if) the "literature of our childhood" nurtures early reading ability and attitude, we ask our undergraduates to think about three pieces of literature that held a strong influence during their childhood (e.g., a book read to them, one they requested repeatedly, one that could have been their undoing as a reader, or maybe one they hope to introduce to their classmates, their students, even their children). We ask for book titles and what made the books appealing. We also ask them to think about the literature in light of their lives at the time. What they tell us reveals some common wisdom about the early influence of literature to create readers: Literature read aloud lingers positively; we remember the books, the people who read them, and the feelings they elicited.

- ◉ Personal relationships associated with literature (whether read aloud "with voices" by Mom or Dad, received as a gift from a beloved aunt or older sister, or recommended by someone who knows what you love) are trusted and treasured.

- ◉ Literature that connects to our lives, emotions, interests, and tastes makes sense and often prompts rereading.

- ◉ Favorite stories and poems that we listen to repeatedly rarely grow old and often become the first literature we read independently.

- Literature we read without having to prove, justify, or defend is worth our time.

- Literature becomes our favorite, not necessarily because of literary quality or awards, but for reasons of taste and relationship.

Assured by the experiences of students who loved literature and who viewed themselves as readers early on, we consider how to adapt these truths in the classroom, not only to teach children how to read but perhaps more importantly to create active readers who discover literature to inspire, connect, engage, teach, and rekindle their sense of wonder.

Reading aloud

The power of the read-aloud is humorously portrayed in Laura Numeroff's picture book *Beatrice Doesn't Want To* (2004). As the story opens, the last place Beatrice wants to be is in the library. But when her older, exasperated brother (who is trying to complete a report on dinosaurs) drops her off in the story time room while he works, Beatrice becomes enamored with a read-aloud book about a roller-skating mouse. The expressive librarian makes the story come alive for Beatrice, and when her brother returns to pick her up, she is quietly ensconced in a chair with the book that has captured her interest and invited her to read.

Reading aloud may be our most valuable tool for both teaching and creating readers. The Commission on Reading supports this belief by stating, "The single most important activity for building the knowledge for eventual success in reading is reading aloud to children. . . . It is a practice that should continue through the grades" (Anderson et al. 1985, 23, 51). Sometimes there is a notion that we should stop reading aloud to students once they have become readers themselves. We've been asked, "But if the *teacher* is reading, how do children learn the skills and strategies they need to improve *their* reading ability?" While the sole purpose of the read-aloud isn't to teach reading, we can't deny the opportunity it offers students to experience the pleasures of reading and to develop the art of listening from a capable and skilled reader.

When teachers read aloud, they apply reading strategies and demonstrate what good readers do: They slow down the pace or reread interesting sentences or paragraphs; they read with expression and may create voices for characters; and they linger over illustrations that are visually appealing and deserve a longer look. At times, they pause to think about what they have read, what predictions they have, and what connections are emerging. Through reading aloud, they reinforce concepts of print and story, enrich vocabularies, and offer their students vicarious experiences. Reading aloud also introduces various genres and motivates students to read stories they may never have attempted on their own. Books, then, become accessible to all readers regardless of ability or interest. In addition, Jim Trelease's *The New Read-Aloud Handbook* (2006) contends that reading aloud

- increases independent reading
- stretches attention spans
- stimulates imagination
- fosters critical-thinking skills
- improves reading comprehension
- establishes a reading-writing connection

Through the read-aloud we can also emphasize, just as the librarian did in *Beatrice Doesn't Want To*, the criteria to use when choosing books. When we seek an engaging read-aloud, we keep our audience in mind and select books that tell an interesting story, contain appealing illustrations, portray a multidimensional character, or offer up delicious language. And we always choose books we like. As we read aloud, it's not uncommon for us to tell our students why we selected the book. This highlights and confirms for children how books can be carefully chosen for the purpose we have determined. Since we choose books for various reasons, our read-alouds become the primary means to reveal how we make these decisions.

When we step into the classrooms of any of the teachers we have profiled in this book, we see how reading aloud serves as an integral component of their reading instruction. They make conscious decisions about which books to read aloud: they consider if students will like the story, how it might support their curriculum, and if it's something they enjoyed reading themselves. They seek books that are meaty, engaging, and likely to foster response. The read-aloud sets the tone and serves as the foundation and heart of everything that happens in these classrooms. And just like Beatrice, their students discover that reading is an enjoyable and pleasurable way to spend their time.

Because we are readers, we know there are inherent rewards from reading. But we also know there are children who haven't yet discovered how books can be their friends. Therefore we feel compelled to invite them to know a full range of books and to experience intrinsic pleasures and rewards that come from them. Reading aloud allows us to make this introduction. As we read aloud, those rewards are further illustrated by how we respond to books ourselves. Mem Fox echoes our strong belief about how teachers exhibit the many rewards from reading.

We need, as teachers, to be seen reading and loving to read *in class*, in front of the children. We need to be seen laughing over books, being unable to put books down, sobbing over sob stories, gasping over horror stories, and sighing over love stories—anything, in fact, that helps our students to realize that there is some reward, that there are *many* rewards, to be had from the act of reading. (1993, 63)

As Mem Fox so passionately states, reading and reading aloud promise those *aah*s that denote active response and participation. We sigh with relief when Winn-Dixie returns to Opal Buloni in Kate DiCamillo's *Because of Winn-Dixie* (2000) because the author has kept us on edge, not knowing where Opal's beloved dog has gone during an awful thunderstorm. Cyndi's voice trembles every time she reads aloud this part of the story; her students sense the realistic drama and feel Opal's palpable grief over her missing pooch. When Megan Sloan shares *All the Places to Love* by Patricia MacLachlan (1994), she reads it aloud more than once, inviting students to join her in reading specific lines. That taste of language will entice them to revisit the book and repeat the phrases again and again. And as Kate Norem chuckles with her students while reading aloud with gusto and expression Judy Schachner's *Skippyjon Jones* (2003) and *Skippyjon Jones in the Doghouse* (2005), she's laying a foundation for literary memories that will last long after fifth grade ends.

Shared reading

In 2005 we heard Regie Routman speak about the importance of shared demonstration, a key component in her optimal learning model. We understood even more clearly why we promote opportunities for shared reading when she said, "Shared demonstration is a form of hand-holding; it says to students, 'I am not going to let you fail.' It lets the learner relax." We learn with support and we succeed more readily in the company of those who believe in us. Teachers like Megan concur. As she shows her students the cover of Denise Fleming's *In the Small, Small Pond* (1993), all eyes are riveted to the vivid illustration depicting a child surprised by a leaping frog. As she reads, "In the small, small pond . . . / wiggle, giggle, tadpoles wriggle / waddle, wade, geese parade . . ." the students know they will be invited to read along. They recognize Fleming's distinctive collage in this book from previous shared book experiences of *Where Once There Was a Wood* (1996) and *Barnyard Banter* (1994). Megan knows Fleming's books are perfect for shared reading because the text is brief, the language is appealing, and the illustrations are vibrant. She also selects poems by Jack Prelutsky,

Douglas Florian, and Karla Kuskin that contain content and language appropriate and engaging for primary-grade students.

The shared reading model, developed by Don Holdaway (1979), attempts to replicate storybook reading between parent and child. This process enables children to first observe an expert read with fluency and expression and then participate in the reading. Over time and with predictable literature, children become coreaders as they develop a sense of story and narrative. Margaret Mooney suggests that shared reading provides opportunities to

- create a welcoming and supportive climate that encourages children to participate in supported readings

- acknowledge children's contributions as those of readers

- model strategies children may need in guided and independent reading

- introduce new, memorable, and more complex language

- increase familiarity with book language through texts beyond a child's level of independent reading

- model fluent, expressive reading that creates interest and invites participation (1994, 70–72)

While shared reading is typically used with emergent readers, it is also effective with older students, particularly those who are struggling with fluency and comprehension. In primary grades, teachers choose big books, songs, rhymes, and patterned language books (see Figure 4.2 for Megan's recommendations). Predictable books, such as Eric Carle's *Today Is Monday* (1993), *Possum Come A-Knockin'*, by Nancy Van Laan (1990), *Good Night, Gorilla*, by Peggy Rathmann (1994), and the perennial favorite *Brown Bear, Brown Bear, What Do You See?* by Bill Martin Jr. (1992), work well for shared reading as they enable readers to foretell how the story will develop and end, through text organization (rhythm, rhyme, repeated lines) or connections to reader experiences. Intermediate teachers might use poetry with rhythm, rhyme, and kid appeal. Shel Silverstein and Jack Prelutsky are big favorites, but don't miss Alice Schertle, Kristine O'Connell George, and Janet Wong.

Partner reading

Partner reading isn't difficult to define—it involves sharing the reading experience with a partner. This informal approach to reading offers students the opportunity to listen to fluent readers, participate in authentic discussions, build

Click, Clack, Moo: Cows That Type, by Doreen Cronin. Illus. Betsy Lewin. New York: Simon and Schuster, 2000.

Do You Want to Be My Friend? by Eric Carle. New York: HarperCollins, 1971.

Don't Let the Pigeon Drive the Bus, by Mo Willems. New York: Hyperion, 2003.

Is Your Mama a Llama? by Deborah Guarino. Illus. Steven Kellogg. New York: Scholastic, 1989.

Jump, Frog, Jump, by Robert Kalan. Illus. Byron Barton. New York: Greenwillow, 1995.

Time for Bed, by Mem Fox. Illus. Jane Dyer. San Diego: Gulliver/Harcourt, 1993.

Where the Wild Things Are, by Maurice Sendak. New York: Harper and Row, 1963.

Who Is the Beast? by Keith Baker. San Diego: Harcourt, 1990.

FIG 4.2 *Megan Sloan's Recommended Books for Shared Reading*

meaning, and learn from each other. An important quality of partner reading is how it acknowledges and honors the social nature of reading.

Partner reading typically involves an older student reading to a younger child who is an emerging or reluctant reader. However, students in the same class can find pleasure and benefit from partnering as well. The reading can be structured so that one child reads the entire book to the other or the partners alternate the reading of pages. We have also observed echo reading, where one partner begins by reading a sentence or paragraph and then the other partner reads the same sentence or paragraph. This strategy works best on subsequent readings rather than the initial reading, so that fluency and the construction of meaning are not lost in the process of echo reading.

Megan introduces partner reading to her students by talking about both roles in the partnership: the reader (to read with expression) and the listener (to listen for fluency and understanding). She then asks two students to sit knee-to-knee as they model what partner reading looks like and sounds like. Periodically, Megan will stop the reading to ask the class what strategies they notice the partners are using. She records these observations on chart paper so that students can reference them when they begin their own reading partnerships. Megan also introduces how to select books for this activity, suggesting this might be the time to choose a book that's a bit more difficult than what they've chosen in the past for independent reading because now they'll have someone to help them read. She encourages the children to articulate their purpose for the reading before choosing their book or their partner. Is it to listen for fluency? Is it to read and learn new information? Is it to read and discuss a story? Or it is to enjoy a book with a friend? All reasons are valid and all are encouraged as one component of reading workshop in Megan's classroom.

To prepare her fifth graders for reading to their kindergarten buddies, Kate takes her students to the school library, where they spend time choosing and reading picture books. The kindergarten teacher has requested fifth-grade reading partners to extend opportunities for her students to listen to fluent reading. She also values the chance for young children to meet students they would not normally encounter in the school day. Kate knows there is great value for her students as well, especially in the experience it provides them to model fluent, expressive reading. She also hopes to boost the self-esteem of her struggling readers who will select and rehearse a book they will read with confidence, and she is committed to prepare them for success.

Before the initial meeting between the two classes, Kate's students read their picture books numerous times, eventually pairing with a classmate who will critique them on their technique (Do I pause at the right places? Does the story sound interesting? Can you hear my voice?) and offer constructive suggestions. In between rehearsals, Kate inserts focus lessons on fluency, setting a purpose as they prepare for partner reading, and reflecting on how fluent reading isn't just an in-school skill. Kate uses anecdotes from her own life to illustrate this point. "Just last week, while reading a newspaper, one of my friends said, 'Here's something interesting. Let me read it to you,' and when he did, it was interesting and made sense. That's because of *how* he read it. Keep that in mind when you read your book today."

Kate includes literary demonstrations to support her focus lessons. For several weeks, the fifth graders listen to books on tape, watch film excerpts of children's books, and hear Kate read aloud daily. After each listening event, the students gather and debrief what they notice while Kate serves as scribe (see Figure 4.3). As in Megan's class, the students' ideas are transcribed onto chart

Expressive face	Made it fun
Voice got louder for mad or exciting parts	Stayed on pages so partner could see the pictures
Voice got quieter for calm parts	Reading flowed
Used different voices	Spoke clearly
Involved the audience	Used different tones
Paused for effect/drama	

FIG 4.3 *Strategies for Reading Aloud with Fluency*

paper to become a reference for their reading partnerships. Kate asks: "What did you notice about the voice of the reader? How did she keep you interested in listening? How did his voice help you understand what the story was about?" Again, teacher and students take the time to observe and talk about what good readers do.

In partner reading, literature is the essential companion. Readers select stories they like, often starting with their favorite books or authors. They learn to consider the appropriateness of the book for their audience. After the initial meeting with their partner, students may conduct an informal interview to discover their partner's interests, what type of stories she likes, whether he has a favorite author—all useful information that will help guide book selection for future readings.

Choral reading

In what has become an annual ritual, Christine Jordan introduces her fifth graders to Paul Fleischman's Newbery Medal–winning *Joyful Noise: Poems for Two Voices* (1988). In this collection of insect poetry, some lines are read simultaneously, and others require a call-and-response format, which naturally lends itself to choral reading. As she places one poem on the overhead projector, Christine encourages students to discuss its unique format and work on how to read it collaboratively.

In many ways, choral reading is a close relative of shared reading and a natural next step after (or in concert with) partner reading. Similar to a musical chorus, the purpose of choral reading is to create music in listeners' ears by lifting the words off the page with life, beauty, and expression. Performing a choral reading is the result of rehearsal, decisions about expression and meaning, and collaborative accomplishment. Whether with two voices, ten voices, or the combined chorus of an entire class, some of the many benefits of choral reading are that it

- offers practice in oral reading and supports comprehension development
- strengthens speaking and listening skills
- promotes articulation, expression, and fluency
- enhances vocabulary and encourages punctuation use
- encourages discussion and interpretation
- necessitates social interaction, compromise, and decision making

One of the most important aspects to remember when choosing literature for choral reading is to keep the selection relatively short. This is critical when small groups or even the whole class reads the piece in unison so that the reading can remain smooth. Longer pieces often fall apart before the end. Play with the pace of the reading—alternate slow and fast lines. Try on different voices—loud or soft, high or low. Are there key words that should be emphasized? Are there pauses that should be incorporated into the reading? The focus should be on fluently reading aloud together an interesting text with vivid language that enables all children to participate.

When Megan involves her students in choral reading, she provides each student a copy of a poem rather than enlarging it on chart paper or on the overhead projector. This decision is intentional as it encourages readers of all abilities to follow along with the text in front of them. The first few times the children read together it's often halting and requires the support of Megan's voice to keep things going. Repeated readings allow them to feel the rhythm and the flow of the lines and to play around with pacing and voice level.

Poetry isn't the only literature Megan chooses for choral reading (see Figure 4.4 for suggestions for choral reading poems). After reading aloud Bill Martin Jr.'s *Beasty Story* (1999), she hands each student a copy of the text. They practice using their spooky voices as they read, "In a dark, dark wood there is a dark, dark house." Sometimes Megan will divide up the class and alternate reading different pages, but the whole class always joins in to read the final lines, "In the dark, dark box there was a GHOST!" with dramatic flair.

Big Talk: Poems for Four Voices, by Paul Fleischman. Illus. Beppe Giacobbe. Cambridge, MA: Candlewick, 2000.

Color Me a Rhyme: Nature Poems for Young People, by Jane Yolen. Photo. Jason Stemple. Honesdale, PA: Wordsong/Boyds Mills, 2000.

Farmer's Dog Goes to the Forest: Rhymes for Two Voices, by David L. Harrison. Illus. Arden Johnson-Petrov. Honesdale, PA: Wordsong/Boyds Mills, 2005.

Handsprings, by Douglas Florian. New York: Greenwillow, 2006.

Lemonade Sun: And Other Summer Poems, by Rebecca Kai Dotlich. Illus. Jan Spivey Gilchrist. Honesdale, PA: Boyds Mills, 1998.

Oh No! Where Are My Pants? And Other Disaster Poems, by Lee Bennett Hopkins. Illus. Wolf Erlbruch. New York: HarperCollins, 2005.

Toasting Marshmallows: Camping Poems, by Kristine O'Connell George. Illus. Kate Keisler. New York: Clarion, 2001.

Zany Zoo, by William Wise. Illus. Lynn Munsinger. Boston: Houghton Mifflin, 2006.

FIG 4.4 *Poetry Books for Choral Reading*

Readers' theatre

Readers' theatre offers students another opportunity for interpretive oral reading as they use voices, facial expressions, and hand gestures rather than costumes and stage sets to interpret characters in scripts and stories. We've found choral reading a valuable rehearsal for readers' theatre because students have already experienced using strategies to create a lively reading. Whether students participate as readers or audience members, they encounter literature presented in an entertaining and interesting manner, often creating new or renewed interest in a book or an author's work. The many benefits of readers' theatre include that it

- builds readers' confidence
- brings stories to life
- animates content areas
- allows students with differing reading abilities to participate
- improves reading ability and quality of oral reading skills (fluency, expression, intonation, inflection)
- improves comprehension because the focus is on interpretation rather than performance

Literature that lends itself to readers' theatre adaptation includes stories or excerpts with exciting plots, compelling characters with lots of dialogue, and descriptive language that enables listeners to create visual images. It is advisable that students already be familiar with a story before you adapt it for a readers' theatre script. While there are numerous websites that offer ready-made scripts, we've found transforming a favorite book or chapter into a script surprisingly easy. By creating your own script, you can link readers' theatre to the books, topics, and interests of your students and your curriculum. If you choose a passage (or complete story) with lively dialogue and interest, the character parts will neatly fall into place. Then either delete or summarize long descriptive passages and create narrator parts to deliver this description and provide necessary context. This attention to dialogue with narration that links characters to plot will make a well-selected text readily adaptable as a script. Then it's time to practice and discuss what's happening in the story and about the characters' intentions, personalities, relationships, and behaviors. This can guide students in how to use voices to interpret the characters. While it's fun to offer different scripts for different groups in your class, it's not necessary. As with choral reading, when multiple groups perform the same selection, it opens up discussion of the different ways a text can be read and interpreted.

We also value the process that students engage in when they write readers' theatre scripts themselves, determine how to read them, and negotiate the staging. It's fascinating to observe the teamwork required as readers gather in small groups to bring the story alive. The decisions they make about what to include in the script and what characters should sound like put social skills to work as students develop the voice of the literature.

After Kate's students finished reading Jerry Spinelli's *Maniac Magee* (1990) in their literature circles, they began writing readers' theatre scripts as an extension project. To guide them in this unique form of writing, Kate demonstrated the process for transforming a story into a script. She copied some pages from a chapter in the novel that served as a stand alone story, put these on the overhead, and talked with the students about what was important to include in the script and what was not. Using an overhead pen, she showed how to cross out "he said" and "she said" lines, how to delete or rewrite lengthy descriptions, how to add a narrator to keep the story's pace moving, and how to rearrange the text into a script for ease of reading. Then students worked in their literature circle groups to select a scene from *Maniac Magee* and rewrite it as a script. This process, including rehearsal and presentation, took approximately two weeks to complete, much longer than Kate had planned.

While there were benefits from this experience, Kate made some different decisions about how and when to involve students in readers' theatre the following year. She realized that the time invested in students writing their own scripts caused her focus on fluency to get lost. Keeping in mind the paired reading relationships between the fifth graders and kindergartners and her commitment to keep students invested in purposeful (and enjoyable) learning toward the end of the school year, the next year Kate revised her focus for readers' theatre. "It occurred to me that picture books were a perfect avenue for readers' theatre, especially if they were books we'd already fallen in love with. It was natural to choose books that my students *felt* something for and it created a real purpose for the students to rehearse (and improve their fluency) because they wanted the classes they visited to become mesmerized by the books they loved so dearly."

Kate sought ready-made scripts for some of her class favorites—Kevin Henkes' *Owen* (1993) and *Wemberly Worried* (2000) and Judy Schachner's *Skippyjon Jones* (2003)—finding success online and with scripts prepared by Nancy's undergraduates. These books represented complete stories and contained more dialogue than the descriptive passages from *Maniac Magee*, and since Kate had read the books aloud earlier in the year, her students had already developed an ear for the story language. With the goal of "going on the road" to perform their scripts in other classrooms the last week of school, Kate's fifth graders had a real reason and audience for their rehearsals, and they took this reading work seriously.

Rarely have we been in classrooms where children were not eager to participate in readers' theatre. There's something about performance that piques interest and involvement. Perhaps because they are supported by a script and given time to rehearse, instead of feeling pressured to memorize, most students find success and fun in readers' theatre. The performance aspect carries over into other areas of reading and writing as students aim to make characters come alive and plots interesting. Since one of the purposes for readers' theatre is to read for an audience (classmates, younger children, parents—at an assembly, for open house, even for Grandparents' Day), students are compelled to practice their lines repeatedly, which reinforces fluency, expression, and comprehension. Readers' theatre also contributes to building community among the students and within the school as the traveling troupe performs in classroom after classroom.

Book talks

In *Wild About Books* (2004), Judy Sierra spins the tale of librarian Molly McGrew, who mistakenly drives her bookmobile into a zoo. The animals become attracted to books through her read-alouds, and soon she is giving book talks and suggesting titles that each "reader" might enjoy. Molly becomes so successful that the zoo creatures no longer depend on her as they develop their own zoobrary. Getting books into children's hands (or into animals' paws, claws, and trunks) is a goal for both Molly McGrew and Miss Malarkey in *Miss Malarkey Leaves No Reader Behind* (Finchler 2006). One strategy for this is book talking.

Librarians are often known for their enthusiastic and informative book talks. When a grade level is studying a content area topic, a genre, or even an author's or illustrator's work in Lisa Williams' school, she gathers library books, shares them with teachers, and then introduces them to students through book talks. Afterward, Lisa tucks the books into a large basket or onto a rolling cart that is shared between the classes. It's not uncommon to see teachers incorporating these books into their read-alouds and students selecting them for independent reading. The school librarian becomes the book expert, both inside and outside the library, informing students about books that might spark their interest, support an inquiry study, or serve as good selections for partner reading.

Book talks are often underutilized in classrooms, yet they are one of the most effective strategies to entice readers. Spontaneous book talks can occur at any time during the day, including the spare minutes students find as they line up for lunch or wait for the bus. It can result from the question "Read anything good lately?" Planned book talks are effective to introduce students to books in the classroom library, book choices for literature circles, text sets about a topic or theme, books by an author or illustrator, or books they might choose for independent reading.

Kate is an avid reader and naturally talks about the book she is currently reading, the next book she hopes to read, and books that have been suggested to her. Many of Kate's book recommendations occur during reading conferences and in response to her students' literary letters. Kate pays attention to the choices her fifth graders make for independent reading, using these to inform her of their interests and tastes so she can make strategic recommendations, either face-to-face or in writing. It's not uncommon for her to suggest books by the same author, about a similar topic, or written in a style the student enjoys reading. And as evidenced by the written conversation that evolves through literary letters, students reciprocate with their own advice—"You should read this book. I think you'll like really it."

Teachers and librarians aren't the only book talkers. Students also "sell" books to their peers all the time, usually with a quick "I think you'd love this one" comment. When students perceive themselves and each other as readers, they are apt to strike up a conversation about a favorite or shared piece of literature. They trust each other to know what's worth reading; often their book recommendations hold more immediate appeal than those from adults.

On the front wall of Megan's classroom is a chart where students record book recommendations for others—including their teacher. Sean articulates how he loves the language in Douglas Florian's poetry books. Lauren thinks Mo Willems' books are really, really funny and she's written her own pigeon book to mimic his ideas. Mackenzie has learned something new about Harriet Tubman from Glennette Tilley Turner's *An Apple for Harriet Tubman* (2006) and wants everyone to know about that book. Students listen closely to each other as they reveal their reading interests and recommend books their classmates will like (see Figure 4.5).

Independent reading

As teachers, we must determine what we value about reading as well as the attitudes and behaviors we want our students to exhibit. In *The Art of Teaching Reading*, Lucy McCormick Calkins relates, "Children can't learn to swim without swimming, to write without writing, to sing without singing, or to read without reading. If all we did in the independent reading workshop was to create a structure to ensure that every child spent extended time engaged in reading appropriate texts, we would have supported readers more efficiently and more effectively than we could through any elaborate plan, beautiful ditto sheet, or

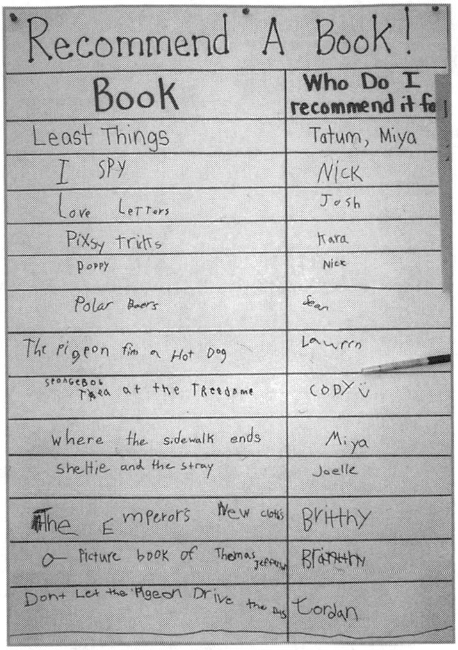

FIG 4.5 *Wall Chart of Primary Students' Book Recommendations*

brilliant lecture" (2001, 68). One of our goals as teachers of reading is to create readers—students who can and want to read independently. Our partner in accomplishing this task is literature.

Independent reading is time to just read. Readers determine their interests, purpose, and taste and they choose a book accordingly. No one assigns it; no one requires a book report; no one checks on comprehension. We know that for anyone to become a proficient reader, she must have time to practice and apply what she is learning. It's important, however, to provide students with strategies for selecting books to read independently. This can be accomplished explicitly through focus lessons on choosing books and implicitly through book talks and the selections we make for read-alouds and literature circles. As we talk about what we enjoy about a book—the type of writing that appeals, the style of illustrations that catches our eye, characters that remind us of people we know, a plot that holds our interest—we demonstrate for students the thinking that is involved in selecting books.

As Megan establishes her reading workshop at the beginning of the year, she takes time to teach the children how to determine a read-to-self book. Not surprisingly, she turns to children's literature for support. Toward the end of

Petunia, by Roger Duvoisin, the main character finally understands how reading is much more than holding a book:

> "Just the other day I heard Mr. Pumpkin telling Bill that Books are very precious. 'He who owns Books and loves them is wise.' That is what he said."
>
> "He who owns Books and loves them is wise," repeated Petunia to herself. And she thought as hard and as long as she could. "Well, then," she said at last, "If I take this Book with me, and love it, I will be wise, too. And no one will call me a silly goose ever again."
>
> So Petunia picked up the book, and off she went with it. (1950)

Reading this book aloud leads to a discussion of how to choose a book that is just right for independent reading. The class creates a list of suggestions to guide their choices (see Figure 4.6). *Petunia* offers an example of the type of reading Megan expects (and the type of reader she promotes). She tells her students, "I don't want any Petunias during read-to-self time," and references this story and the students' suggestions as they choose books that aren't too difficult, books they can read and understand.

Significant to independent reading is book selection and our need to respect what students choose, including magazines, nonfiction, joke or riddle books, series books, poetry, even books written by their classmates. Our actions reflect how we honor these choices. For Megan it means occasionally reading aloud from a series (like Pee Wee Scouts, Junie B. Jones, Horrible Harry, and the Magic Tree House) or books she knows are not meaty but will inspire students to read. She values student choices and knows how motivating it is when they discover books they are interested in, can read on their own, or can read with a friend. For Kate this means actually reading some books that her students recommend in their literary letters.

How to Pick a "Just Right" Book

- ⊡ when you can read most of the words
- ⊡ when the pictures help you
- ⊡ when you like the topic—when you have an interest in it
- ⊡ when you can tell about it after you read it
- ⊡ when you understand the book

FIG 4.6 *Wall Chart on Choosing Just-Right Books*

If we told the real truth about our reading choices as kids, many of us would admit to the pleasures of series books. We hankered for another swell Hardy Boys mystery, modeled our friendship clubs after those in the Baby-Sitters Club, or gulped down episodes of Goosebumps. We related to the cubs in the Berenstain Bears series and were amazed by the spectacular feats in each year's volume of *The Guinness World Book of Records*. It seems we couldn't get enough of books that were part of a series. Today's readers are enamored with them too. So what's the fuss? Authors recognize that series books are part of our literary heritage and they treat them as such. As Avi stated during a presentation at the 2004 American Library Association Annual Conference, "Series books are more 'children's literature' than anything because kids never see adults reading them. Kids treat them as *their* 'literary family.'" Author Bruce Colville refers to series books as training-wheel books and assures concerned adults of their importance in reader development. They give kids the confidence to eventually take on stories that have more complex language and greater length.

Literature circles

There is no doubt that Oprah's televised book clubs have elevated a community of readers to a higher level. Readers across the nation trust Oprah's choices, find ways to get their hands on the books, and tune in to participate as viewers in the televised literary discussions. Anyone who has participated in a book club, whether in person or vicariously, knows how his understanding of the literature grows, changes, evolves, and sometimes becomes more complicated when others bring their interpretation, experience, and opinion to the discussion. Literature circles (or book clubs or literature discussion groups) capitalize on the social nature of learning by honoring talk and shared experiences as valuable ways to respond to a book. Children who participate in literature circles have discovered this as well.

Literature circles are "small groups of students who gather together to discuss a piece of literature in depth. The discussion is guided by students' response to what they have read" (Schlick Noe and Johnson 1999, ix). Literature circles are not intended as *the* reading or literacy program; rather, they provide natural ways for readers to apply the skills and strategies acquired through the read-aloud and learned from shared, guided, and independent reading. Literature circle involvement benefits all students, regardless of age or ability, because it supports and encourages readers to "discuss insights, raise questions, cite related experiences, wonder about or puzzle over situations prompted by what they read" (2).

As a primary-grade teacher, Megan knows she is responsible for teaching her emergent and developing readers the skills and strategies they need to be successful. She devotes time each day to work with small groups of students on areas of need that she has identified through assessment and observation. To do this, Megan makes appropriate choices by using books her students want to read and will become successful in doing so. When a group of students selected *Baseball Saved Us*, by Ken Mochizuki (1993) as their text for guided reading, Megan started with a picture walk. Because good readers often make predictions or generate questions based on what they observe in the illustrations, she took time to begin reading this book visually. Megan then read the first page aloud to establish a purpose, generate questions, and discern the kinds of support the children might need in reading this particular book. She asked, "What images were created in your mind as you read? What questions do you have? What are your connections?" Once students read a few pages of *Baseball Saved Us* on their own, they paused to talk about what they understood and then continued reading the story independently until they reached the end and discussed the book as a whole. To some this might look more like a guided reading lesson than a literature circle. But until her students have experience responding in small groups, Megan supports, demonstrates, and participates with guidance as they read and discuss a book together. She knows that students need to cultivate an understanding and structure for literature circles as well as develop the skills needed for discussion. She begins this process in September and continues demonstrating strategies for reading, discussing, and responding, gradually reducing her role as the year progresses.

One year Kate's fifth graders participated in four rounds of literature circles, each taking approximately three weeks to complete. The first began in mid-October with every group reading Jerry Spinelli's *Maniac Magee* (1990). Kate chose this novel for a number of reasons: she had access to a whole-class set; she knew the characters and themes would interest her students; and most of her students could read the book without support. During this literature circle experience Kate had two goals. One was to teach her students how to talk to each other. She explained, "I assume they don't know how to do so respectfully or with much substance. So I do lots of modeling and we develop a chart of 'conversation changers' to keep the discussion going." The other goal was a focus on reading as thinking. Kate developed this goal through focus lessons on how to mark thinking. She started small: "Put sticky notes on two places where you're predicting something." Then she added other thinking tools during follow-up focus lessons, such as using quick codes written onto sticky notes and attaching these to the pages where the thinking occurred: P for prediction, Q for question, C for connection, and GL for golden line. These thinking flags directly aligned with reading strategies that Kate addressed at other times in the year (e.g., when students responded to the read-aloud and during her guided reading instruction).

The fifth graders' second round of literature circles started in January and included five different novels that Kate selected because her school's book room had multiple copies. Her choices were *How to Eat Fried Worms* (Rockwell 1973), *Because of Winn-Dixie* (DiCamillo 2000), *My Side of the Mountain* (George 1988), *Number the Stars* (Lowry 1989), and *The Time Warp Trio: Knights of the Kitchen Table* (Scieszka 1991). In March the literature circle focus was a genre study of historical fiction. The literature choices included *Fever 1793* (Anderson 2000), *The Captain's Dog: My Journey with the Lewis and Clark Tribe* (Smith 1999), *My Brother Sam Is Dead* (Collier and Collier 1974), *Esperanza Rising* (Ryan 2000), and *Bud, Not Buddy* (Curtis 1999). This round of literature circles evolved into mini-inquiries as each group became steeped in a time period it knew little about. During discussions students raised questions that necessitated a quick Internet search for background information and responses to their wonderings ("What is yellow fever? Does it exist today?"). This literature circle focus developed students' abilities and willingness to raise questions as they sought to clarify and construct factual understandings in order to better understand the characters' thoughts, feelings, and actions in their novels (see Figure 4.7).

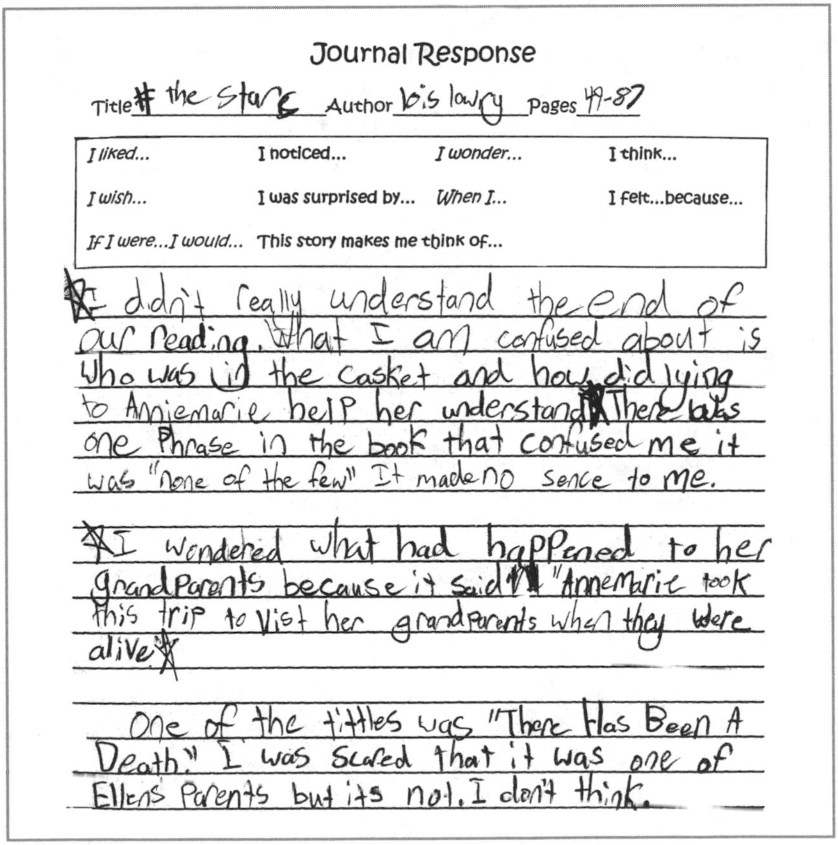
Journal Response

Title # the Stars Author lois lowry Pages 49-87

I liked...	I noticed...	*I wonder...*	I think...
I wish...	I was surprised by...	*When I...*	I felt...because...
If I were...I would...	This story makes me think of...		

I didn't really understand the end of our reading. What I am confused about is Who was in the casket and how did lying to Anniemarie help her understand. There was one Phrase in the book that confused me it was "none of the few" It made no sence to me.

I wondered what had happened to her grandParents because it said "AnneMarie took this trip to vist her grandParents when they were alive"

One of the tittles was "There Has Been A Death." I was scared that it was one of Ellens Parents but its not. I don't think.

FIG 4.7 *Bri's Journal Response to* Number the Stars

The last month of the year featured an author's study on the life and writing of Roald Dahl. Kate started reading aloud Dahl's memoir, *Boy: Tales of Childhood* (1984) a week before she gave book talks on the literature circle books. She wanted to introduce the author's childhood and offer students an ear for some of the personal experiences that Dahl wove into his fiction. The books for this round included *The BFG* (1982), *The Witches* (1983), *Matilda* (1988), *The Twits* (2002b) and *George's Marvelous Medicine* (2002a) (one group read both books), and *James and the Giant Peach* (1996).

How Do Children's Book Authors and Illustrators Become Our Teaching Partners?

As avid readers, we love to talk about our favorite authors and illustrators—about who they are, but mostly about what they create. Now that we've read Avi's *Crispin: At the Edge of the World* (2006), we wonder what will happen in the third book of the trilogy. We're curious about the inspiration behind Mo Willems' hilarious Pigeon books. We indulge in the language in *Out of the Dust* (1997) and other novels written by Karen Hesse that beg to be read aloud.

Children are also intrigued by authors and illustrators. They wonder: What do they look like? Where do they live? How old are they? Do they have any pets? Where do they get their ideas? Sometimes children's questions reflect wonderings unrelated to craft but inspired by their burning interests and genuine curiosity. "One little boy looked as if he would burst if I didn't choose him so I did, and his question was: 'Where did you get your earrings?'" shared Mem Fox on her author's blog about an incident that occurred during a recent author's visit (www.memfox.com). Perhaps adults in the audience were wondering the same thing!

Answers to readers' inquiries about authors and illustrators can be found in the many biographies and autobiographies available in books and other media. A majority of authors, illustrators, and poets now have websites containing interesting biographical information, details about their process for writing and illustrating, questions from readers, and notices about upcoming books. And blogs by authors and illustrators such as Mem Fox, Jane Yolen, Jack Gantos, and J. K. Rowling cause readers (including us) to invest hours reading about the travels and travails of these fascinating individuals. The possibilities for inviting an author or illustrator for a classroom visit—real or virtual—are abundant and provide valuable resources. (See Figure 4.8.)

How can we learn even more about the authors and illustrators who are our partners in creating readers? One strategy for delving deeper into the artistry of

The Author and You series. Portsmouth, NH: Libraries Unlimited.

Caldecott Celebration: Six Artists Share Their Paths to the Caldecott Medal, by Leonard S. Marcus. New York: Walker, 1999.

Children's Books and Their Creators, ed. by Anita Silvey. New York: Houghton Mifflin, 1995.

Good Conversations video series. Scarborough, NY: Tim Podell Productions. www.goodconversations.com/index.htm.

Meet the Author series. Katonah, NY: Richard C. Owen.

Pass It Down: Five Picture Book Families Make Their Mark, by Leonard S. Marcus. New York: Walker, 2006.

Side by Side: Five Favorite Picture-Book Teams Go to Work, by Leonard S. Marcus. New York: Walker, 2001.

Talking with Artists: Volume III, by Pat Cummings. New York: Clarion, 1999. (See also Volumes I and II.)

FIG 4.8 *Resources About Authors and Illustrators*

these individuals is to conduct a focused study. Author studies deepen understanding and appreciation as students read books by the same author, discuss connections within and across books, and develop and offer reasons for personal reading preferences. As they explore an author or illustrator, students discover tidbits of information and begin to view that individual as a real person. After spending time at www.chrisvanallsburg.com, we discovered the reason Chris Van Allsburg includes all or a portion of a white dog in his picture books and we feel like we've been let in on a little secret. Recently, we have enjoyed frequent visits to www.loislowry.com to read Lowry's blog about the latest exploits of her new puppy, Alfie, and her disastrous incident involving a passport photo. Lowry allows us a glimpse into her life through personal, interesting, and humorous anecdotes that often relate to the books she has written. These insights help us realize that her stories are not far removed from her personal life.

During an author study students might examine the writer's craft in depth as they identify elements of the author's writing style that they may emulate themselves. Studying an illustrator teaches about artists' techniques and deepens appreciation for the story that has been told through art. It's not uncommon for us to share snippets of information about authors and illustrators before beginning the read-aloud. Literature circles focused on the author's or illustrator's books can also be conducted. Learning centers, bulletin boards, mini-inquiries, writing craft lessons, and art studies focused on style and media offer other strategies to introduce and extend students' knowledge about authors and illustrators.

One other way authors and illustrators are our teaching partners in creating readers is by revealing their experiences as readers, reminding us of the essence of learning to read. Beverly Cleary comes to mind, not because of her beloved character Ramona, but rather because of the early experiences in Cleary's own reading life. In her memoir, *A Girl from Yamhill* (1988), Cleary relates that she was placed in the Blackbird reading group in first grade, where she was hopelessly lost. "The worst part of the day was the reading circle, where the Blackbirds in turn had to read words from the despised and meaningless word lists: 'shad, shed, shod, shin, shun, shut, shot, ship, shift, shell.' We all feared and hated our turns at that circle of chairs . . . as much as we dreaded saying the words on flash cards" (80). Cleary was "passed on trial" to second grade and eventually encountered teachers who didn't give up on her as a reader. She also discovered literature that interested her, including series books. Literature not only found a key place in her reading life, but in her career too. She was a librarian first, and later became a children's book author. And it's in her life as a writer that she has created such an important place in our students' lives.

Professional Literature Cited

Anderson, Richard C., Elfrieda H. Hiebert, Judith A. Scott, and Ian A. G. Wilkinson. 1985. *Becoming a Nation of Readers: The Report of the Commission on Reading*. Washington, DC: National Institute of Education.

Avi. 2004. American Library Association Annual Convention. June, Orlando, FL.

Calkins, Lucy McCormick. 2001. *The Art of Teaching Reading*. New York: Longman.

Fountas, Irene C., and Gay Su Pinnell. 1996. *Guided Reading*. Portsmouth, NH: Heinemann.

———. 2001. *Guiding Readers and Writers, Grades 3–6: Teaching Comprehension, Genre, and Content Literacy*. Portsmouth, NH: Heinemann.

Fox, Mem. 1993. *Radical Reflections: Passionate Opinions on Teaching, Learning and Living*. San Diego: Harvest/Harcourt.

Holdaway, Don. 1979. *The Foundation of Literacy*. Portsmouth, NH: Heinemann.

Krashen, Stephen D. 2004. *The Power of Reading: Insights from the Research*. Portsmouth, NH: Heinemann.

Mooney, Margaret. 1994. "Shared Reading: Making It Work for You." *Teaching PreK-8* 25: 70–72.

Paterson, Katherine. 1981. *Gates of Excellence: On Reading and Writing Books for Children*. New York: Lodestar.

Peck, Richard. No date. "Sharing the Truth with the First Citizens of the 21st Century." Accessed at www.highlightsfoundation.org/pages/current /sharingTruth.html.

Routman, Regie. 1996. *Literacy at the Crossroads: Crucial Talk About Reading, Writing, and Other Teaching Dilemmas*. Portsmouth, NH: Heinemann.

———. 2005. Association for the Advancement of International Education Conference. July, Seattle, WA.

Schlick Noe, Katherine L., and Nancy J. Johnson. 1999. *Getting Started with Literature Circles*. Norwood, MA: Christopher-Gordon.

Smith, Frank. 1988. *Joining the Literacy Club*. Portsmouth, NH: Heinemann.

Trelease, Jim. 2006. *The New Read-Aloud Handbook*. 6th ed. New York: Penguin.

Conversation with . . .

Author Lois Lowry

Before reading this conversation, you can gain an insider's perspective about Lois Lowry's life by perusing her collected memories included in *Looking Back: A Book of Memories*. We suggest beginning with "Absolute Innocence," "Opening a Trunk," or "Naming."

Your memoir* Looking Back *reminds us that a lot of fiction has roots or inspiration in our own lives. Are there other revelations or back stories since you published that book?

When I went to first grade, I could already read because my sister taught me when I was three and four. I had a wonderful first-grade teacher who dealt with that by giving me books while she was teaching the rest of the class to read. I remember sitting separately from the rest of the class, however. It was kind of an isolated experience. At the end of the year they just put me into third grade. I never went to second grade. The second-grade room was right across from my first-grade room and the kids were always having fun in there. I even remember the second-grade teacher's name. She lived on a farm and at the end of the year she took all the kids out to her house and they rode ponies. I was so looking forward to second grade because they would be doing stuff I hadn't learned yet and I wouldn't be sitting in the corner by myself and I would get to ride a pony. And yet, at the end of that year, and the beginning of the next, I had to walk right past that second-grade room and on to third grade, which was horrible. I always had this feeling of missing out on something wonderful—it was second grade. I think that's why I set the Gooney Bird Greene books within a second-grade classroom.

I was also a self-conscious, shy, introverted child and I envied the children that commanded the stage. I think writers often reshape their own lives in writing to com-

mand the stage. We re-create what we wish we could have gotten or been or done. I did that in my first book, *A Summer to Die*, when I took a family experience and made it better by giving the girl different parents and an elderly friend who was wise, wonderful, and supportive—none of which I had. My parents were kind of stunned into muteness after my sister's illness. So I gave this girl some parents who talked about and dealt with it. I did the same thing in the Gooney Bird books by creating second-grade experiences I'd never had and by creating a little girl I had never been.

Is this true for Gathering Blue *or any of your other books?*

Somebody once said that all fiction is autobiography and all autobiography is fiction. I think that is true. In my fiction there will always be autobiographical elements. In *Gathering Blue* there is a solitary girl, and that was me, and also a very creative and artistic girl, and that was me as well. For *The Silent Boy*, I used family photographs for ideas. Some of the photographs in the book are of my mother as a child. And even though the town is not named, in my mind it's the town where my mother grew up and where I spent my childhood. Although I didn't live in it, when I was a child I knew which house had been my mother's. It was on the same street as the one I put in the book. *Gossamer* involves a character slightly older than I am, but not a whole lot. This unnamed woman would clearly be me. I spend a lot of time in my old house in Maine alone with my dog. That's just what I was picturing when I was creating that woman and her life.

How did Looking Back *originate?*

I was the family recipient of photographs and one day I discovered a funny little book about clothing, accompanied by vignettes. So I looked through my own old photos with clothing in mind. Originally I was going to write anecdotes related to photographs of me wearing hideous clothing throughout my life. There was a photograph of me at age twelve in a red plaid taffeta dress. I remember that dress clearly. We were living in Tokyo after World War II, and we couldn't buy American-style clothes. We used to order clothes through the Sears Roebuck catalog. I fell in love with this dress in the catalog, so my mother gave it to me for Christmas. But I hadn't realized what taffeta was. It was this shiny rustling dress that made too much noise. I couldn't stand the dress. I was almost afraid of it. So that ended up in *Looking Back.* I don't think the text ever refers to the clothing, but many of the photographs in there have to do with what I was wearing back then. So that was the origin, but the book became more than that because I began to see that my memories of those particular photographs worked their way somehow into the fiction that I later wrote.

You create believable characters that readers seem to connect with. How do you do this?

I am a very visual writer. Not only can I see characters, sometimes they tell me their names. As I start writing, I begin describing them physically. But I am not so completely aware that I sit down and say, "She was five feet four inches tall." It's kind of a magical process—it just happens—and it is usually the thing that begins the book for me. The strong feeling of a character seems very real. This is the voice I can hear. Then the dialogue almost writes itself.

Your characters become so real, readers can see them and hear them. Have any surprised you?

Although I generally know how a book is going to end, I don't know how the character is going to achieve that ending. Sometimes it takes me by surprise. I'm not sure that I knew in advance that the main character in *Messenger* was going to die at the end of the book. Yet when I got to that point, it seemed that no other thing could happen.

What are the easiest and hardest parts of writing?

The easiest part is starting something. I could sit and write twelve book beginnings every week. And the endings, once I sort them out in my mind, are also easy. It becomes harder as it goes along, and I'm sure every writer would say the same thing. There is an analogy in *The Giver* in the scene where Jonas is on a sled and he goes through snow. It describes how snow accumulates on the runners of the sled and the sled gets harder and harder to propel. That's what writing a book is like because when you add more characters the plot gets more complicated, it accumulates and accumulates, and pretty soon you really have to push your way through and make everything connect.

Gathering Blue, by Lois Lowry. Boston: Houghton Mifflin, 2000.

The Giver, by Lois Lowry. Boston: Houghton Mifflin, 1993.

Gooney Bird Greene, by Lois Lowry. Illus. Middy Thomas. Boston: Houghton Mifflin, 2002.

Gooney Bird and the Room Mother, by Lois Lowry. Illus. Middy Thomas. Boston: Houghton Mifflin, 2005.

Gooney the Fabulous, by Lois Lowry. Illus. Middy Thomas. Boston: Houghton Mifflin, 2007.

Gossamer, by Lois Lowry. Boston: Houghton Mifflin, 2006.

Looking Back: A Book of Memories, by Lois Lowry. Boston: Houghton Mifflin, 1998.

Messenger, by Lois Lowry. Boston: Houghton Mifflin, 2004.

The Silent Boy, by Lois Lowry. Boston: Houghton Mifflin, 2003.

A Summer to Die, by Lois Lowry. Boston: Houghton Mifflin, 1977.

Side by Side by Side
Literature/Teacher/Learner: Chapter Book Read-Alouds

Book

O'Brien, Robert C. 1971. *Mrs. Frisby and the Rats of NIMH*. Illus. Edward S. Gaza. New York: Atheneum.

Poor Mrs. Frisby! Not only is she recently widowed, but one of her four mouse children is sick with pneumonia and she must allow her natural enemies to come to her aid. The rats of NIMH's exceptional breeding make them highly intelligent, an ideal trait to assist Mrs. Frisby and her children as they travel to their summer quarters safely, but not without suspense, risk, and hold-your-breath adventure.

Related literature

Because of Winn-Dixie, by Kate DiCamillo. Cambridge, MA: Candlewick, 2000.

Charlotte's Web, by E. B. White. Illus. Garth Williams. New York: Harper and Row, 1952.

Did You Carry the Flag Today, Charley? by Rebecca Caudill. Illus. Nancy Grossman. New York: Holt, 1966/2007.

The Enormous Egg, by Oliver Butterworth. Boston: Little, Brown, 1993.

The Green Dog, by Suzanne Fisher Staples. New York: Farrar, Straus and Giroux, 2003.

Henry Huggins, by Beverly Cleary. Illus. Louis Darling. New York: HarperCollins, 1990 (reissue).

Love That Dog, by Sharon Creech. New York: Joanna Cotler/HarperCollins, 2001.

The Mouse and the Motorcycle, by Beverly Cleary. New York: HarperTrophy, 1965.

Poppy, by Avi. New York: Orchard, 1995.

Poppy and Rye, by Avi. Illus. Brian Floca. New York: HarperCollins, 1998.

Ramona the Brave, by Beverly Cleary. Illus. Allan Tiegreen. New York: HarperCollins, 1975 (reissue).

The Tale of Despereaux: Being the Story of a Mouse, a Princess, Some Soup, and a Spool of Thread, by Kate DiCamillo. Illus. Timothy B. Ering. Cambridge, MA: Candlewick, 2005.

Teaching Response

It's the first month of school and the first and second graders in Megan Sloan's class are fully engaged in listening to Robert O'Brien's novel *Mrs. Frisby and the Rats of NIMH*. Each afternoon begins gathered on the carpet, where Megan's voice brings the adventures of Mrs. Frisby to life in this classic Newbery Medal winner. The children are captivated by this story, a book made accessible because it is read aloud, discussed, and imaginatively comprehended orally, visually, and in writing.

While it's not uncommon to hear daily read-alouds of picture books in a primary classroom, what is less common is including novels as part of this repertoire. But Megan knows the power of a good story, no matter the length. She is determined to introduce her students to a rich variety of literature, including books they aren't yet able to access independently.

As Megan considers which chapter-length books to read aloud, she wonders:

Does the novel have rich vocabulary and great language?

Is it a story with interesting characters or about a captivating topic? Will it draw students in?

Will they want me to keep reading? Will they beg for more?

Does it elicit rich response (high-level questions, prediction, connection, visualizing)?

Will it encourage students to read another book in the series or another book by the same author?

How does Megan nurture understanding, individually and collaboratively? Most days this occurs during the follow-up discussion as the children talk aloud, often turning to a classmate to discuss their thinking about the book. Capitalizing on this initial response, Megan might also guide students toward further reflection, sometimes through writing, other times by sketching.

Mrs. Frisby and the Rats of NIMH isn't the only novel Megan will read aloud this year. They'll fall in love with Avi's characters in *Poppy* and *Poppy and Rye*, prompting students like six-year-old Jordan to reread them, even though the books are too challenging for her to read independently ("I love Poppy. I'm going to read all the Poppy books."). They'll become inspired to write poetry, sympathetic to Jack's dilemmas as

a poet in *Love That Dog* (Creech). And personal connections will fly when Megan reads aloud *Ramona the Brave* (Cleary).

How do we know? Children tell us and show us and remind us of the ways they get it—not only intellectually, but in their hearts.

Student Response

Figure 4.9 shows Luca's response to *Mrs. Frisby and the Rats of NIMH*.

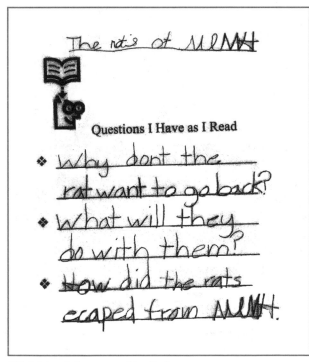

FIG 4.9 *Luca's Response to* Mrs. Frisby

November 9

Dear Miss Norem,
Today, I finished <u>Absolutely Normal Chaos</u>, by Sharon Creech. I don't realy like
the ending. But most of all I don't like that it ended. It was such a good book.
I think that the book should of ended when MaryLou kissed Alex, (which I think
she is a little too obssesed with Alex) or when Carl Ray gets all better and they
go to wind rock and then when they come home she says "School starts tomorrow,
uggggg. I got to stop writing because, it's a school night and I have got to go to
sleep." Something like that anyways.

   You know what I've been thinking? I've been thinking that maybe I should get
a journal. Well, actually I have one, but may be I should actuall start writing in it.
MaryLou reminds me of me. She has so much going on in her life, just like me.
That's what I've been thinking.

   I am going to miss the book <u>Absolutely Normal Chaos</u>! I am so glad Terra, Ali,
and Briana recomended it or eles I wouldn't have read it. This amazing book would
make a good read aloud. I know that because <u>Walk Two Moons</u> is an amazing book
that is just like this one, and my teacher last year read it to us.

With love from Alpha and Omega,
and the people all around,
Monica

November 11

Dear Monica,
I love, love, love Sharon Creech, too! It's always hard for me when a
book I love ends with an ending that I am unsatisfied with.
   I usually do exactly what you did and imagine alternative endings!
   I am so excited to hear about your idea to keep a journal. I have a
journal that I take everywhere with me so that I can write whenever I
feel like it. I also put special things in my journal like tickets and
pictures! I'm sure that if you kept a journal it would fill up with ideas
really fast! Plus, sometimes it feels good to just get your thoughts
down on paper!
   Monica, thank you for sharing your thinking with me. Keep me
posted on your journal.

Love,
Miss Norem

The Presence of Literature to Inspire Writing

Special to
THE AURORA COUNTY NEWS
(Mr. Johnson, this is for
the September 4 early afternoon edition.)

Yet Another Untimely Death
at Snowberger's!!!
Life Notices by Comfort Snowberger:
Explorer, Recipe Tester, and Funeral Reporter

Grab your handkerchiefs! Eggs Florentine Snowberger, Matriarch of the Snowberger's Funeral Home Empire, has died at the ripe old age of 94 after a long and (extremely) colorful life.

She was born into a chicken-farming family, the Petersons, of Halleluia, Mississippi. Her older brother, Benedict, moved to nearby Snapfinger to work at Snowberger's Sawmill when it opened, and that's how Florentine, while visiting Benedict, met Allagash. They fell in love, married, and moved into the old sawmill boardinghouse that became Snowberger's Funeral Home. It's a long story and too much to go into here.

Today the entire Snowberger family lives above Snowberger's Funeral Home in more rooms than this reporter can count. Florentine decorated every room with lavender (her signature herb) and made it her business to sample all funeral food on funeral days. With her favorite niece, Comfort Snowberger, she was compiling a cookbook called *Fantastic (and Fun) Funeral Food for Family and Friends*. . . .

The viewing will be held at 7 pm on Fri., Sept. 4. The funeral will be at 4 pm on Sat., Sept. 5, with visitation for an hour before the service. It's Labor Day weekend, but don't let that stop you. Y'all loved Florentine Snowberger as much as we did, and (as Florentine always said) a funeral offers the perfect time to study geography. So get in the car and come on to the funeral.

—DEBORAH WILES, *Each Little Bird That Sings*

omfort Snowberger is a writer. At ten years old she yearns for publication, crafting ideas on her daddy's Royal typewriter and submitting "life notices" to the editor of the *Aurora County News*, the local newspaper edited by her best friend's father. Comfort is not only a funeral reporter but also a collector and tester of recipes (with plans for cookbook publication until her great-great-aunt Florentine's death), a writer of letters, and a list maker of helpful hints. Her "Top Ten Tips for First-Rate Funeral Behavior," as well as everything else she writes, is grounded in what she knows—and what Comfort knows is life and death, family and friends. Readers of Deborah Wiles' novel *Each Little Bird That Sings* become acquainted with everyday life in Snapfinger, Mississippi, where they meet an assortment of memorable characters (including a loyal shaggy dog named Dismay) and implicitly discover the ways that writing fits into one child's life, for purposes as varied as celebrating, venting, and memorializing, and for audiences as diverse as subscribers to the *Aurora County News*, aggravating cousins, and a spurned best friend.

Learning to write in the presence of literature is about as natural as it comes. Nearly every published writer we know is emphatic about the role of reading in a writer's life. This makes good sense. If we read recipe after recipe after recipe, we internalize the format, as well as the voice of recipe writing. The same is true for all genres. However, reading the literature of what we write isn't enough. We still have to write. But we don't have to do it alone. Writing "under the influence" (Harwayne 1992) of literature is present in the life and work of all published writers. It also can be—and should be—a dominant presence in the life and work of our students. If we revisit Sharon Creech's *Love That Dog* (2001b), we can't miss Jack's partnership with literature during his writing development from September through June. His process, the poetry he writes, even the discoveries he makes about writing all take place in a classroom where students are "marinated" (Fletcher and Portalupi 2001) in literature and supported by a classroom teacher who plays an active role in the writing-literature partnership.

As we mentioned in Chapter 1, we're fully aware that *Love That Dog* is fiction. But our experience in real classrooms in which literature and writing function in tandem convinces us that Ms. Stretchberry's philosophy and pedagogy are valuable and doable. And this makes us wonder:

- ▣ What do we know about teaching writing, and how does literature influence the writer?

- ▣ How does literature serve as a catalyst for student writing?

- ▣ What can we learn from authors and illustrators to inspire writing and teach writers?

What Do We Know About Teaching Writing and How Does Literature Influence the Writer?

Many years ago Donald Graves spoke at a National Council of Teachers of English convention about his research examining the writing instruction in elementary classrooms that culminated in *Writing: Teachers and Children at Work* (1983). One key finding was the difference between processes used by real writers and the ways writing curriculum has been designed. Nearly twenty-five years later, many classrooms have revised writing instruction into workshops that nurture, nourish, and support what real writers do. One element of this, Graves claims, is creating predictable, consistent opportunities for children to write, *no less than* three days a week. When writers know there is time carved out to write—time they can count on—they not only come prepared to write, they also think about and often rehearse their writing even when they're not in the workshop. Without consistent, reliable time to write, there is no momentum and no development of the rhythm that propels ideas and builds confidence.

As we worked on this book, heading to our desks every morning intending to write, Graves' research was confirmed for us. We write in our heads all the time—when we walk, when we read, even when we sleep (and sometimes interrupting our sleep!). We sort and discover ideas at odd moments: waiting in line at the coffee shop, blow-drying our hair, reading a magazine on the airplane. We're on the lookout for insights and examples every time we visit a classroom or talk with a teacher. We live in the middle of our writing even when there's no computer screen or paper or pen at hand, so much so that we've found ideas in unexpected places.

In the winter of 2006, while perusing the *Alaska Airlines Magazine*, Nancy's attention was drawn to an interview with a television actor from a medical drama in which he explained how he prepared for his role playing a cardiac-thoracic surgeon. This included spending more than one year shadowing doctors and performing tasks such as changing bedpans and holding wounds together as a doctor sutured them closed. He observed closely, but he also participated. "'In order to be credible . . . I have to study people who do it for real. It just makes me have to pretend less'" (Bhatt 2006, 23).

An actor's apprenticeship to a certified doctor isn't that different from the teaching and learning process we create for the writers in our classrooms. We study the people who write for a living, cognizant of how an active presence of literature makes this possible. When we do, we understand what Graves claims: when we write for real—for real purposes and real audiences—the need and the desire to learn from our mentors increase.

Early each year Kate Norem guides an introductory focus on writing by asking her fifth graders, "*What* do people write?" She turns to a fresh page of chart paper and jots down ideas as students scan the classroom for evidence. Books, posters, dictionaries, T-shirt slogans make their way onto the chart. Kate sends her students home that afternoon to do some detective work, to notice the myriad forms of writing that exist in their world. She suggests they look around their home with their family and create a list together, perhaps collecting examples of writing they find intriguing and bringing these to class. When the students gather the next day, Kate writes rapidly, tabulating the ideas that come in: menu, voter's guide, cartoon, grocery list, jokes, newspaper article, recipe, advertisement, cereal box, email, baseball statistics, and so on. Writing forms fill up the chart paper, with some writing examples taped next to ideas for evidence. Then Kate asks, "*Why* do people write?" and invites her students to scan the list they've just created to see what they can infer ("Why does someone write an advertisement? Why do people write a grocery list, a joke, an email?"). This second question becomes homework; students must do more sleuthing, on their own and with their families, and return the next day to create a companion list.

Kate wants her students to know and appreciate authentic writing. She wants them to realize there are many purposes that motivate writers and richly diverse audiences associated with those purposes. She also wants them to look closely at what they read (from advertisements to email, from poetry to picture books) so that they'll learn not only about topics and ideas but also about what inspires writers in the first place. Kate wants her students to read with a writer's eye, growing aware of the possibilities they can try out themselves, gleaned from every book (or letter or pamphlet) they read.

Because we intend to teach students not only how to write but also to become skilled, proficient, confident writers, we've made a commitment to remain open to the world of writing around us as our teaching partner. We savor what we learn about writing from the literature we read to and with our students, but we also relish the literature-writing understandings we glean from professional books such as Katie Wood Ray's *Study Driven: A Framework for Planning Units of Study in the Writing Workshop* (2006), Ralph Fletcher and JoAnn Portalupi's *Craft Lessons* (1998) and *Nonfiction Craft Lessons* (2001), Shelley Harwayne's *Novel Perspectives: Writing Minilessons Inspired by the Children in Adult Fiction* (2005), and Megan Sloan's *Trait-Based Mini-Lessons for Teaching Writing in Grades 2–4* (2005). No matter what we read—from professional books and articles, to novels and picture books, to magazine and newspaper articles—we're being taught about writing by the experts. It's good to know we're not alone as we develop relationships between literature and writers.

How Does Literature Serve as a Catalyst for Student Writing?

"Where do you get your ideas?" must be the most common question asked of an author. Those whose lives are invested in writing find ideas anywhere and everywhere. Hungering for rain to relieve summer's heat led to Karen Hesse's picture book *Come On, Rain* (1999), as well as her Newbery Award–winning *Out of the Dust* (1997). Paying close attention during a morning walk inspired the poetry in Ralph Fletcher's *Ordinary Things: Poems from a Walk in Early Spring* (1997). Seeking to cope following a year filled with loss evolved into a tribute to new beginnings in Deborah Wiles' *Each Little Bird That Sings* (2005). The literature we read to our students, as well as the literature they read on their own, holds rich potential to demonstrate the countless topics to write about, to reveal choices writers make regarding genre and format, and to reflect qualities of writing such as word choice and voice.

Literature inspires and demonstrates. And it does so in lively, meaningful ways when teachers make time for wisdom from the resident authors they bring into their classrooms through the literature they read aloud, through author and genre studies, and through focus lessons on topics as broad as where ideas come from and as specific as using verbs for description.

So, where do authors get their ideas? Quite often they tell us, sometimes directly, other times through hints or metaphor. For example, in the author's note to *Color Me a Rhyme: Nature Poems for Young People*, Jane Yolen reveals: "When Jason Stemple and I discussed this book, I said, 'Find me colors in nature!' He laughed. He knew as I did that there are colors everywhere. The problem, of course, was not finding the colors, but isolating them" (2000). Like colors, ideas are also everywhere. Because of that, it's easy to feel overwhelmed by all that's possible. When we suggest that our students choose their own topics, we assume this freedom and openness will result in personal investment in their writing. Yet this anything-is-possible freedom can be overwhelming. As Yolen suggests, the key is in isolating what's possible.

Resident author to inspire ideas

It's nearly 11 A.M. in Portable A. School has been in session for three weeks and today Kate interrupts the two-hour literacy block by gathering her students on the rug to listen to a few pages from Ralph Fletcher's *A Writer's Notebook: Unlocking the Writer Within You* (2003). For the next month, the students will hear excerpts from different chapters in this book, writing in response to some of

Fletcher's ideas and building their endurance and confidence by writing for ten, fifteen, maybe even twenty minutes following each read-aloud. But today is about introductions—to literature about writing, to keeping a writer's notebook, and to what will become the writing portion of their daily literacy block. Kate has chosen Fletcher to craft these beginnings with her.

"This year's writing workshop will probably be a little different from what you've done before," she acknowledges and then reads aloud "What Is a Writer's Notebook, Anyway?" in which Fletcher introduces himself and shares insight into his work as a writer:

> Writing is what I do for my job. I've written books for adults and books for young readers. I've published a novel, several books of poetry, short stories, and books for teachers on how to teach writing. In this book I want to explore with you the most important tool I use: my writer's notebook. Keeping a writer's notebook is one of the best ways I know of living a writing kind of life. (1998, 2)

Fletcher's conversational tone and his shared anecdote about seeing an unusual rainbow and trying to capture the wonder of it in his writer's notebook captivate Kate's students. They begin to know this writer and his experiences. They don't feel intimidated. Rather, they sense a kinship with Fletcher even though they will probably never meet him face-to-face. As she closes the book, Kate inquires, "What are some things from this chapter that excite you, or maybe make you nervous about writing?" She knows that writing can result in emotional involvement and she believes there will be days when writing will feel exhilarating as well as frustrating.

Monica asserts, "This kind of writing sounds like fun."

Chelsea reveals how she's excited to write more poetry.

Even Jacqylyn responds: "It feels good to write stories."

There are just a few comments today, no lengthy discussion. Kate's intention for this focus lesson is introductory, and that's what transpires.

For the next month Kate's focus lessons center around discovering and generating ideas, and Ralph Fletcher is by her side. She reads aloud the chapter titled "Unforgettable Stories" and follows with time for the class to respond orally, first in pairs, then as a whole group. They like Fletcher's suggestion to use their writer's notebook as a place for mental placeholders to remind them of what they might want to return to and write about some other time. They comment on examples from the chapter of everyday, this-happened-to-me events and how stories can have an emotional tug. They point out some of Fletcher's thoughts about writing the stories that keep "tumbling through your mind even when you try not to think about them" (12–13). By the time Kate distributes paper and suggests that they create a list of some unforgettable moments in their lives, everyone has something to write (see Figure 5.1).

When Kate's students receive their writer's notebooks in early November, they have compiled six or seven pages of ideas, all inspired by chapters from *A Writer's Notebook*. The chapters "Seed Ideas" and "Lists" capitalize on students' own interests, as well as events from their lives. "Writing That Scrapes the Heart" reinforces how honest writing takes courage and may tap into emotions. Six, seven, eight pages of possibilities, specific to the each fifth grader's life, are saved and tucked into individual notebooks. The day Kate distributes their writer's notebooks the first time, more than blank paper greets the students. Focus lessons follow on how to use their lists to select or isolate one idea to write about. These young writers are acquiring valuable strategies for idea generating, and they continue this discovery throughout the year.

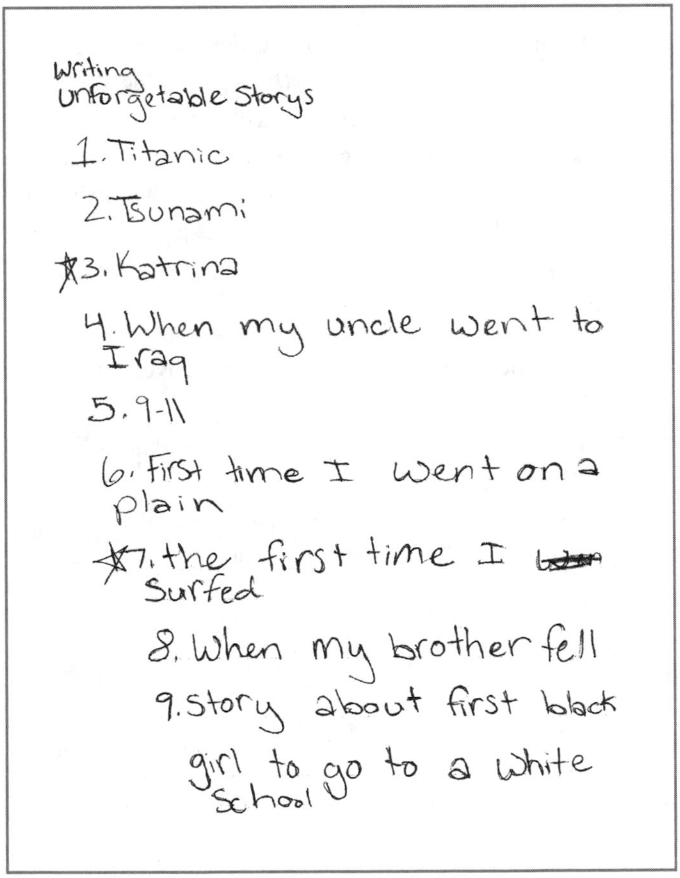

> Writing
> Unforgetable Storys
> 1. Titanic
> 2. Tsunami
> ⭐3. Katrina
> 4. When my uncle went to Iraq
> 5. 9-11
> 6. First time I went on a plain
> ⭐7. the first time I ~~started~~ Surfed
> 8. When my brother fell
> 9. Story about first black girl to go to a white School

FIG 5.1 *Michaela's "Unforgettable Moments" List*

Gradually and purposefully, Kate builds anticipation for the writer's notebook. By taking time to linger together, developing a rich cache of writing topics, and by creating a space and desire to discover them, she helps students' ideas percolate, generate, and bubble up to a point of tantalizing desire. "Will we get our writer's notebooks today?" they beg. And when they do, these children are more than ready to write.

Resident author to demonstrate possibilities

In June, Megan Sloan reads poetry from Fletcher's *A Writing Kind of Day: Poems for Young Poets* (2005) to her first and second graders. As is her ritual, she reads aloud to offer ideas, language, formats, and the inspiring and creative writing of authors whose work she reveres. The students in Megan's class are not new to poetry, not in June. They've heard poetry read since the first day of school. They've read poetry during independent reading. They've written poems in response to their class inquiry about Harriet Tubman and to reflect their intrigue and new understandings following a study of the desert. They've also written nature poetry to accompany images from magazines, following an introduction to Jane Yolen's *Color Me a Rhyme* (2000). This is a class where the presence of poetry has permeated reading and writing all year long. When Megan reads from *A Writing Kind of Day* she's not assigning poetry writing. She's aware that her students have already developed a keen eye and ear for poetry. So it's no surprise when Mason writes "It's a Writing Kind of Night," inspired by Fletcher's poem with nearly the same title.

It's a Writing Kind of Night

It's a writing kind of night.
A galaxy is near,
made of words and minds.
Look! The stars
are falling, each
making a word
of a poem.
—Mason Caldwell

A Writing Kind of Night

It is clear tonight,
a writing kind of night.

There's a moon stirring up
mysterious metaphors
in my imagination.

The heavens are jam-packed
with planets and black holes
that are still undiscovered,

and magnificent poems
that are still unwritten.
—Ralph Fletcher

Both Kate and Megan understand the benefits of inviting an author like Ralph Fletcher to take up virtual residence in their writing classrooms for a week, a month, or all year long. This residence provides inspiration and instruction, whether through the author's or illustrator's written exploration of craft or through the indirect lessons that are gleaned from thoughtfully reading their work. Neither teacher wastes energy trying to choose authors who best match their students' age or grade level. Instead, they trust how almost any author's writing can provide ideas, understandings, and demonstrations for their students, and they prove how the same author can become a mentor, no matter how old the writer is.

"What can I write about?" Inspiration from literature

Both of us started teaching writing with little experience as writers ourselves and with limited education about writing instruction. We modeled our teaching on the patterns of our own education. Creating writing topics for our students fell to us—or so we thought—and this task was both perplexing and daunting. At times we relied on story starters and topics culled from how-to books with reproducible worksheets. Other times we racked our brains for topics we thought our students would find exciting, such as magic or outer space or even "the day I woke up as a pencil." Not only was our students' writing lifeless and unremarkable, but there was little ownership of their work and no match between what they wrote and what they liked to read. What's more, they hated writing and we dreaded our role as creator of topics. We now know this doesn't have to happen.

When Kate reads aloud *All the Places to Love* by Patricia MacLachlan (1994), she has chosen this book intentionally. She knows it will spark a conversation about how authors write what they know and care about and will also allude to place as a worthwhile topic for a writer. Following the read-aloud, the students talk in pairs about places they have some feelings about, places they know well enough to describe not only visually but also using other senses. Kate rereads the book, this time suggesting they attend to MacLachlan's description. "How does she use smell, sound, and taste words or phrases to let us know this place she loves?" As students prepare to write that day, Kate offers MacLachlan's idea as a possibility: "Let's take about five or ten minutes to try this out. Write about a place you know well and try to describe it in ways a reader will know not only what it looks like but also how you feel about it."

Kate chooses picture books as springboards, not as story starters. She doesn't expect polished pieces with every quick-write that's ignited by an idea an author introduces, nor does she expect the writing will directly replicate the literature

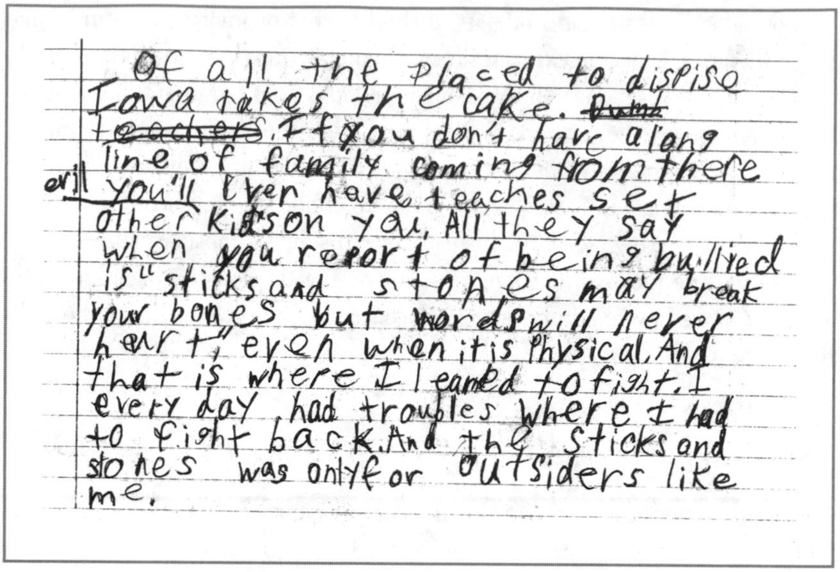
Of all the Placed to disPise Iowa takes the cake. ~~Dumb teachers~~. If you don't have a long line of family coming from there you'll ever have teaches set other kids on you. All they say when you report of being bullied is "sticks and stones may break your bones but words will never hurt," even when it is Physical. And that is where I learned to fight. I every day had troubles where I had to fight back. And the sticks and stones was only for outsiders like me.

FIG 5.2 *Stuart's Writing Inspired by* All the Places to Love

(see Figure 5.2). That's not her intent. Whenever she selects literature to raise the awareness of writing—from ideas to word choice to format—she does so to get her students' thoughts rolling and their ideas flowing.

"The bones of good writing can be found in a picture book," suggested Laurie Halse Anderson at a conference for teachers and writers. This advice is confirmed for us with each piece of student writing, reflecting ideas gleaned from picture books such as Patricia MacLachlan's *All the Places to Love*, Mem Fox's *Wilfrid Gordon McDonald Partridge* (1985), and Janet Wong's *You Have to Write* (2002). The more we read and write ourselves, the more easily we can discern a book's potential to inspire writing.

Discovering where ideas reside is like going on a fantastic treasure hunt. We peruse books, taking time to read aloud authors' notes, acknowledgments pages, and afterwords. We realize how these components can deepen understanding and appreciation for the book and serve to uncover riches for teaching and writing. For example, the author's note in David Shannon's *No, David!* (1998b) hints at how this picture book is literally a remake of one he created as a five-year-old, using the very same title. Apparently Shannon's mother mailed him a copy of his child-created book, liberally illustrated and using only the words he could spell (*no* and *David*). So he simply remade that book, using full sentences ("Don't play with your food!" and "Stop that this instant!") and wacky illustrations.

The afterword to Christopher Paul Curtis' *Bud, Not Buddy* (1999) reveals that a number of characters in the novel were based on family members. He relates how when he was a child and the older folks would talk about their lives during the Depression, his "eyes would glaze over and [he'd] think, 'Oh, no, not those boring tall tales again!'" (242). Curtis admonishes, "Be smarter than I was: Go talk to Grandma and Grandpa, Mom and Dad. . . . Discover and remember what they have to say about . . . growing up" (243). The idea for Pam Muñoz Ryan's *When Marian Sang* (2002) was also sparked by a family story, but her inspiration was less direct. Ryan's previous picture book, *Amelia and Eleanor Go for a Ride* (1999), prompted her readers to share Eleanor Roosevelt stories, including one passed along by the uncle of Brian Selznick (the illustrator of *Amelia and Eleanor* as well as *When Marian Sang*). His story about Eleanor Roosevelt, Marian Anderson, and the Lincoln Memorial concert intrigued Ryan and led to research, fascination, and the feeling of being "introduced to someone who was a kindred spirit to other characters about whom [she'd] written. . . . It was with that passion and conviction that [she] set out to write this book" (2002).

Newspaper clippings can also provide fodder for ideas. The author's note at the end of Jeanette Winter's *The Librarian of Basra: A True Story from Iraq* (2005) acknowledges Shaila K. Dewan, a *New York Times* reporter who uncovered the story of librarian Alia Muhammad Baker. Winter read Dewan's newspaper article about how this city librarian saved nearly 70 percent of the library's collection before it burned during the invasion of Iraq, and she felt compelled to recast the story as a picture book, certain that this *real* story would interest young readers.

Whenever we read these inside stories, we're reminded that topics for writing can come from anywhere. There's no magic formula for discovering writing ideas; often they are as close as our own experiences or our family's lives. They're as present as what we read in the newspaper or hear in the news. And we can research them by talking to family members as we discover and then uncover stories that might wind their way into memoir, biography, or poetry or even become reimagined as fiction.

In addition to reading the front and back matter in literature, we recommend visiting authors' websites for additional inspiration for ideas. Avi's website (www.avi-writer.com) reminds us that ideas don't belong only to writers:

Everybody has ideas. The vital question is, what do you do with them? My rock musician sons shape their ideas into music. My sister takes her ideas and fashions them into poems. My brother uses his ideas to help him understand science. I take my ideas and turn them into stories. Now, what do you think you'll do with your ideas?

Teaching students how literature can inspire ideas for their writing has become some of the most exhilarating work we do, especially because we do it in the company of these fine writers. Discovering unforgettable stories and ideas that writers care enough to write about doesn't require any special talent or worksheet or writing prompt. Our discoveries can be supported by the literature itself, the wisdom of authors who encourage us to mine the experiences and feelings from our own lives, keep our eyes wide open when we read or watch television or listen to music, and then actually do something with them.

Leaning on literature to learn about and celebrate writing formats

One pure pleasure of our work is filling kids up with authors all year long. When we do so, we discover there are writing lessons available with every book we read. When Megan introduces literature to her students, she invites them to "stand on the shoulders of the author" to learn about ideas, mimic the writer's style, and borrow her technique. Whether the invitation is one all students will accept, or whether it's intended purely as inspiration, we're reminded once again of the valuable presence of literature as our teaching partner.

Young children don't think twice about adapting an idea or format they've picked up from authors and illustrators. In May, first grader Joelle used her reading journal to record information about birds that interested her, organized in a question-answer format. When asked to share her journal with the rest of the class, Joelle revealed how the question-answer design of the book *Why?* (Prap 2005) inspired her format. *Why?* features a question on each page, such as "Why do kangaroos have pouches?" and then offers humorous answers ("To hide their bellybuttons. To put their toys in. So they don't lose their babies when they jump"). Prap states in the book's introduction: "Dear Curious Friends: Some of the answers to the questions in this book are silly, some are sensible, and some are scientific. (Those are the ones marked by an asterisk *.)" Since *Why?* provided a doable structure with both silly and serious facts, Joelle chose to model her own writing after what she was reading. A book became Joelle's teacher as she learned a new format to share facts, and then she became a teaching partner for her classmates as they guessed their way through her questions about birds.

Kate introduces books with riddle poems, such as *When Riddles Come Rumbling* (Dotlich 2001) and *Butterfly Eyes and Other Secrets of the Meadow* (Sidman 2006) to ponder how and why a writer might choose this form. This lesson is enough to tease some students into trying the technique themselves, as Brickell and Monica did to create a collaborative collection of riddles called *Guess What It Is . . .*

Put your feet up and relax
I am here to save you from trouble and exhaustion
One long load and I'll sink to the ground
Don't worry
I won't let you down
Add a pillow
I'm as comfy as can be
[*chair*]

A slip of memories
Ghostly and vital
But lovely pieces of art
Come and create!
[*paper*]

Since literature is present all day, every day in these classes, evidence of it appears in students' writing notebooks and reading journals. So when both Kate and Megan read aloud books with an intriguing format, such as *Dear Juno*, by Soyung Pak (1999), and *Plantzilla*, by Jerdine Nolen (2002), picture books written through letters, their students follow suit (see Figure 5.3 for lists of literature written as letters, postcards, diary entries, and travel logs). It doesn't always take a well-honed craft lesson to inspire writing. What it does take is the presence of literature, someone to give it life and voice, time to read and write, and audiences and purposes to celebrate both the false starts and the final products.

One winter Kate's fifth graders were eager to share their poetry with a wider audience, so they organized the Class Café—Poetry Reading, an evening event for their families. They designed the invitation, secured help from parents for table decorations and refreshments, selected one poem each to read aloud, and practiced, practiced, practiced. There was standing room only in the library for the very first student poetry reading in the history of Geneva Elementary School, and the audience was treated to a full range of poetry, from Dustin's heart-wrenching "What Happened" to Jacqylyn's "Julya," a four-line tribute to her sister, and from Cameron's unrhymed "Love Is a Power" to Stuart's celebration of fireworks in "Poppers."

Leaning on literature to demonstrate genre and traits

Nearly every classroom teacher we know faces curricular requirements regarding the teaching of writing genres and traits. While there are numerous resources

Picture Books That Include Letters, Postcards, Notes, or Memos

Click, Clack, Moo: Cows That Type, by Doreen Cronin. Illus. Betsy Lewin. New York: Simon and Schuster, 2000.

Dear Mrs. LaRue: Letters from Obedience School, by Mark Teague. New York: Scholastic, 2002.

Detective LaRue: Letters from the Investigation, by Mark Teague. New York: Scholastic, 2004.

The Gardener, by Sarah Stewart. Illus. David Small. New York: Farrar, Straus and Giroux, 1997.

I Wanna Iguana, by Jerdine Nolen. Illus. David Catrow. New York: Putnam, 2004.

Messages from Mars, by Loreen Leedy and Andrew Schuerger. New York: Holiday House, 2006.

One Thousand Tracings: Healing the Wounds of World War II, by Lita Judge. New York: Hyperion, 2007.

Stringbean's Trip to the Shining Sea, by Vera B. Williams and Jennifer Williams. New York: Greenwillow, 1988.

Novels That Include Letters, Memos, and/or News Journalism

Beany Goes to Camp, by Susan Wojciechowski. Illus. Susanna Natti. Cambridge, MA: Candlewick, 2002.

Dear Mr. Henshaw, by Beverly Cleary. Illus. Paul O. Zelinsky. New York: HarperCollins, 1983.

Dear Papa, by Anne Ylvisaker. Cambridge, MA: Candlewick, 2002.

The Landry News, by Andrew Clements. Illus. Salvatore Murdocca. New York: Simon and Schuster, 1999.

Letters from Camp: A Mystery, by Kate Klise. Illus. M. Sarah Klise. New York: HarperCollins, 1999.

Little Wolf's Book of Badness, by Ian Whybrow. Illus. Tony Ross. Minneapolis: Carolrhoda, 1999.

Love from Your Friend, Hannah, by Mindy Warshaw Skolsky. New York: DK Publishing, 1998.

Love, Ruby Lavender, by Deborah Wiles. San Diego: Harcourt, 2001.

Nothing But the Truth, by Avi. New York: Scholastic, 1991.

Picture Books That Include Diary Entries, Journals, Travel Logs, or Notebooks

Amazon Diary: The Jungle Adventures of Alex Winters, by Hudson Talbott. New York: Putnam, 1996.

Amelia's Notebook, by Marissa Moss. Middleton, WI: Pleasant, 1999.

Amelia's School Survival Guide, by Marissa Moss. New York: Paula Wiseman/Simon & Schuster, 2006.

Diary of a Fly, by Doreen Cronin. Illus. Harry Bliss. New York: Joanna Cotler/HarperCollins, 2007.

Diary of a Spider, by Doreen Cronin. Illus. Harry Bliss. New York: Joanna Cotler/HarperCollins, 2005.

Diary of a Worm, by Doreen Cronin. Illus. Harry Bliss. New York: Joanna Cotler/HarperCollins, 2003.

The Journey, by Sarah Stewart. Illus. David Small. New York: Farrar, Straus and Giroux, 2001.

My Season with Penguins: An Antarctic Journal, by Sophie Webb. Boston: Houghton Mifflin, 2000.

Novels That Include Diary Entries, Journals, Travel Logs, or Notebooks

Catherine, Called Birdy, by Karen Cushman. New York: Clarion, 1994.

Don't You Dare Read This, Mrs. Dunphrey, by Mary Peterson Haddix. New York: Simon and Schuster, 1996.

A Gathering of Days: A New England Girl's Journal, 1830–1832, by Joan W. Blos. New York: Scribner's, 1979.

Melanie in Manhattan, by Carol Weston. New York: Knopf, 2005.

Pedro's Journal, by Pam Conrad. Illus. Peter Koeppen. Honesdale, PA: Boyds Mills, 1991.

The Private Notebook of Katie Roberts, Age 11, by Amy Hest. Illus. Sonja Lamut. Cambridge, MA: Candlewick, 2005.

The True Confessions of Charlotte Doyle, by Avi. New York: Scholastic, 1990.

The Wanderer, by Sharon Creech. Illus. David Diaz. New York: Joanna Cotler/ HarperCollins, 2000.

FIG 5.3 *Books with Interesting Formats*

available that capitalize on these expectations, we believe the truest resource comes from immersion in the genre or trait we're teaching students. We've seen students become skilled writers through intentional teaching that includes reading and rereading well-crafted literature in that genre (or using specific traits), discovering what can be inferred from the writing, and partnering this examination with wisdom from the authors themselves.

Both Megan and Kate choose to focus on poetry every year, not because it's poetry month or because their school district mandates that genre for their grade level, but because they know that an investment in poetry will reap rewards that seep into other reading and writing work they do. They read poetry aloud. They invite students to discover poetry written about nearly any topic imaginable. They focus on ways to pay attention to words, layout, and rhythm (and maybe also rhyme). They discover how the genre of poetry allows them to notice word choice and line breaks, as well as pay attention to mind pictures and metaphors. These teachers rely on insight from professional books like Georgia Heard's *Awakening the Heart: Exploring Poetry in the Middle School* (1998) and Sara Holbrook's *Practical Poetry* (2005) and interviews with poets in *Poetry Matters: Writing a Poem from the Inside Out*, by Ralph Fletcher (2002). They savor suggestions for poetic play from Jack Prelutsky's *Read a Rhyme, Write a Rhyme* (2005) and *Scranimals* (2002) as well as other collections of poetry written for children. And they also discover poets' advice written exclusively for young writers, such as in Paul Janeczko's *The Place My Words Are Looking For* (1990) and *Seeing the Blue Between: Advice and Inspiration for Young Poets* (2002).

When Megan reads aloud the poems from Jane Yolen's *Color Me a Rhyme* (2000), she lingers over each page, making sure her students notice not only the poem and the accompanying photograph but also the way the photo on each page is framed with color words that illuminate the poem. The words *apricot, pumpkin, tangerine, copper,* and *carrot* frame a photograph of lichen opposite the poem titled "Orange." "Green" is accompanied by a photo of a sword fern and set inside the words *ivy, verdure, grass, olive, leek,* and *emerald.* Yolen's collection of poetry varies in pattern and form. Some pieces are short, some are long, and all paint pictures with color words.

Megan doesn't race through this collection. She reads aloud just one or two poems a day. Then at week's end she brings large sheets of colored construction paper to the writing workshop. On each page she's printed the corresponding color words that Yolen used to complement her poems. The focus lesson this Friday is on word choice, specifically how writers paint pictures with words. First, Megan and the children read through the word lists on each sheet of construction paper before she writes. Then she explains how a daffodil blooming at the edge of the playground caught her eye that morning and how this might make a good idea for a poem. As Megan talks, she drafts words and phrases onto chart paper, trying out alternatives for the color yellow—lemon, saffron, canary—borrowed directly from the construction paper list, eventually composing a short, visually descriptive poem. Before the children leave the carpet area to write, Megan places the color charts and a box of nature photographs clipped from *National Geographic* and *Zoobook* onto a centrally located desk. She suggests students might want to focus their writing that day on using descriptive color words, perhaps to write about something they notice in their world or about something in a photo that inspires them. Miya's attention is drawn to a photo of underwater sea creatures, while Sydney crafts a haiku based on a memory of autumn harvest.

Green, Purple, Orange

Orchid sea stars
leap over pumpkin tentacles,
Emerald plants sit by a rainbow,
underwater
miracles
sitting together
Best friends forever.
—Miya

Orange

A pumpkin breeze floats
Among us, through horizons
Tangerine air rises.
—Sydney

Because Megan's students read and write poetry from September through June, they know the possibilities and the pleasures this genre holds. A few years ago, her class was particularly on fire as poets. They saw poetry everywhere, even in each other's experiences. One morning Jordan shared some photos she'd taken of a garter snake in her backyard tree. Hardly a minute passed before Joelle approached Megan, begging to write about her classmate's snake (see Figure 5.4). "Ms. Sloan, Ms. Sloan," Joelle exclaimed, "I'm burning up with a poem." This wise teacher's response? "By all means, go write."

Kate also begins the writing portion of each morning's literacy block with a focus lesson. Usually it incorporates literature and often she reads aloud a story, a poem, or even a short passage to demonstrate writer's craft. Kate's school district evaluates student writing using a trait rubric, so it's not unexpected to observe

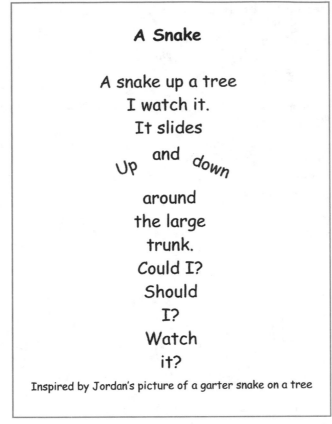

A Snake

A snake up a tree
I watch it.
It slides

UP   and   down

around
the large
trunk.
Could I?
Should
I?
Watch
it?

Inspired by Jordan's picture of a garter snake on a tree

FIG 5.4 *Joelle's Poem, "A Snake"*

her weaving the language of the traits into her focus lessons. She does so not to teach to the test, but rather because the traits serve as a common vocabulary about the qualities and elements of writing found in everything she reads. Like Megan, Kate supports students' poetry writing with plenty of poetry reading. She also teaches ways of slowing down an idea, techniques for creating surprise and connection with metaphor and simile, and strategies for working out line breaks. Today the focus lesson is on simile, and Kate has adapted an idea called Spinning Metaphors and Similes from Georgia Heard's *Awakening the Heart* (1998) to guide her lesson. Kate reads aloud "Safety Pin" and "Asparagus" from Valerie Worth's *All the Small Poems and Fourteen More* (1994). A discussion ensues about how a poet can start with an ordinary object, look at it in a whole new way, and then use that to create a poem. On a fresh sheet of chart paper, Kate and her students search the room for something ordinary, and then they look closely for other ways, unexpected ways, to describe it. Using the frame "A _____ is like . . . ," Monica comes up with three similes for her topic, a paper lantern.

A paper lantern is like . . .

1. a tiny globe hanging from a blanket of sky
2. a ball of fire reaching out to the ground
3. a ball of snow floating in the air

Then she sorts and sifts, drafts and revises until an unexpected description is created:

Paper lanterns hang like tiny beehives
clinging to a tree.
A glimpse of light peeks from the
bottom of the swinging ball.
Above, a blanket of twinkling sky
below, a ground of earth and moisture.
Delicate as a crystal, shining like the moon.
—Monica

What Can We Learn from Authors and Illustrators to Inspire Writing and Teach Writers?

If we learn to write from literature, we should capitalize on every opportunity to introduce our students to the many literary mentors who can teach them not only where ideas reside but also about living a writing life. This includes learning from authors and illustrators, editors and art directors, and even the writerly characters in children's literature.

In the previous chapter we suggested bringing books and resources about writers and illustrators into the classroom, such as Richard C. Owens' superb Meet the Authors series. These short autobiographical books read like intimate conversations with friends. They are replete with photographs, showing the writer at work in her own home or studio and revealing aspects of her personal life that weave a way into her writing. In *Firetalking* (Polacco 1994a) we meet Patricia Polacco's family, learn about her Russian heritage, and discover that her book *Mrs. Katz and Tush* (1992) was written to honor a beloved pet cat, Tush, who died just a year earlier. When we read Jane Yolen's *Letter from Phoenix Farm* (1992b), we take a walk with her along the Connecticut River, observe her writing routines, and unearth her inspiration for *Owl Moon* (1987). It's really the story of her husband taking their daughter, Heidi, out owling.

Two other resources we recommend are "Meet the Author/Illustrator," available on the *Children's Book Council Magazine* website (www.cbcbooks.org/

cbcmagazine/meet), which has an archive of articles that go back to 1996, and the author/illustrator interviews in each issue of *Book Links*, a publication of the American Library Association. While both resources are written for adults, we've shared revelation gleaned from their interviews with our students. Figure 5.5 lists additional literature and resources we suggest that showcase authors and illustrators writing about their craft.

Children's book authors have created what must surely constitute an entire classroom of characters who write (see Figure 5.6 for some examples). From Comfort Snowberger's recipes and life notices in *Each Little Bird That Sings* (2005) to Ruby Lavender's letters to her grandmother, Miss Eula, in *Love, Ruby Lavender* (2001), Deborah Wiles introduces characters who reveal themselves, their friends and enemies, and small-town life in Mississippi through their writing. In *Hey World, Here I Am!* (1986), Jean Little's writerly character is Kate Bloomfield, a poet, journal writer, and keen observer of the world, her family, and her feelings. Helen Frost's *Spinning Through the Universe* (2004) and Nikki Grimes' *Bronx Masquerade* (2001) take readers into two classrooms, introducing

---

Author: A True Story by Helen Lester. Boston: Walter Lorraine/Houghton Mifflin, 1997.

Booklinks: www.ala.org/ala/productsandpublications/periodicals/booklinks/booklinks.htm.

"Creative Collaboration: Author-Editor Dialogues." *CBC Magazine.* Children's Book Council Website: www.cbcbooks.org/cbcmagazine/dialogues/.

From Pictures to Words: A Book About Making a Book, by Janet Stevens. New York: Holiday House, 1995.

How a Book Is Made, by Aliki. New York: Crowell, 1986.

If You Were a Writer, by Joan Lowery Nixon. Illus. Bruce Degen. New York: Four Winds, 1988.

Look at My Book: How Kids Can Write and Illustrate Terrific Books, by Loreen Leedy. New York: Holiday House, 2005.

Poems from Homeroom: A Writer's Place to Start, by Kathi Appelt. New York: Holt, 2002.

Seeing the Blue Between: Advice and Inspiration for Young Poets, compiled by Paul Janeszko. Cambridge, MA: Candlewick, 2002.

What Do Authors Do? by Eileen Cristelow. New York: Clarion, 1997.

What Do Illustrators Do? by Eileen Cristelow. New York: Clarion, 1999.

What's Your Story? A Young Person's Guide to Writing Fiction, by Marion Dane Bauer. New York: Clarion, 1992.

You Have to Write by Janet S. Wong. Illus. Teresa Flavin. New York: Margaret K. McElderry/Simon and Schuster, 2002.

FIG 5.5 *Children's and Young Adult Authors Writing About Craft*

Novels Featuring Characters Who Write

Bronx Masquerade, by Nikki Grimes. New York: Dial, 2001.

Catherine, Called Birdy, by Karen Cushman. New York: Clarion, 1994.

Dear Max, by Sally Grindley. Illus. Tony Ross. New York: Margaret K. McElderry/Simon and Schuster, 2006.

Hattie Big Sky, by Kirby Larson. New York: Delacorte, 2006.

Olive's Ocean, by Kevin Henkes. New York: Greenwillow, 2003.

Pieces of Georgia, by Jen Bryant. New York: Knopf, 2006.

Project Mulberry, by Linda Sue Park. New York: Clarion, 2005.

Sahara Special, by Esmé Raji Codell. New York: Hyperion, 2003.

The School Story, by Andrew Clements. Illus. Brian Selznick. New York: Simon and Schuster, 2001.

Spinning Through the Universe, by Helen Frost. New York: Farrar, Straus and Giroux, 2004.

Picture Books Featuring Characters Who Write

The Boy Who Loved Words, by Roni Schotter. Illus. Giselle Potter. New York: Schwartz and Wade, 2006.

The Day of Ahmed's Secret, by Florence Parry Heide and Judith Heide Gilliland. Illus. Ted Lewin. New York: HarperCollins, 1990.

Giggle, Giggle, Quack, by Doreen Cronin. Illus. Betsy Lewin. New York: Simon and Schuster, 2002.

Letters from a Desperate Dog, by Eileen Christelow. New York: Clarion, 2006.

Matilda's Humdinger, by Lynn Downey. Illus. Tim Bowers. New York: Knopf, 2006.

Max's Words, by Kate Banks. Illus. Boris Kulikov. New York: Farrar, Straus and Giroux, 2006.

Mr. Putter and Tabby Write the Book, by Cynthia Rylant. Illus. Arthur Howard. San Diego: Harcourt, 2004.

Nothing Ever Happens on 90th Street, by Roni Schotter. Illus. Kyrsten Brooker. New York: Scholastic, 1997.

Patches Lost and Found, by Steven Kroll. Illus. Barry Gott. New York: Winslow, 2001.

A Splendid Friend, Indeed, by Suzanne Bloom. Honesdale, PA: Boyds Mills, 2005.

Wild About Books, by Judy Sierra. Illus. Marc Brown. New York: Knopf, 2004.

FIG 5.6 *Characters Who Write*

them to individual students through their poetry and revealing first-person prose. Reading aloud a novel like Andrew Clements' *The School Story* (2001) will answer students' questions about the publishing world and encourage future novelists, agents, and editors.

A number of irresistible picture book characters reflect equal skill as writers. Reading these books aloud once, twice, even three times will add new voices to the classroom, voices of storytellers, picture writers, letter writers, and poets. Doreen Cronin's *Click, Clack, Moo: Cows That Type* (2000) introduces remarkably literate cows who use the influence of writing notes to Farmer Brown to get their needs met. When Duck finds a pen in *Duck's Tale*, by Harmen van Straaten (2007), he is convinced that he can write because his friend Toad can "read" after he finds a pair of glasses. After proudly scribbling a story onto paper and giving it to Toad to read, Duck discovers there is often more to writing (and reading) than meets the eye. Laurie Halse Anderson relates the power of the pen through her picture book *Thank You, Sarah: The Woman Who Saved Thanksgiving* (2002). This biography tells the dynamic story of Sarah Hale, a little-known poet, novelist, and magazine editor who wrote thousands of letters asking politicians to make Thanksgiving a national holiday and finally convinced Abraham Lincoln to say yes! And the animals in *Wild About Books*, by Judy Sierra (2004), teach us about writing as they first devoured books as readers and then "made up adventures so thrilling and new / that the others decided to be authors, too." All are characters that children will delight in as they find support to participate as writers too.

Professional Literature Cited

Bhatt, Robert N. 2006. "Character Study: *Grey's Anatomy's* Isaiah Washington." *Alaska Airlines Magazine* (January): 23–24.

Fletcher, Ralph J., and JoAnn Portalupi. 1998. *Craft Lessons: Teaching Writing K–8*. York, ME: Stenhouse.

———. 2001. *Writing Workshop: The Essential Guide*. Portsmouth, NH: Heinemann.

Fox, Mem. 1993. *Radical Reflections: Passionate Opinions on Teaching, Learning, and Living*. San Diego: Harvest/Harcourt.

Graves, Donald H. 1983. *Writing: Teachers and Children at Work*. Portsmouth, NH: Heinemann.

Harwayne, Shelley. 1992. *Lasting Impressions: Weaving Literature into the Writing Workshop*. Portsmouth, NH: Heinemann.

———. 2005. *Novel Perspectives: Writing Minilessons Inspired by the Children in Adult Fiction*. Portsmouth, NH: Heinemann.

Heard, Georgia. 1998. *Awakening the Heart: Exploring Poetry in the Elementary and Middle School*. Portsmouth, NH: Heinemann.

Holbrook, Sara. 2005. *Practical Poetry: A Nonstandard Approach to Meeting Content Area Standards*. Portsmouth, NH: Heinemann.

Portalupi, JoAnn, and Ralph Fletcher. 2001. *Nonfiction Craft Lessons: Teaching Information Writing K–8*. York, ME: Stenhouse.

Ray, Katie Wood. 2006. *Study Driven: A Framework for Planning Units of Study in the Writing Workshop*. Portsmouth, NH: Heinemann.

Sloan, Megan. 2005. *Trait-Based Mini-Lessons for Teaching Writing in Grades 2–4*. New York: Scholastic.

Conversation with . . .
Author Linda Sue Park and editor Dinah Stevenson

Linda Sue Park and her editor Dinah Stevenson reveal the process of working together on several of Park's books including the Newbery Award winner ***A Single Shard*** as well as ***Seesaw Girl***, ***When My Name Was Keoko***, ***Project Mulberry***, and ***Archer's Quest***.

We're curious about the relationship and the conversations that an author and her editor have as they negotiate a piece of writing.

PARK: All editors are different and probably work differently with each of their writers. Dinah rarely gives me a suggestion. Instead, she asks questions. With *Seesaw Girl*, she asked, "The wedding seems to be an important part of the story. Do you think you handled it too perfunctorily?" As a new writer, this was extremely frustrating. I was like a little kid. Tell me what to do and I'll do what you want. But she wouldn't because it's my book and she wanted the ideas to be mine. Eventually I understood that, after I finished slamming my head against the wall and cursing her! This process has become important and valuable to me. I recognize that I need her to ask the questions that tell me where something isn't clear. It is my job to find the answer. I understand how much Dinah has helped me grow as a writer.

Dinah, do you ever make suggestions to other writers whose work you edit?

STEVENSON: Rarely, because I don't think that is my function. I'm not the person that makes it up; I'm the person who sees that it works. One of the analogies I like to use is going for a ride. The story should be a smooth ride that takes you where you want to go. If it's bumpy, you call attention to the bumps and say there's a bump here that threw me off the road for a little bit. Maybe it was something that wasn't clear or maybe it was something that

didn't seem to have anything to do with the direction I thought we were going—here's a bump and another bump. I thought we were going to the amusement park, but you've taken me to Death Valley. I just want to be able to take my ride and have it be smooth and exciting. The writer's job is to do that.

And maybe different from a ride you've taken before?

STEVENSON: Maybe, although emotionally I think there aren't that many rides—you just want to feel emotionally satisfied. If it's a funny story, you want to be amused. If it's sad, you want to be moved. You want to be taken away by the story to wherever the writer wants to take you.

***When My Name Was Keoko** is historical fiction, told through two voices and also not necessarily what readers might expect.*

PARK: I was pretty far into the writing process before it became two voices. The first twelve drafts were only the girl talking. I had difficulty with the plot when the brother goes away to become a kamikaze because I wanted Sun-hee to experience her brother's army training. So, I made several adjustments such as having them write letters, but that didn't work. I finally junked the whole thing. Then Tae-Yul spoke to me and said, "No, you can't do this, this is my story too"; at that the point it became a dual narrative. In hindsight it was the most difficult of my books.

Dinah saw more revisions of *Keoko* than she'd seen of any of my books before or since.

STEVENSON: On the other hand, I think that this was something we had to go through in order for me to be able to say, "OK, if you feel strongly about it, go ahead and make it work." There were times when neither of us saw daylight at all, but finally we came out of the tunnel.

So no matter what genre you're writing, you trust your editor's feedback if you realize that it is coming from someone who's a real reader, but not your only reader.

PARK: There's this huge X factor in anything, which is a personality thing. Even when Dinah and I are disagreeing, there is never any doubt that she is on my side, or that we are both on the book's or story's side. It becomes a common goal that we're working on together, not in opposition.

Linda Sue, did you take a risk in writing Project Mulberry *in such a unique style, where the protagonist holds a conversation with you, the author?*

PARK: I didn't think of it as a risk at all. The first three books I wrote were historical perspective, third person, past tense, and pretty traditional stories. After *A Single Shard* I thought I had that style down (but of course you never do entirely). And I was ready to try something new. *When My Name Was Keoko* was written as a dual narrative. I like to read different kinds of books and then I want to try and write them. *Project Mulberry* probably felt like a risk to Dinah, but that's partly my fault because the first version she saw was such a wreck.

Did the first version talk to the reader?

PARK: It did, but not in the format that it's in now. There was a lot of talking on almost every page.

STEVENSON: There was also a lot of interruption.

PARK: Dinah was always very polite and very professional, but basically she said, "I can't stay with the story if you interrupt me every scene." I sensed the talking was a distraction and the reader couldn't connect with the characters if something tricky was going on with every page. But, I so wanted to keep those author-character exchanges. Finally, I wrote a draft where I pulled it all out. Based on the millions of school visits I've done, I knew that kids were interested in the kinds of things the character Julia was asking. She was the kid who was always in the audience asking questions about my work. Dinah told me that if I wanted to keep the exchanges, I had to figure out a way to make them work that didn't drive her crazy.

STEVENSON: The risk aspect was more from the point of view of the publishing business. Here we have this award-winning, well-esteemed author who writes historical fiction and now she's writing this other stuff. People will expect it to be extraordinary because she gave up writing stories in a way that she does exceedingly well. If she's going to do something new, it has to really be special. And it was.

How does Archer's Quest *differ from your other novels?*

PARK: I've thought a lot about boys and the kinds of books they pick up. My feeling is, if you can get a kid to pick up a book and if it is going to be one of only ten books that child reads in three years, it has to be a great story. There needs to be action-packed books, but with really good writing. That's what I wanted from *Archer's Quest*. Dinah told me to beef up the action if that's what I wanted, but she always made sure the writing was at the top of its game.

How do you go about completing the final editing of a book?

PARK: We usually edit by phone. We might spend four to five minutes talking about a comma, which is something I just love because I feel we're at a point where we're making it as perfect as it can possibly be. Sometimes this conversation can take an hour or an hour and a half. I'm always sorry when we're finished and I ask her, "Is that all? Don't you have anything more?"

STEVENSON: There are some writers [who] find this irritating and don't want anything to do with it. They say, "You fix it; it's OK. I'm done with this. If you want to put in a comma, fine. If you don't, fine, I won't notice." There are people who don't notice and there are people who care very much about commas and word choice. And then there are authors who say, "No, I wrote that comma. I want that comma. Put it back."

PARK: I actually think it might be fun one day to record a portion of our conversation. I'm sure some people would think it's insane that we enjoy it so much, at least I do. We enjoy that stage and discussing that semicolon for so long.

Linda Sue, are you more secure in your writing since receiving the Newbery Award?

PARK: Every time I give Dinah a manuscript I tell her, "This is the last one." I'm sure every book I write will be my last.

STEVENSON: And I'm equally sure that it won't.

Archer's Quest, by Linda Sue Park. New York: Clarion, 2006.

Project Mulberry, by Linda Sue Park. New York: Clarion, 2004.

Seesaw Girl, by Linda Sue Park. New York: Clarion, 1999.

A Single Shard, by Linda Sue Park. New York: Clarion, 2001.

When My Name Was Keoko, by Linda Sue Park. New York: Clarion, 2002.

Side by Side by Side
Literature/Teacher/Learner: Writing About Memories

Book

Fox, Mem. 1985. *Wilfrid Gordon McDonald Partridge*. Illus. Julie Vivas. New York: Kane/Miller.

> Wilfrid, a small boy with four names, befriends the old folks who live next door, including his favorite friend of all, ninety-six-year-old Miss Nancy Alison Delacourte Cooper. When Wilfrid overhears his parents' worries that Miss Nancy has lost her memory, he sets out to remedy it. He asks each elderly neighbor, "What's a memory?" and, taking their advice, gathers favorite memories of his own to share with Miss Nancy.

Related literature

All the Places to Love, by Patricia MacLachlan. Illus. Mike Wimmer. New York: Joanna Cotler/HarperCollins, 1994.

Amelia's Road, by Linda Jacobs Altman. Illus. Enrique O. Sanchez. New York: Lee and Low, 1993.

Betty Doll, by Patricia Polacco. New York: Philomel, 2001.

The Hundred Penny Box, by Sharon Bell Mathis. Illus. Leo Dillon and Diane Dillon. New York: Viking, 1975.

The Rag Coat, by Lauren A. Mills. Boston: Little, Brown, 1991.

Salsa Stories, by Lulu Delacre. New York: Scholastic, 2000.

Teaching Response

Megan teaches her primary writers how their lives are ripe with potential writing ideas by reading aloud books that reflect family stories, feature special artifacts, and highlight personal experiences, places, or feelings. Using Mem Fox's *Wilfrid Gordon McDonald Partridge*, Megan demonstrates how to choose an idea and narrow the focus. She reads the book aloud all the way through, first allowing her students to appreciate the story's intergenerational relationships and Wilfrid's growing understanding of the concept of memories. Then she guides the children to notice how memories aren't always the same size or shape. As the old folks in the story suggest, a memory can be something from long ago, something that makes you laugh or cry, something that keeps you warm, and something as precious as gold. These different qualities serve as valuable suggestions for students to brainstorm the many memories they have.

Following this discussion, Megan asks the children to make a list of at least five different memories. To help generate their ideas, she suggests they talk with a partner. As the children create their lists, she compiles her own on chart paper. Then she talks through her ideas, modeling how she chooses which memory she'd like to write about. Because she knows that good writing comes when writers help narrow their focus, Megan encourages her students to "write a lot about a little." She shows them how to do this by talking about one of her own memories, then drafting a short piece of writing on chart paper. The students' memory writing inspired by *Wilfrid Gordon McDonald Partridge* is compiled into a class book. Their lists of ideas are stapled inside their writing folders so they can add to them whenever they think of others.

Student Response

Figures 5.7 and 5.8 show two students' memory writing.

I have a memory of last year in baseball. My team was the udafeated champoons. My favrit pishon's were pitcher and cecher. My team name was the twins and I never wanted the seasin to end. It was ecstordinary!

Andy

4-20-95

FIG 5.7 *Andy's Memory of Baseball*

A special memory I have is one that is happening right now. It is vary sad. My Grandma has all timers. Alltimers is a sickness. I feel cind of sad about it. My dad is a srgen and he can't do anything. Alltimers is a sickness in the head. She can't remember any more. Scienticets are exporing the sea bottom for any cure for alltimers.

Christopher

4-20-95

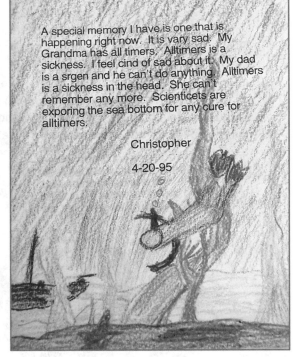

FIG 5.8 *Christopher's Memory of His Grandma*

3·21

Dear Miss Norem,
I am reading <u>Rose's Journal</u> by Marissa Moss. It is about a girl who lives in a Depression time. (which I still think is a Depressing time.) I like how only just a little girl (Mariss Moss) is writing it. It so far is a very good and reviling book. The thing now is, what kind of Genre is it? I'm thinking It is Historical fiction but I put it as biogrophy. The Author makes it so it looks like everybody fights all the time. When they say the <u>great</u> Depression Do they mean the biggest Depression ever? if so how big? if no why do they call it that? Whould people like fight over thing because everything was needed? Why dose it talk about money if it is all about water being gone. I mean you don't need water to make money. I am happy you are happy to read my letters. I am very glad to read yours too!

Love,
Jazlyn

3/26

Dear Jazlyn,
I think that this book is actually a historical biography. That is, if the girl in the story is a real person. If she is made up, then it is a historical fiction book. Please let me know in your next letter.

Jazlyn, I am so impressed by the big questions you ask as you read. Perhaps you could do some more research on The Great Depression to answer your questions.

The reason people needed money when there was no water is a <u>big</u> one! Why don't you come talk to me during class and we can talk about it.

Love,
Miss Norem

The Presence of Literature to Promote Inquiry

Dear Readers,

When we began to work on this book, we found there was so much to learn about ancient Rome. We knew about the gladiators and Pompeii and other things. But suddenly the story of 2,000 years of Roman history had to be told!

We got big, thick notebooks. We grabbed our pencils and headed to the library. Whole shelves of books on ancient Rome were waiting for us. We learned about the great Roman army. We read about the rulers and heroes of Rome. We even looked at pictures that showed old Roman roads . . . some are still used today.

Then we went home and sat down at the computer. There were great Web sites just waiting to be explored. So put on your gladiator's helmet and come join us. We're off to ancient Rome!

Jack   Annie

—Mary Pope Osborne and Natalie Pope Boyce, *Magic Tree House Research Guide: Ancient Rome and Pompeii*

Jack and Annie, the adventurous duo in Mary Pope Osborne's Magic Tree House series, display their enthusiasm to learn more about ancient Rome, as explained through the introductory letter in *Magic Tree House Research Guide: Ancient Rome and Pompeii.* They discover that learning about one topic raises further questions, motivating them to trek to the library, search the Internet, talk to experts, and use whatever resources they can locate. As readers and researchers, we can infer that the actions of these fictional characters mirror author Osborne's own process of inquiry into historical time periods and events.

On her website, Osborne exclaims, "I love using my imagination. I love doing research and learning new things. I love old stories about magic and fantasy. And I love kids. So if you combine all these things—I love writing books filled with imagination and real life and fantasy" (www.magictreehouse.com). When her avid readers declared their fascination for the facts woven into Jack and Annie's adventures, Osborne took out her notebooks and reshaped them into companion nonfiction research guides. She wanted to share facts but also hoped to launch readers into their own research, generated by inquiry.

What is inquiry? Inquiry is ripe with wonder. Questions and curiosity propel exploration, allow space for serendipity and surprise, fuel inspiration and imagination, and motivate us as learners. Children's natural curiosity leads them to ask questions of who, what, where, when, how, and why. They wonder how something will feel if they touch it or what it will taste like if they put it in their mouth. Toddlers often ask "Why?" repeatedly when an adult tries to explain something or to answer their question. Everything seems to fascinate children as they continually question and learn.

Kate Norem understands that students enter her fifth-grade classroom possessing an ardent desire to know about the world around them. "Everything we do is inquiry. I want my students to be lifelong learners." Kate recognizes that inquiry isn't restricted to school, but it influences and informs the ways in which we live. She consciously makes use of morning quotations, newspaper and magazine articles, books, field trips, the Internet, and even mandated curriculum to spark inquiry in her classroom. Personal observations or experiences also prompt students to want to know more about different topics, issues, and questions. For example, one day Kate's students begged to take their books outside and read. She told them that when she was their age, she hated doing that because allergies made her eyes swell shut. Her students were intrigued by why this would happen and wanted to know more. Kate and her students performed a quick search on the Internet to find information about pollen. Monica became so interested in this phenomenon that she conducted her own research and took it upon herself to announce each morning whether the pollen count made it safe to go outside. This spontaneous whole-class ministudy was based on curiosity and evolved into personal inquiry for one student. It wasn't expected, assigned, or evaluated, but it did engage and inform students.

Questions that students generate from observation, reading, or personal experience can be integrated into the curriculum; they can also become the curriculum. Paulo Freire (1985) contends that inquirers must be problem posers, not just problem solvers. This belief is supported by John Dewey's (1938) view of education that placed an emphasis on the development of problem-solving and critical-thinking skills, beginning with the learner's curiosity. Building from these philosophies, we consider how the presence of literature promotes inquiry by wondering:

- How does literature create a foundation that promotes inquiry?
- How do teachers partner with literature to implement an inquiry-based curriculum?
- What can we learn from authors and illustrators about inquiry?

How Does Literature Create a Foundation That Promotes Inquiry?

In classrooms where inquiry thrives, literature is a primary resource as well as a teaching partner, companion, informant, and question poser. In addition, it offers published examples of authors' or illustrators' inquiries, as evidenced by Mary Pope Osborne's Magic Tree House series, as well as her historical novels, Norse myths, and fairy tale retellings. Literature naturally triggers readers' questions because of its interesting topics, intriguing language, and captivating illustrations. Students' wonderings are sparked by a desire to discover more as they read and respond to the books that are read aloud, discussed during literature circles, and selected for independent reading.

Creating a foundation for inquiry must be an intentional decision made by the teacher that will influence how she will develop and teach the curriculum. To demonstrate the inquiry process, Kate's fifth-grade class became buddies with Amy Tisdale's first graders. When the buddies met for the first time, they discussed Kevin Henkes' *Chrysanthemum* (1991) and *Owen* (1993) to begin community building and make connections through literature. Following this initial getting-to-know-you activity, a yearlong study of the arts was launched, which was based on the two teachers' backgrounds and interests: Amy was an art major in college and Kate plays drums in a band on weekends. For one hour each Friday, the classes explored visual artists such as Georgia O'Keefe, Frida Kahlo, and Monet. The teachers read aloud literature related to each artist: *My Name Is Georgia* (Winter 1998), *Frida* (Winter 2002), and *Linnea in Monet's Garden* (Bjork 1987). Following each read-aloud, Kate and Amy recorded on chart paper what students had learned. Kate brought in art prints and accessed museum sites on the Internet for additional photos of art. Students also emulated each artist's style of painting. During the year, local artists visited the classroom and shared their techniques and art with the students. Kate also invited musicians, who demonstrated how they write music and lyrics. These visits allowed students to meet real artists and musicians and learn about their creative process.

This intentional exploration of art and music provided a foundation for future inquiry studies. Students participated in research, raised questions, and compared and contrasted artistic styles and media. While the study of art was teacher directed, Kate's students knew they could conduct additional research about an artist that might interest them. What Kate and Amy began in September continued throughout the school year and enabled students to learn not only about artists and musicians but also about the inquiry process.

Interactive read-alouds

A valuable strategy for laying the foundation for inquiry is through the interactive read-aloud. We have intentionally discussed the role of the read-aloud in previous chapters, but this time our focus is on the potential of both fiction and nonfiction to promote question posing. Interactive read-alouds set the stage for inquiry. Teachers such as Kate and Megan Sloan rely on the read-aloud to demonstrate their own process of thinking and questioning because they believe when they read with true wonder by raising questions, students will see it as something they can do as well.

To initiate this process, Megan asks students to pose questions before, during, and after the read-aloud. She records these on a chart or distributes sticky notes for students to write down their questions and post them in their reading journals. One September, Megan chose *Mr. Lincoln's Way*, by Patricia Polacco (2001), to demonstrate this process. Polacco's picture book tells the story of Eugene "Mean Gene" Esterhause, who is not only the school bully but also calls Principal Lincoln a racist name. But "the coolest principal in the whole world" discovers Eugene's interest in birds and attempts to find a way to make a connection with him while enlisting his help. Before beginning the read-aloud, Megan showed her students the book's cover, read the title and author's name, and then asked the students to write some initial questions. "What are you wondering? What are you curious about?" Then she paused at several points in the story so they could record additional questions. When the book ended, students had a third opportunity to record their questions. First grader Emelia couldn't wait to share her questions about *Mr. Lincoln's Way* and had several wonderings about the story:

Before:	Who is Mr. Lincoln?
	What is *his* way?
During:	Why didn't Eugene like the cool principal?
	Does Mr. Lincoln like children?
	Does Eugene like birds?
	Why isn't he mean anymore?
After:	Will Eugene stay out of trouble?

Megan encourages students to use this questioning strategy as they read independently during reading workshop. She advises them not to stop the flow of reading, but to record the wonderings that seem interesting or important. Megan reminds them that once the reading of their book is complete, they can go back and see which questions were answered by the text or illustration or inferred from the story and which questions still linger inside their heads.

Nonfiction read-alouds

In many, perhaps most classrooms, the majority of books selected for reading aloud are fictional stories. Teachers seldom choose nonfiction. One reason is the format poses a fluency challenge. Numerous captions, speech bubbles, or sidebars seem to complicate the reading process. Cyndi recalls her first attempt at reading aloud a Magic School Bus book. After she read a few pages, the first graders were squirming and she was exasperated. At that point, she realized she should read the narrative text in its entirety, then the speech bubbles, and then the characters' reports. When she tried reading everything on each page, the story line got lost and so did her students' attention. Once Cyndi understood how to read books with nonnarrative formats, they became an integral part of her read-alouds.

Since nonfiction begs to be read differently than fiction, teachers need to adjust their read-aloud strategies. Sometimes one paragraph or a single caption can be read, as in Eyewitness series books with their information-filled pages or Ernest Drake's *Dragonology: The Complete Book of Dragons* (2003), which captures children's interest because of its topic and format. Some nonfiction is written in short sections or chapters, such as *Girls Think of Everything: Stories of Ingenious Inventions by Women* by Catherine Thimmesh (2000) or Katherine Gibbs Davis' *Wackiest White House Pets* (2004). These books allow teachers to read aloud a particularly appealing section without needing to read the book from beginning to end.

Other nonfiction books can be read in their entirety because of the text's narrative structure. We recently observed a sixth-grade teacher reading aloud Jennifer Armstrong's lengthy *Shipwreck at the Bottom of the World: The Extraordinary True Story of Shackleton and the* Endurance (2000). This book held students' rapt attention because of the adventurous scenes and unbelievable unfolding of events. In addition, picture books by Lois Ehlert (*Planting a Rainbow* [1988] and *Leaf Man* [2005]) and Shelley Rotner (*Parts* [2001] and *Lots of Feelings* [2003]) also engage students in listening because of their vivid illustrations and appealing text. Other nonfiction authors who write in a narrative style effective for reading aloud include Gail Gibbons, Lynn Curlee, Jean Craighead George, Seymour Simon, Sandra Markle, and Russell Freedman. Nonfiction books that have received the Orbis Pictus Award or the Robert F. Sibert Award are worth investigating for their potential as read-alouds.

Literature circles

In Chapter 4 we highlighted the role of literature circles to create readers. Literature circles can also play an important part in nurturing the inquiry process. Students might engage in discussions about books on a curricular topic such as geology. When Kate's students read *Everybody Needs a Rock*, by Byrd Baylor (1974), and *If You Find a Rock*, by Peggy Christian (2000), as part of a text set, they learned about igneous, sedimentary, and metamorphic rocks ("How do wishing rocks get those perfectly white stripes around them?") and also discussed how important it was to slow down as they read and use their observational skills during their geology investigation.

Various time periods and historical events can also be explored through literature circles. A novel like Karen Hesse's *Out of the Dust* (1997) ignites numerous questions about the Oklahoma dust bowl and the 1930s and sparks discussion that results in reading nonfiction books and accessing the Internet to discover additional information. And sometimes literature circles are based on student appeal, such as children's interest in pirates. Students in Christine Jordan's fifth-grade class couldn't wait to talk about *Peter and the Starcatchers*, by Dave Barry and Ridley Pearson (2006), as they encountered the stinky rogues, possible cannibals, and biting mermaids in this swashbuckling prequel to Peter Pan. Additional books about pirates, including *How I Became a Pirate* (Long 2003), *Pirate Girl* (Funke 2005), and *Pirates* (Matthews 2006), had students scrambling to the library for more pirate books. A personal inquiry for two students who were spellbound by the literature resulted in a debate and subsequent research to determine if pirates were real or fictional.

Independent reading

As a former school librarian, Cyndi remembers students rushing to the nonfiction shelves to locate books about every topic imaginable—dinosaurs and sharks; motorcycles and racing; drawing and cooking. They wanted to know more about something they had seen on television or heard someone talk about, or simply wanted to explore a topic with their best friend. Students were enthralled by illustrations, mesmerized by format, or intrigued by captions. And often they asked, "Do you have more books about . . . ?" Students select a nonfiction book for independent reading because the interest is there and they want to know more. The opportunity for students to choose books that interest them is the key to independent reading and it also plays a role in furthering inquiry.

How Do Teachers Partner with Literature to Implement an Inquiry-Based Curriculum?

As Kate reminds us, inquiry isn't assigned to a certain time of the day. It should not be confined only to a focused study or to a content area such as social studies or science. It stems from the curriculum and from students' own questions. Of course, it also emerges from the literature that is present in our classrooms.

Pappas, Kiefer, and Levstik (1999) suggest that teachers build curriculum and focus studies around critical questions that engage children with important ideas and multiple points of view. They believe that all children are "active, constructive meaning makers" (3) who learn best when they participate and engage in the pursuit of essential questions and ideas. Inquiry studies provide students with authentic purposes for reading and writing. Literature affords an opportunity to generate meaningful questions and serves as a resource for response to their inquiry.

At times it's difficult to determine how to adopt an inquiry stance amid mandated curriculum and time constraints placed upon us. We recognize that true inquiry comes from within, but sometimes we struggle to honor this belief. Once we recognize and experience the value of inquiry in our classrooms and the ways it grows naturally from the curriculum, then our hesitation and fears can diminish.

There is a misconception that inquiry is a free-for-all approach to teaching and learning—students make all the decisions about what they want to learn with little input from the teacher. In an inquiry-based classroom, teachers provide important guidance for learning because of the literature selected to generate questions and the topics that are introduced. Intentional decisions are made every day about what students will do and learn. We recognize learning opportunities and know what to do with them. Unless teachers lay the foundation for question posing, teach the skills necessary to access and discover new information, and provide strategies to reflect or opportunities to present ideas and projects, student inquiry will likely not occur.

We take you into three classrooms at the primary, intermediate, and middle school levels to discover how the presence of literature supports inquiry. Here we highlight the intentional decisions each teacher makes to promote questioning, research, and response within the context of the curriculum.

Megan's primary classroom

When you walk into Megan's classroom, it is evident that students are actively involved in learning. Students are seated around the room in table groupings, hunched over a small stack of picture book biographies. Around the room are charts that provide a record of student thinking over the course of the past few months. Megan keeps these charts on the walls for as long as they are useful, but even after she takes them down they are still accessible. Throughout the year, her students engage in shared and guided inquiry. Sometimes this involves required components of the district curriculum that all students must learn. Other times, Megan creates baskets of books related to a broad theme that her students will read and discuss. Her process is not random; she has a clear purpose for the curricular decisions that she makes.

Megan listens to and values the questions her students ask. "They are both learners and questioners. I love when they are the leaders of our learning." As part of her curriculum, Megan often explores the broad theme of courage, dedication, and acting as a change agent. As students read literature to support these themes, one group became curious about Harriet Tubman after reading Catherine Nichols' biography (2002). They wondered who she was as a person. When they brought their questions to Megan, she recorded them on a chart and shared them with the rest of the class. Other children became intrigued by these questions, and this focus evolved into whole-class inquiry. Megan encouraged and supported their interest by reading aloud *A Picture Book of Harriet Tubman*, by David Adler (1992). Students wondered how Tubman related to other people in history they had learned about, such as Martin Luther King Jr. and George Washington, so they made a time line. Megan also wanted students to understand that Adler's biography presented only one perspective. She gathered more books about Harriet Tubman for additional read-alouds and shared reading, including *Aunt Harriet's Underground Railroad in the Sky* (Ringgold 1992), *Minty: A Story of Young Harriet Tubman* (Schroeder 1996), and *Moses: When Harriet Tubman Led Her People to Freedom* (Weatherford 2006). These books produced more questions, which students recorded in their reading journals.

Eloise Greenfield's poem "Harriet Tubman," from *Honey, I Love and Other Love Poems* (1978), sparked further questions. As Megan read the poem and as students read it aloud again for choral reading, the language resonated with them, especially the lines:

> Nineteen times she went back South
> To get three hundred others
> She ran for her freedom nineteen times
> To save Black sisters and brothers.

Megan asked what her students learned and could infer about Tubman from the poem. They remembered the nineteen times more readily than they had when that same information was presented in a nonfiction book. They responded, "She was courageous because she helped so many people," and "She must have been scared when the dogs chased her. I would be scared if that happened to me." Then they made a list of other names for Tubman—risk taker, daughter, saver of people, women's rights activist, slave, and escapee. First grader Courtney demonstrated her learning about Harriet Tubman through a written response that illustrated both the impact of Greenfield's poem and also the inconsistency of researched facts:

> Let me tell you about a special person named Harriet Tubman. Harriet was born in either 1820 or 1821. She was born a slave. She didn't like it one bit. One night she went to go to freedom (although she was sad to leave her friends and family).
>
> Once she was at the free land, she went back 19 times to get 300 others. She helped them escape on the Underground Railroad. They called her Moses. Harriet Tubman died after helping many people. She was a very great person.

Over the course of several weeks the children wrote journal entries illuminating information they learned, connections they made, and questions that still lingered. Megan then structured an assessment of what they learned from this inquiry study. She demonstrated how to select interesting information and synthesize that into a cinquain. The children reviewed their journals and wrote individual cinquains about Harriet Tubman (see Figure 6.1). The inquiry culminated when Megan asked her students to consider how they might become risk takers and courageous people who help others.

Kate's intermediate classroom

Kate's classroom walls are also filled with charts of student thinking, responses to literature, and learning demonstrations. Each year, Kate is faced with the challenge of teaching the required fifth-grade curriculum about North American history, from Aztecs to the tragedy of 9/11. It's impossible to study this broad time period, so she considers how to approach the mandated curriculum in a way that is both accessible and engaging. Kate initiates a class mini-inquiry by reading aloud Pam Conrad's *Pedro's Journal: A Voyage with Christopher Columbus August 3, 1492–February 14, 1493* (1991). Along with this short chapter book, she reads picture books about Columbus, including Jane Yolen's *Encounter* (1992a), and shows a video created by Disney. Some of the students are intrigued, even shocked, by what they discover:

> SHANE: I always thought Columbus was a good guy.
> KATE: Did anyone else think Columbus was a good guy? Is this the first time you've heard this?
> MONICA: Why didn't the natives say, "You can't do this to us"?

FIG 6.1 *Brittney's Cinquain on Harriet Tubman*

As each book is read, additional questions emerge and students seek answers to some while discussing others. The insights students gain and the responses and questions they generate require them to determine if the facts and "myths" are accurate. This leads them to wonder about other historical figures.

To address curriculum requirements about the "discovery" of North America, Kate pairs students up to research different explorers. Since this inquiry will involve accessing multiple resources, she wants at least one student to be a competent reader. Kate provides a list of explorers, and the class uses the WebQuest program to gain some information about each person. Because few students have even heard of these explorers, they make their choices randomly, except for those with "cool" names. Not surprisingly, Marco Polo is a popular choice; students know the game, but not the explorer. As they work in pairs and jot down questions and findings about their selected explorer, they search through information from books and other resources and analyze who wrote each source, the author's motive, and whether the information is consistent with other books and resources. They ask if the author is biased in the reporting, something that Kate demonstrated during the reading of *Pedro's Journal*. Once students determine what information is important, they create explorer brochures that are posted on a hallway bulletin board for others in the school to read.

Georgia's middle school classroom

At the beginning of the year, middle school teacher Georgia Connor Schultzman frames her curriculum around a broad theme such as humanity, human rights, courage, or journeys. To initiate thinking with her seventh-grade students, she uses a web to model her thoughts about the theme. Since her goal is student-generated inquiry, Georgia feels "the teacher must, must, must give up control over the look of the outcome and the direction each student takes while on the inquiry journey."

As mentioned in Chapter 3's discussion of response, our different lives and literary experiences influence our interpretation of both text and illustrations. These diverse responses also impact our questions. As Georgia's class read the historical novel *Beyond the Divide*, by Kathryn Lasky (1983), as part of their thematic focus on human rights, they paused to investigate the impact of a rape that occurred in the story and considered how it reflected society's view and treatment in 1849. They discussed how this stigma continued well into the late twentieth century and to some degree is still present in today's society. A number of her students, both female and male, reread the scene in Lasky's novel to investigate the manner in which the community responded to the rape. Many shared personal experiences from their families and friends. Those who had knowledge of other cultures and beliefs contributed that knowledge to the inquiry. Some read the newspaper, looking for current examples to further the discussion. The reading of *Beyond the Divide* sparked the questions and, in turn, created this inquiry.

Independent inquiry

We know it is impossible to explore every topic or question that intrigues children—there just isn't time. Students in classrooms where inquiry is valued and encouraged know that they can engage in their own inquiry. Some of the questions that students share with Megan will prompt her to respond, "That would make a really good research question. Why don't you read more about it during reading workshop?" It's no surprise that Emelia chose to learn more about

Benjamin Franklin following her class focus on biographies, then later in the year pursued questions about bats such as Is the skin on the wings see-through? and Do all bats have rabies? Emelia and her classmates know that they can learn about whatever they are interested in whenever they want because student choice is key to Megan's reading and writing workshop.

To introduce personal inquiry, Kate asks her students, "Who is interested in learning about giraffes?" Three or four hands eagerly shoot up in the air. Then Kate informs the class they won't be studying giraffes this year, but they *can* study them or *anything* else on their own. Kate wants students to understand that their questions and interests are important, but there just isn't time to explore everyone's individual questions during the school day. She encourages personal inquiry by asking students to sign contracts indicating their questions and setting a time line to investigate it. She also makes time for presentations of independent inquiries. Recently, two girls became experts on hippos and created a PowerPoint presentation that incorporated elements of readers' theatre to share the information they discovered.

Georgia encourages independent inquiry as well. Since she is restricted to fifty-five minutes per class, she incorporates these studies into her curriculum. In her seventh-grade classroom, she furthers the theme of humanity through literature circles and independent reading, selecting books such as *A Break with Charity: A Story About the Salem Witch Trials* (Rinaldi 1992), *Party Girl* (Ewing 1998), *The Cage* (Sender 1986), *The Upstairs Room* (Reiss 1972), *The Great Gatsby* (Fitzgerald 1996), *The Devil's Arithmetic* (Yolen 1988), *Somewhere in the Darkness* (Myers 1992), *Toning the Sweep* (Johnson 1993), and *Speak* (Anderson 1999). Personal inquiries that have evolved focused on issues of gender, power, acceptance, justice, and the American dream. Students read nonfiction, tapped personal experiences, and responded through literature letters and discussions to extend their knowledge. Their inquiries culminated in a scrapbook format that included poetry, graffiti pages, letters to characters and letters as characters, character journals, comic representations, and artistic renderings. The students also depicted historical events through time lines.

Borrowing from literature to report inquiry

Since literature provides a rich variety of formats for presenting knowledge and information, we rely on it to demonstrate how research can be presented. One morning, Kate gathered her students on the carpet and pointed to a book cart loaded with nonfiction books. "I know that many of you are at the point in your research where you are ready to present what you've found. You probably wonder how authors share their research." She then selected three books and proceeded to walk through each, indicating text features that she found distinctive or attention grabbing. When she had finished, Kate gave each group of students a pile of nonfiction texts from the book cart to browse and examine. She instructed them not to spend time reading, but rather to write down what they observed about how the information was presented. When the class gathered again, the students shared their findings, which Kate recorded on a piece of chart paper: table of contents, glossary, index, headings, speech bubbles, title page, information box, and bar graphs, as well as the use of color, varying sizes of print, and font differences.

We consistently turn to our literary partners to introduce appealing formats to present research (see Figure 6.2). Alphabet books published today rarely depict sound-symbol relationships but rather present information about various topics, such as Wendell Minor's *Yankee Doodle America: The Spirit of 1776 from A to Z* (2006) and Pat Mora's animal names in English and Spanish from *¡Marimba!: Animales from A to Z* (2006). Students devour books with unusual formats, including Robert Sabuda and Matthew Reinhart's *Encyclopedia Prehistorica Dinosaurs: A Definitive Pop-Up* (2005) and Mordicai Gerstein's *The Man Who Walked Between the Towers* (2003), with its expansive gatefolds. We enjoy sharing poetry that presents information about geology in *Earthshake: Poems from the Ground Up*, by Lisa Westberg Peters (2003), as well as J. Patrick Lewis' *A Burst of Firsts: Doers, Shakers, and Record Breakers* (2001), with its snappy verses about quirky events and endeavors. We take delight in introducing how poetic prose can tell a story, such as Karen Hesse's *Out of the Dust* (1997), and how *The Trial*, by Jen Bryant (2005), describes a child's-eye view of the trial of the Lindbergh baby kidnapping.

Ah, Music, by Aliki. New York: HarperCollins, 2003.

Don't Know Much About Planet Earth, by Kenneth Davis. Illus. Tom Bloom. New York: HarperCollins, 2001.

Egyptology, by Emily Sands. Cambridge, MA: Candlewick, 2004.

Field Trips: Bug Hunting, Animal Tracking, Bird-Watching, Shore Walking, by Jim Arnosky. New York: HarperCollins, 2002.

Ice Cream: The Full Scoop, by Gail Gibbons. New York: Holiday House, 2006.

An Island Scrapbook: Dawn to Dusk on a Barrier Island, by Virginia Wright-Frierson. New York: Simon and Schuster, 1998.

Prehistoric Actual Size, by Steve Jenkins. Boston: Houghton Mifflin, 2005.

The Roman News: The Greatest Newspaper in Civilization, by Andrew Langley and Philip de Souza. Cambridge, MA: Candlewick, 1996.

Summer: An Alphabet Acrostic, by Steven Schnur. Illus. Leslie Evans. New York: Clarion, 2001.

What You Never Knew About Fingers, Forks and Chopsticks, by Patricia Lauber. Illus. John Manders. New York: Simon and Schuster, 1999.

FIG 6.2 Unusual Formats and Designs That Present Inquiry Findings

Following their second-grade inquiry study on spiders, two of Nancy's teacher education students borrowed the poetry structure from Paul Fleischman's Newbery Award–winning *Joyful Noise: Poems for Two Voices* (1988) to collaboratively present some of the information the class had learned. What resulted was a rousing choral reading of their poem:

Spiders

All spiders have	All spiders have
Eight legs	
	Eight eyes
Some spiders make webs	Some spiders make webs
	Some webs are soft.
There are orb webs,	
	And sticky parts in webs;
	They catch bugs in there.
Some spiders live underwater.	Some spiders live underwater.
A fishing spider catches her air,	
	Pushing water
	Out of her bubble.
Some spiders are poisonous.	Some spiders are poisonous.
Like Black Widows	
	And Wolf Spiders.
We think spiders are cool.	We think spiders are cool.

What Can We Learn from Authors and Illustrators About Inquiry?

Children's book authors and illustrators share their inquiries through rich, descriptive language and eye-catching artistic interpretations. Their books are often the result of extensive and intensive research that may have been propelled by a wondering from daily life, family stories, newspaper articles, conversations, or their own imaginations. Many times, authors and illustrators inform readers about the origins of an idea or a story. This information may be conveyed through an author's note, expressed within a blog, articulated in an interview, or revealed in a speech.

When poet Kristine O'Connell George realized that a mother hummingbird was building a nest in the potted tree on her patio, she became mesmerized by her "very own private nature show, live and in full color!" (www.kristinegeorge.com).

She spent weeks writing observations in her journal ("After his 'solo' the tiny bird sat on a branch and chirped piteously; I was *so* relieved to see mom return. Thank goodness!"). She conducted further research ("One of the many things I learned about hummingbirds is that the mother cares for her fledglings for a few days after they leave the nest."). Finally, George made a decision to use poetry to share what she had learned, resulting in the publication of *Hummingbird Nest: A Journal of Poems* (2004), a text that documents this extraordinary experience, from nest building to watching the baby hummingbirds complete two successful solos.

At times, authors mine their own family for memories and stories. Avid readers of Patricia Polacco's fictional picture books know these are generally rooted in family stories. Her research involves collaborating with family members to verify factual issues such as the birth order of the nine children in her grandmother's family, which is portrayed in *An Orange for Frankie* (2004) (www.patricia polacco.com). As Polacco wrote *Pink and Say* (1994c), she needed to determine what division Great-Great-Grandpa Sheldon Curtis (Say) served in the Union Army and how old he would have been during the Civil War. Again she checked with relatives. While Polacco doesn't rely on her family for artistic input, she does seek their assistance to make sure family facts and details are accurate. For autobiographical books such as *Thank You, Mr. Falker* (1998), Polacco relies on her own memories, while other stories, such as *My Ol' Man* (1995) and *My Rotten Redheaded Older Brother* (1994b), are inspired by family photographs, which she often weaves into her illustrations.

Similar to Polacco, Pam Muñoz Ryan has been intrigued by family stories. She explains in her author's note how the novel *Esperanza Rising* was inspired: "When I was a young girl, Grandma used to tell me what her life was like when she first came to the United States from Mexico" (2000, 255). While this fictional story is loosely based on Ryan's grandmother's immigration, it details events of the early 1930s, when many strikes occurred in the California agricultural fields. Not all the needed information could be gleaned from family stories, so Ryan conducted extensive research at the Beale Library in Bakersfield, California, interviewed many people who lived in the Mexican camp at DiGiorgio Farms (the same camp as her grandmother), and visited the sheds and the area of Arvin, California. Ryan used family names in the book, but those characters are composites of who she imagined they might have been. *Esperanza Rising* has its roots in both family stories and historical events.

An author's inquiry about one topic might evolve into writing about another. When Karen Hesse was writing a picture book featuring a character longing for rain, fellow author Eileen Christelow questioned her about the child's motivation. This query, coupled with Hesse's car trip through Kansas several years earlier, planted the seed for the eventual Newbery Award–winning *Out of the Dust*

(1997). Not only did Hesse research newspapers and other accounts of the Oklahoma dust bowl, but she also determined how to share the story of protagonist Billie Jo Kelby. The result was an entrancing novel written in free verse because "the frugality of the life, the hypnotically hard work of farming, the grimness of conditions during the dust bowl demanded an economy of words" (Hesse 1998, 426). A few years later, she returned to her initial inquiry and wrote the text for the picture book, *Come On, Rain!* (1999).

While the stories in the Magic Tree House series are often the product of Mary Pope Osborne's inquisitive nature and subsequent research, her readers also influence the choices of topics. In *Blizzard of the Blue Moon* (2006), Jack and Annie go back in time to New York City during the Great Depression. A terrible snowstorm rages, and to stop the blizzard the two children must save the unicorn made famous in the Cloisters' medieval tapestries. Osborne's research involved spending time at the Cloisters to study the tapestries and reading numerous resources. This focus on the Great Depression, as with topics of other Magic Tree House books, developed from questions that readers asked as well as Osborne's own wonderings about the past. She is known to throw herself into a subject, having the time of her life. Because she values her readers, they know she will listen to them and consider their topic suggestions, especially when they make good sense. Once, during an appearance at a bookstore, one child commented to Osborne that the working title of her next book, *Vacation on the Volcano*, didn't make sense. "No one could vacation *on* a volcano." Osborne quickly changed the title to *Vacation Under the Volcano*.

Following the 2004 tsunami in the Indian Ocean, several authors and illustrators embarked on a quest to tell the true story of the amazing friendship between a baby hippo (Owen) and a 130-year-old tortoise (Mzee). This poignant account about Owen's loss of his mother and the tortoise's unofficial adoption of this 650-pound baby was featured on the evening news, in newspapers, and on the Internet. Author-illustrator Jeanette Winter chose to tell the story *Mama* (2006) through minimal text and acrylic paintings featuring winsome animals and thickly applied jewel tones. Marion Dane Bauer's *A Mama for Owen* (2007) offers a rhythmic presentation of the same event, illustrated by John Butler's soft colors and optimistic tone. Writer Craig Hatkoff decided on narrative text and crisp photographs by Peter Greste to document his version of the story, *Owen and Mzee: The True Story of a Remarkable Friendship* (2006). Essentially all three books tell the same story, but two do it primarily through illustrations while the other presents Owen and Mzee through photographs and informational text. These books provide an excellent example of how authors and illustrators discover ideas for stories and how they choose to share their inquiry through different formats. Just because an author's book is published doesn't mean the inquiry is complete. Hatkoff remained interested in Owen and Mzee and followed their situation, resulting in the sequel, *Owen and Mzee: The Language of Friendship* (Hatkoff, Hatkoff, and Kahumba 2007).

While observation, conversation, family stories, and news reports inspire inquiry and research, sometimes imagination is what is needed most. Children's book author and illustrator Peter Catalanotto reveals that his stories often begin by asking, "What if . . . ?" What if a Dalmatian fantasized in black and white about a soccer game between skunks and penguins (*Dylan's Day Out* [1989])? What if you asked for a dozen bagels and the shopkeeper gave you a dozing beagle instead (*Mr. Mumble* [1990])? What if all the children in your first-grade classroom had the same first name (*Matthew A.B.C.* [2002])? Catalanotto's curiosity about the possible and the improbable fuels his inquiry, which results in text and art in picture books.

Professional Literature Cited

Dewey, John. 1938. *Experience and Education*. New York: Collier.

Freire, Paolo. 1985. *The Politics of Education*. South Hadley, MA: Bergin and Garvey.

Hesse, Karen. 1998. "Newbery Medal Acceptance." *The Horn Book Magazine* 422–27.

Pappas, Christine C., Barbara Z. Kiefer, and Lynn S. Levstik. 1999. *An Integrated Language Perspective in the Elementary School: An Action Approach*. 3d ed. New York: Longman.

Conversation with . . .
Author-illustrator Brian Selznick

Brian Selznick engaged in extensive research before illustrating the picture book biographies ***Walt Whitman: Words for America***, ***When Marian Sang***, ***The Dinosaurs of Waterhouse Hawkins***, and ***Amelia and Eleanor Go for a Ride***. In this conversation, Brian illuminates his process and his curiosity about people and places.

What is your research process?

It's a lot like treasure hunting. Many times I know a little bit about the subject I'm starting to research. Or, I might even think I know a lot about it. Once I dive in, I find myself constantly discovering things that I had not known about the subject, the person, or the time period. That is when it gets exciting. Part of my research process is to travel to where the story takes place or where the person lived. Since I have a large book collection, I also turn to the books on my shelves. When I need more specific information, I turn to the library or use the Internet. My process may involve tracking down an expert on that topic—asking him or her how I should do research, what I should see, what I should read. When I illustrate, I want to illustrate for the seven or eight people in America who will actually know if I got it wrong.

When initially working on the Walt Whitman book, I illustrated the type case wrong. Someone at the typography museum had given me specific information about the type of case used during Whitman's time. When I finished the art—but luckily before the book was published—I met a typographer who looked at my painting and said, "Oh no, that's a Hamilton type case. It was not invented until the 1890s." I realized that was not going to work because the scene in my illustration is set in the 1830s. She told me not to change it—"No one's going to know!" But I'll know and I needed to have it right.

One of the exciting perks of being an author and an illustrator is meeting people who are experts. When I conducted research for *When Marian Sang*, I met a woman who played piano as a child at Marian Anderson's house. She now runs the Marian Anderson historical society out of her home. I also met a man who is an expert on Waterhouse Hawkins. He's the one who gave me the metal bolts from the Crystal Palace that I treasure now.

You've illustrated books about Amelia Earhart, Eleanor Roosevelt, Marian Anderson, Waterhouse Hawkins, and Walt Whitman. Did you feel a responsibility to make sure the illustrations were accurate?

I definitely want to be accurate. But illustration is always an interpretation. It is interesting to see biographies of people and how they are retold. It can be very complicated to be factually accurate. Since there are a million different ways to present facts, I have to decide my focus. I can't cover somebody's entire life in thirty-two pages of a picture book. I have to figure out what aspect of their life to represent. In researching *Walt Whitman: Words for America*, I had to contend with a life that encompassed nearly the entire nineteenth century, the Civil War and slavery, and the birth of America. What do I do? Where do I begin? Barbara Kerley's idea for the book was to focus on Whitman's work during the Civil War, which included his life from childhood to old age. If someone else was doing a biography for kids about Walt Whitman, they might choose something else. That was the other complicated factor. This was a book about someone whose work is not read by children. The themes in his work are typically not for children at all. So, for me, part of the process was figuring out Why are we telling this story? What is there for kids?

How do you make that decision of how to tell a story through art?

Usually when I work on a book, I don't question whether it is appropriate for kids. If it's something that strikes me as right for me, then I trust that it will be right for an audience of young readers. When my editor, Tracy Mack, told me the story of Waterhouse Hawkins over the phone, I didn't even have to read the manuscript. I said, "Yes, I'm going to illustrate that book." It was the same with *Amelia and Eleanor Go for a Ride*. I didn't know that Amelia and Eleanor were such good friends. As soon as I found that out, I got pretty excited and knew I wanted to work [on] that book. But the first time I heard about the Whitman book, it was much more complicated to respond. I loved the idea of Whitman but had never read much of his work. I knew who he was and what he represented, but that wasn't enough.

Everything starts with text. I have to figure out the relationship of the pictures to that text so that it illustrates what is there and what is not there. It is the difference between illustrating and illuminating a text, shedding another kind of light on it that you can only get by looking at the combination of the words and the pictures. That can come from research or gut instinct about what the story means to me.

You are an illustrator, but you are also an author. How does your research differ when you write?

It is much easier to do research when I illustrate because the author has already done half of it. She sends me everything she has collected so far. Then I need to do visual research, to find images from the 1880s, or photographs, or look at the kind of shoes kids were wearing, which sometimes the author has touched on. Often the research they've done can lead me quickly to where I need to go because they've contacted a librarian for assistance, or found experts. When Pam Muñoz Ryan was writing *Riding Freedom*, she took stagecoach lessons. I was able to call the person who gave her the lessons. I generally don't talk to authors about any creative decisions. That all gets filtered though the editor. But for research questions, I will talk directly to the author.

When it's something I'm writing, it means I have to start from scratch. When I was writing *The Houdini Box*, I still lived at home with my parents. I was in college at the time so I started my research at the public library. Eventually I went to the New York Library of the Performing Arts, where they had a huge file about Houdini. They even had clippings of all of his obituaries. There's a scene at the end of *The Houdini Box* that takes place at his grave, so I needed to find out what the grave looked like. Through this file I found out where he was buried. I visited the grave and took photographs. The main difference between *The Houdini Box* and the books I have illustrated is that this one is historical fiction. So, while Houdini is real, the story is about Victor, a ten-year-old boy. I was more concerned about telling Victor's story. If I needed to change something about Houdini's real life, I did it because the story was Victor's. For instance, at the end of the book, Victor needed to be in New York on Halloween, the day Houdini died, but in real life he died in Chicago. I included an author's note saying what I changed and why I changed it, because accuracy is important to me even in a work of fiction where I purposefully change the facts. I would not, could not, do that in a work that is labeled nonfiction.

Amelia and Eleanor Go for a Ride, by Pam Muñoz Ryan. Illus. by Brian Selznick. New York: Scholastic, 1999.

The Dinosaurs of Waterhouse Hawkins, by Barbara Kerley. Illus. by Brian Selznick. New York: Scholastic, 2001.

The Houdini Box, by Brian Selznick. New York: Atheneum, 2001.

Riding Freedom, by Pam Muñoz Ryan. Illus. by Brian Selznick. New York: Scholastic, 1998.

Walt Whitman: Words for America, by Barbara Kerley. Illus. by Brian Selznick. New York: Scholastic, 2004.

When Marian Sang, by Pam Muñoz Ryan. Illus. by Brian Selznick. New York: Scholastic, 2002.

Side by Side by Side
Literature/Teacher/Learner: Author's Notes

Books

Greenfield, Eloise. 2004. *In the Land of Words: New and Selected Poems*. Illus. Jan Spivey Gilchrist. New York: HarperCollins.

Kurtz, Jane. 2000. *River Friendly, River Wild*. Illus. Neil Brennan. New York: Simon and Schuster.

Wong, Janet. 2003. *Knock on Wood: Poems About Superstitions*. Illus. Julie Paschkis. New York: Margaret K. McElderry/Simon and Schuster.

Related literature

Brown Angels: An Album of Pictures and Verse, by Walter Dean Myers. New York: HarperCollins, 1993.

Poems to Dream Together: Poemas Para Soñar Juntos, by Francisco X. Alarcón. Illus. Paula Barragán. New York: Lee and Low, 2005.

Snow, Snow: Winter Poems for Children, by Jane Yolen. Photo. Jason Stemple. Honesdale, PA: Boyds Mills, 1998.

Teaching Response

The fifth graders in Kate Norem's class are nearly done writing poetry about their self-selected inquiry studies. Their topics vary widely: There's Michael's poetry about the desert, written to pay tribute to a region he loves and misses since moving away from Albuquerque. Jacob's poetry reflects his intrigue with the solar system, and Colton's poems reveal his curiosity and discoveries about space. The poems have been revised and typed, one poem per page with illustrations, borders, and images to interest readers and add a visual dimension to the words. Now it's time to compile their individual collections and bind them into handmade books. But there's one item left for the students to write: an author's note.

Kate has pulled a few poetry anthologies from her classroom library to demonstrate the ways individual poets inform their readers and articulate their process and inspiration. Listening to Kate read aloud the author's note is familiar for her students. She reminds them of a discussion following last week's read-aloud of the author's and illustrator's note for *The Magic School Bus and the Science Fair Expedition* (Cole 2006) and suggests they now listen to hear how some poets reveal clues about the inquiry that resulted in their poetry collections.

She selects Jane Kurtz's *River Friendly, River Wild* and reads the two-paragraph author's note that begins the book. The first paragraph chronicles the time line of a major flood that caused nearly all the homes in Kurtz's town to be evacuated. The second paragraph relates the experiences that inspired her to write about this devastating event and who encouraged her to write about this heartbreaking loss. Eloise Greenfield's author's note for *In the Land of Words* also appears at the front of her collection. When Kate reads it aloud, she shows how the illustrator has included a small portrait of the author at the bottom of the same page where Greenfield explains where ideas come from. When Kate reads the last line, "Won't you come with me now for a visit to this land?" she offers another purpose for an author's note— to invite readers to turn the page. Then she reads Janet Wong's note for *Knock on Wood*, which appears as the last page of the book. In it, Wong includes specific references to other people and another book that she turned to as she researched superstitions.

Before returning to their desks to draft their author's notes, Kate invites students to pair up and take a few minutes and talk to each other about some ideas they might include in their notes. She lines the chalk tray with a number of books students can peruse for other demonstrations of author's notes. Kate offers a quick reminder of how this final piece of writing in their poetry anthology can inform readers of their intention, their inspiration, and even their process, and then she suggests they begin writing.

Student Response

Figures 6.3 and 6.4 show two students' author's notes.

Dear Reader,

This collection of poetry called space was picked by me because space is a weird place. Full of mystery and amazement. One thing I want you to notice is that in each poem there is a wince of information. I came up with the idea the day Jacob shared Mars. Then I thought it would be cool to do a collection of space poetry. Some ways my poems have changed is that my poems were dull and not informative. But then I got a book at the library that gave me information I turned into poems. Some important things in my procedure are that I used a thesaurus to get more powerful words. As I said earlier I also use a book called Space for more information. One thing I'd do better next time is I would use a thesaurus before I type up my poem. I would also like to thank some people. Jacob for the inspiration, Space for information, and Miss Norem for helping me along the way.

Enjoy Reading!

FIG 6.3 *Author's Note from Colton*

Author's Note

I wrote my poetry collection about all of the places I love. One of the most important poems to me that I wrote is, The Ocean. It is so important to me because the ocean has always been a big part of my life. I've just always loved the beat and the way it comes in and out, in and out. I chose my title Half Magic because I was trying to think of a title that would fit all of my poems. So I thought of my feelings about all of the poems, I thought of them as magic places, and that is how I got the title. I love all of my poems for several different reasons and I hope you do to!

Michaela

FIG 6.4 *Author's Note from Michaela*

Dear Miss Norem,

I am reading <u>Kennedy assasinated! The World Mourns</u>. By Wilborn Hampton. I can't stop thinking who was Kennedys killer? I am guessing the killer didn't beileve in what Kennedy beileved and was upset that he was elected. It is a pretty wild guess but I wonder if the killer is also the one who shot Lincoln?

I wonder how the wife felt after her husband died. I wonder if she ever wondered would he kill her to, was the bullet ment for her but missed? This is one of my favorite Non-Fiction books, It has showed me Non-Fiction can be fun!

Sincerely,
Anika

April 10

Dear Anika-Banika,
I am so glad that you are discovering that non-fiction can be fun! You are asking some great questions as you read your book. I especially like how you wondered what Kennedy's wife felt like. Did you wonder because you did a report on his wife?

Anika, thank you for your great letter and all of your fabulous thinking!

Love,
Miss Norem

The Presence of Literature to Cultivate Wonder

"Does that book tell what a Wonder really is?"

I thumbed through the pages, back to the introduction. "Here it is. It says, 'a marvel; that which arouses awe, astonishment, surprise, or admiration.' "

Pa scratched his cheek with the dull side of his knife. "I've seen one or two things to admire around here. Maybe if you put out a little effort, you would too."

I closed the book and leaned back on both elbows. "But what's the point?"

"I just think there's no use searching the world for Wonders when you can't see the marvels right under your own nose."

"Amen," said Aunt Pretty.

—BETTY G. BIRNEY, *The Seven Wonders of Sassafras Springs*

Longing to explore places far more wondrous than his own farming community, Eben McAllister, the protagonist of Betty Birney's *The Seven Wonders of Sassafras Springs*, buries his nose in a book about the seven wonders of the world. He sets his sights on seeing important things in faraway places, so he shrugs in disdain when Pa and Aunt Pretty suggest that he take notice of his own community. Handing his son a pad of paper to keep track of local wonders, Pa challenges Eben with a reward that's hard to turn down. If he can find seven wonders in Sassafras Springs in seven days, he'll earn a train trip to the snowy peaks of Colorado to visit some favorite cousins. Eben's a skeptic, unconvinced he'll find anything interesting, let alone wondrous. But since summer's daily life in Sassafras Springs doesn't promise much excitement, he agrees to give it a try. What Eben discovers not only amazes (and annoys) his friends and neighbors, it also takes him on adventures he never imagined possible—at least not so close to home.

Like Eben, many of us find it hard to believe there is much that's wondrous, astonishing, curious, or filled with awe in our daily lives or in our own backyards. Somewhere, somehow, we lose that sense of wonder as we develop a layer of cynicism. Sadly, many of our students do too. Shadow a small child for a few hours. Listen in on her conversations with a friend, adult, or even a beloved pet. What you'll discover from these careful observations is sheer curiosity and awe for a world of marvels right in front of the child's eyes. Young children are known to linger in wonder as they track the glacial pace of a caterpillar. They're famous for layer upon layer of questions, curious about the obvious and the incomprehensible. They need no invitation. To children, wonder resides at the ends of their fingers and curiosity on the tip of their tongue.

We're born with an ability to look at the world with awe and wonder, but for some reason, the natural inclination to ask, "Why?" disappears, or goes underground. Developmentally, some loss of naïveté may be natural as experiences wear away wide-eyed optimism; however, we remember times in our own teaching when the wonder was allowed to be whipped away. Prepackaged questions can do this. So can reliance on scripted curricula and overindulgence on standardized tests that measure only what's measurable. How do we measure curiosity? Evaluate awe? Inspiration? Wonder? Perhaps it's as easy as observing a group of first graders ooh and aah over Steve Jenkins' *Prehistoric Actual Size* (2005) or joining a *l-o-n-g* line of enchantingly garbed readers as midnight approaches the bewitching hour when bookstores open their doors open to sell *Harry Potter and the Deathly Hallows* (2007), or reading a poem, a story, or even an essay that makes us pause, wondering how any writer could weave such magic with words. Or maybe it's in our commitment to nurture what can't be easily measured, as we were recently reminded by Vicki Spandel when she expressed her dismay over teaching that has become automatic and overly concerned with measurable outcomes. Reacting to what she perceives has become a six-trait orthodoxy in writing, Spandel shared some inspiring writing by both children and adults and then cautioned, "We can mechanize anything, including six traits. . . . Remember, surprise and magic are not on that rubric" (2006).

Of the many pleasures we derive from literature, surprise and magic not only foster response but indirectly feed us as humans and as literate beings. We believe that children are entitled to literature that takes their imaginations seriously. The presence of literature unlocks wonder and can cultivate and nurture it as well. And this results in our wondering:

- ⊞ How does literature invite us to recognize and support our students' wonderings?

- ⊞ What we can do to cultivate wonder in our own teaching and learning?

- ⊞ How do authors and illustrators partner with us to nurture wonder?

How Does Literature Invite Us to Recognize and Support Our Students' Wonderings?

We believe our classrooms are filled with wonder not only because of the presence of literature but also by the presence of our students. Evidence of this is obvious when we expect and tune in to it. Wonder is apparent in the books our students choose for independent reading, in their diverse and sometimes surprising responses to literature, in topics they explore through writing, and in their willingness to imagine and raise questions. Throughout this book we've advocated the need to respect children's choices. But it's more than that. When we pay close attention to these choices, we discover how students will reveal and confirm who they are, what matters to them, and what they know and care about. It will also affirm the decisions we make as their teachers, from our read-alouds to the literature we integrate into focus lessons to the informal conversations we hold about authors and illustrators we admire. A commitment to teach children, not necessarily to teach content, relies on this knowledge.

Independent reading choices can reveal wonder

R. L. Stine's Goosebumps books have captivated children for years, as did The Baby-Sitters Club (Ann M. Martin) and Amelia Bedelia (Peggy Parish) books. But why? What's the appeal and how do avid readers of these series reveal what our students know? When Nancy visited a colleague a few years ago, their conversation shifted to kids' reading choices and what appeared to be their indulgence in inferior literature, such as Goosebumps books. At least, that's what her colleague's son inferred from what he overheard. "Have you ever read one?" he inquired. When Nancy sheepishly admitted she hadn't, eleven-year-old Joseph suggested she should and then volunteered to make a recommendation. He scanned his bookshelves carefully, seeking a just-right Goosebumps book for this doubting adult. As Joseph's fingers traced the titles on at least a dozen spines, it became clear he knew and remembered each story, and was determined to match the right book with his intended reader, a responsibility he didn't take lightly. "Start with this one," he said as he offered Nancy his copy of *Monster Blood* (1992), hopeful in his choice.

Asking for students' book recommendations—and then reading them—extends the respectful relationships we aim to cultivate in our classrooms. When Nancy read *Monster Blood*, she discovered plenty to entertain and satisfy Stine's audience: kid characters that repel the bad guys, suspense and action, and a good-defeats-evil resolution. She also discovered Joseph's intimate knowledge of this series and his keen sense of which titles might be most accessible to a Goose-bumps skeptic.

Valuing students' book choices means taking them into consideration when we select books for the read-aloud and for our classroom libraries. Some teachers create opportunities for this by making time for student book talks; others do it by reading aloud excerpts from student-selected books once a week or choosing read-alouds that echo topics, characters, and genres that children enjoy. We know teachers who create book swap tables and others who suggest ways that students can donate books to their classroom library (perhaps books they own but don't reread anymore, or books they'll add to their book order to contribute to the class library, or even books their family might give to the class to honor their birthday). Recently we heard from a fourth-grade teacher who added two questions to her end-of-the-year reflection that she distributes to her students: What book should I buy for next year's class? and What makes it a good addition to our library? Her summer reading and book purchases were guided by these recommendations.

Books and authors that promote wonder

What books and authors do children cite as imaginative and wondrous? Do their choices differ from the literature that teachers mention? Rather than rely on what we *thought* they'd list, we asked teachers to poll their students about the books and authors that instill wonder and that trigger their imaginations. Not surprising, many of the children's choices were books and authors introduced to them through read-alouds and literature circles where there was time and opportunity for response and rereading. In addition, they mentioned books shared during craft lessons for writing and guided inquiry studies. But a fair number were personal choice books, those with appeal not because they'd won an award or because the teacher liked them, but because they were about topics the children found intriguing.

In Megan Sloan's primary classroom, the children listed lots of nonfiction, including Eyewitness Explorer books such as Steve Parker's *Rocks and Minerals* (1993), Judith Draper's *My First Horse and Pony Book* (1995), and Betsy Maestro's *Why Do Leaves Change Color?* (1994). They also chose other genres. The poetry that inspired their curiosity included Douglas Florian's *Autumnblings* (2003) and Jack Prelutsky's *A Pizza the Size of the Sun* (1996). The biography they named was Robert Coles' *The Story of Ruby Bridges* (1995), and they mentioned Faith Ringgold's *Aunt Harriet's Underground Railroad in the Sky* (1992) as a story that made them wonder how much was real and how much was fantasy. But they weren't done. They told Megan she had to include Kate DiCamillo's *The Tale of Despereaux* (2003), E. B. White's *Charlotte's Web* (1952), Robert C. O'Brien's *Mrs. Frisby and the Rats of NIMH* (1971), and Avi's *Poppy* (1999), all books they'd heard her read aloud. The rounded out their list with a mixture of humor, seriousness, and spirited language use when they named *Martha Speaks* (Meddaugh 1992), *Mr. Lincoln's Way* (Polacco 2001), and *In the Small, Small Pond* (Fleming 1993).

When Megan asked, "What authors and illustrators inspire your curiosity?" the first and second graders had no trouble coming up with names. Number one on their list was Avi, known to these children mostly through the read-aloud. They also listed Dr. Seuss, Eric Carle, Kate DiCamillo, Gail Gibbons, Denise Fleming, Shel Silverstein, Dav Pilkey, E. B. White, Eric Kimmel, Kevin Henkes, Jack Prelutsky, and Douglas Florian.

In contrast, Marianne Richardson held a similar conversation with her seventh graders about books and authors that sparked their wonderings. Her question "What creates wonder and how do you really define it?" provoked hearty discussion. Their initial conversation included books that on some level were unexplainable, like Lois Lowry's *The Giver* (1993), but quickly evolved into a discussion about how hard it is to define wonder. Some students were reminded of how they were curious about the kids' exploits in *Harris and Me*, by Gary Paulsen (1993a), especially whether the "me" protagonist was Paulsen himself. Others were more certain that books with wonder meant books that made them think and said Lowry's *Gossamer* (2006), the current read-aloud, did that especially well.

Marianne's middle school students named books that lingered over time, but mostly their choices reflected literature they'd discovered through the read-aloud and stories they could relate to their own lives. Since her language arts classes are divided by gender, their lists are divided similarly. The boys named *Artemis Fowl* (Colfer 2001), *Hoot* (Hiaasen 2002), *Inkheart* (Funke 2003), *Peter Pan in Scarlet* (McCaughrean 2006), *Crispin: The Cross of Lead* (Avi 2002), *Harris and Me* (Paulsen 1993a), and *The Cay* (Taylor 1987) as literature that ignited their imagination and they listed Gary Paulsen, Avi, Lemony Snicket, and Patricia Polacco as the authors that do that the best. When asked about illustrators who promote wonder, the boys named Michael P. White, Bryan Collier, Brett Helquist, and Susan Jeffers. The girls' book choices were *So B. It* (Weeks 2004), *Pictures of Hollis Woods* (Giff 2002), *The Giver* (Lowry 1993), *Gossamer* (Lowry 2006), *The End of the Beginning* (Avi 2004), and *A Corner of the Universe* (Martin 2002). Interestingly, all of these books were read aloud, except *The Giver*.

Their authors list included Lois Lowry, Patricia Reilly Giff, Sarah Weeks, Avi, Patricia Polacco, and Emily Dickinson. They named Eric Carle, Jan Brett, Susan Jeffers, Christopher Myers, and Jerry Pinkney as artists whose illustrations sparked wonder.

Seeing Patricia Polacco's name on both lists caught our attention. Marianne explained that she and a colleague had introduced Polacco's books when they both taught third grade as part of a focus on family and friendship. Many of Marianne's current students were in those classes and claimed they still remembered what they learned about Polacco, including where she acquired the inspiration for her stories and their fascination with how she included family photographs in her illustrations.

Literature to spark students' wonderings

Just recently, a box arrived at our offices full of new books for review. Within those boxes we discovered a number of books with the "oh wow!" factor. If you asked us what we mean by that, we'd find it hard to explain. As Marianne's students discovered, defining wonder isn't easy or exact. It's something we can sense. It hits us emotionally. It teases, excites, and generates response. Upon opening Robert Neubecker's *Wow! School!* (2007), we experienced the first day of school through a child's perspective. This oversized treasure with its bold colors, double-page spreads, and large print transmits the wonder of everything exciting about school—books, art, playground, science, lunch, friends. Any literature that reveals the wonder of place, both familiar and imagined, invites readers to discover close up some marvelous places outside the range of their own backyard (see Figure 7.1).

It didn't take us long to unpack other wow-factor books from our boxes, this time texts featuring characters with vivid imaginations. After their teacher reads a book about dragons in Carole Lexa Schaefer's *Dragon Dancing* (2007), ingenious preschoolers create their own dragon out of feathers, paper, and yarn, then journey into imaginative worlds beyond their playground before returning in time for a birthday celebration. Little Rabbit, in Kate Klise's *Imagine Harry* (2007), has some very nice friends, but his very best friend is invisible. The innocence and charm of this realistic friendship between Little Rabbit and Harry honors the need for imagination in children's lives and the rewards that come from it. *Imagine Harry* also reveals the challenges society can place on too much imagination and a child's clever way to resolve that. Literature that introduces characters with active imaginations not only helps to cultivate wonder through the responses it inspires, it also pays tribute to the power of make-believe (see Figures 7.2 and 7.3).

ABC NYC: A Book About Seeing New York City, by Joanne Dugan. New York: Harry N. Abrams, 2005.

Alphabet City, by Stephen T. Johnson. New York: Viking, 1995.

Angelina's Island, by Jeanette Winter. New York: Farrar, Straus and Giroux, 2007.

Barrio: José's Neighborhood, by George Ancona. San Diego: Harcourt, 1998.

Car Wash, by Sandra Steen and Susan Steen. Illus. G. Brian Karas. New York: Putnam, 2001.

Cloudy with a Chance of Meatballs, by Judi Barrett. Illus. Ron Barrett. New York: Atheneum, 1978.

Comets, Stars, the Moon, and Mars: Space Poems and Paintings, by Douglas Florian. San Diego: Harcourt, 2007.

In the Small, Small Pond, by Denise Fleming. New York: Holt, 1993.

Neighborhood Odes, by Gary Soto. Illus. David Diaz. San Diego: Harcourt, 1992.

The Seven Wonders of the Ancient World, by Lynn Curley. New York: Atheneum, 2002.

Tour America: A Journey Through Poems and Art, by Diane Siebert. Illus. Stephen T. Johnson. San Francisco: Chronicle, 2006.

WOW! CITY! by Robert Neubecker. New York: Hyperion, 2004.

FIG 7.1 Literature to Help Us Experience the Wonder of Place

Ceci Ann's Day of Why, by Christopher Phillips. Illus. Shino Arihara. Berkeley, CA: Tricycle, 2006.

Eddie's Kingdom, by D. B. Johnson. Boston: Houghton Mifflin, 2005.

Harold and the Purple Crayon, by Crockett Johnson. New York: HarperCollins, 1955.

Lily Brown's Paintings, by Angela Johnson. Illus. E. B. Lewis. New York: Orchard, 2007.

Not a Box, by Antoinette Portis. New York: HarperCollins, 2006.

Olivia, by Ian Falconer. New York: Anne Schwartz/Atheneum, 2000.

Roxaboxen, by Alice McLerran. Illus. Barbara Cooney. New York: Lothrop, Lee and Shepard, 1991.

Westlandia, by Paul Fleischman. Illus. Kevin Hawkes. Cambridge, MA: Candlewick, 1999.

Where the Wild Things Are, by Maurice Sendak. New York: Harper and Row, 1963.

The Wise Woman and Her Secret, by Eve Merriam. Illus. Linda Graves. New York: Simon and Schuster, 1991.

FIG 7.2 Picture Books Featuring Fictional Characters with Imagination

When we first saw the cover of Russell Freedman's *The Adventures of Marco Polo* (2006), our questions started popping. Who was this explorer whose name is now associated with a popular children's swimming pool game? How truthful is the story of his twenty-four-year journey to China during which he amassed

The BFG, by Roald Dahl. Illus. Quentin Blake. New York: Farrar, Straus and Giroux, 1982.

Bud, Not Buddy, by Christopher Paul Curtis. New York: Delacorte, 1999.

The Burning Questions of Bingo Brown, by Betsy Byars. New York: Viking Penguin, 1988.

Did You Carry the Flag Today, Charley? by Rebecca Caudill. Illus. Nancy Grossman. New York: Holt, 1966.

Gooney Bird Greene, by Lois Lowry. Illus. Middy Thomas. Boston: Houghton Mifflin, 2002.

Gossamer, by Lois Lowry. Boston: Houghton Mifflin, 2006.

Pippi Longstocking, by Astrid Lindgren. Illus. Louis S. Glanzman. New York: Viking, 1950.

Ramona the Pest, by Beverly Cleary. Illus. Louis Darling. New York: HarperCollins, 1968.

The Talented Clementine, by Sara Pennypacker. Illus. Marla Frazee. New York: Hyperion, 2007.

FIG 7.3 *Novels Featuring Fictional Characters with Imagination*

exotic treasures, fine silk, and jewels? Did he create an imaginative tale of travels so believable that history books credit him for journeys he never took, or were his travels truly factual? Our curiosity about this real person propelled us into Freedman's captivating biography with its unique beginning, where we listened in at Polo's deathbed while his family begged for his true confession. Literature that inspires wonder is often about real individuals whose lives and accomplishments not only elicit our questions but exhibit the many ways that imagination has created their identities (see Figure 7.4).

What Can We Do to Cultivate Wonder in Our Own Teaching and Learning?

In *The Energy to Teach* (2001), Donald Graves argues that we are in charge of our own energy. He reminds us that many of us went into teaching because we are learners and want to instill in students that love of learning. Graves contends that we are most energy filled when we continue to engage in the learning process. Megan echoes this sentiment as she shares with her students her wonderings about how the world works—the sunsets that she sees or the clouds that wisp across the sky. She encourages students to stop, observe, and seek answers to their questions about why the moon can be seen in the daytime or how differently the wind can feel on their faces, or the ways in which flowers change each day. Megan doesn't hesitate to voice her "I wonder why . . ." statements. She believes that it's easy to "hurry, hurry, hurry because we have so much to teach,

Escape! The Story of the Great Harry Houdini, by Sid Fleischman. New York: Greenwillow, 2006.

Girls Think of Everything: Stories of Ingenious Inventions by Women, by Catherine Thimmesh. Illus. Melissa Sweet. Boston: Houghton Mifflin, 2000.

John's Secret Dreams, by Doreen Rappaport. Illus. Bryan Collier. New York: Hyperion, 2005.

The Kid Who Invented the Popsicle: And Other Surprising Stories About Inventions, by Don L. Wulffson. New York: Dutton, 1997.

The Librarian Who Measured the Earth, by Kathryn Lasky. Illus. Kevin Hawkes. Boston: Little, Brown, 1994.

The Man Who Walked Between the Towers, by Mordicai Gerstein. New Milford, CT: Roaring Brook, 2003.

Marvelous Mattie: How Margaret E. Knight Became an Inventor, by Emily Arnold McCully. New York: Farrar, Straus and Giroux, 2006.

Odd Boy Out: Young Albert Einstein, by Don Brown. Boston: Houghton Mifflin, 2004.

Shipwreck at the Bottom of the World: The Extraordinary Story of Shackleton and the Endurance, by Jennifer Armstrong. New York: Crown, 2000.

To Fly: The Story of the Wright Brothers, by Wendie C. Old. Illus. Robert Andrew Parker. New York: Clarion, 2002.

With a Little Luck: Surprising Stories of Amazing Discoveries, by Dennis Brindell Fradin. New York: Dutton, 2006.

FIG 7.4 *Books Featuring Real People Whose Lives Exhibit Wonder and Curiosity*

but we need to slow down and listen to our students and what they wonder about. That way we keep our own wondering alive."

Marianne takes the time to energize her teaching by observing students. She shared with us a recent collaboration between her seventh graders and a class of first graders. The first graders were creating their own versions of Picasso's *Three Musicians* using cut-paper collage. Each seventh grader partnered with a first grader and wrote a poem to accompany the collage. Marianne watched as her students sat head-to-head with the younger children, each awed by the other as they made connections while discussing the art. When the older students returned to their classroom, Marianne was amazed as pens flew across the pages of their writer's notebooks, creating skeletons of poems inspired both by the art and the conversations with their young partners. She recognized that she didn't have to teach voice—it was there. This successful collaboration energized Marianne as she observed her students and as she worked with another teacher.

Both of these teachers, as well as Donald Graves, remind us that wonder probably won't exist unless there is energy to propel it. We are invigorated by observing both the world around us and our students. Wonder is also fueled by reading professionally and holding conversations with colleagues. As Marianne says, "Conversations with others send my mind in a million directions and form a shared community among those of us working together." She also finds that potential lessons emerge from both reading and conversation. Overall, it's Marianne's willingness to discover what cultivates wonder and her desire to pursue it.

Cultivating wonder through literature

If you were to ask one of our undergraduate or graduate students, or even our colleagues, whether we are passionate about teaching and literature, we're pretty sure their answer would be a resounding *yes*! We take delight as we encounter our students the first day of the term, introducing ourselves through the read-aloud. Our offices not only contain piles and piles of books, they also exhibit students' literature responses. We don't attempt to hide the evidence that fuels our passion; we want to share it with those who will listen to us rave about a new book we've just read, share a powerful connection a student made to a literary piece, or relay highlights from a conference presentation by an author or illustrator. What we realized long ago, and what we attempt to instill in our students, is that one of the most important roles of a teacher is to be both promoter and caretaker of wonder.

We aren't alone in the belief that literature provides a source for our wonder. Recently we received an email from Megan asking, "Have you seen the new book about Harriet Tubman, *Moses: When Harriet Tubman Led Her People to Freedom* by Carole Boston Weatherford [2006]? Kadir Nelson's illustrations are amazing!" Discovering a new book on a topic she teaches sparked Megan's enthusiasm to immediately share *Moses* with her students and others. Not only was she intrigued by the story, Megan also knew that the luminous illustrations would captivate her students and generate their questions and wonderings. Christine Jordan eagerly awaits the release of Doreen Cronin and Harry Bliss' newest diary book, *Diary of a Fly* (2007). Based on previous experiences of sharing *Diary of a Worm* (2003) and *Diary of a Spider* (2005), Christine is certain that the humor presented in these books will inspire students' writing. And Kate devours any book written by Patricia Reilly Giff, who became one of her favorite authors after she read *Pictures of Hollis Woods* (2002). Kate's appreciation for Giff's multilayered stories impacts how she reads these books aloud. Giff's characters' face personal struggles that result from challenging circumstances, eliciting powerful oral and written responses from her readers.

Each of these teachers is excited about the books she reads, assured of the potential that literature offers to build community, create readers, inspire writing, nurture response, and promote inquiry. They recognize that literature is a key partner in their teaching and are constantly on the alert for books to read aloud, generate questions, and support students' ongoing literacy development. Literature enhances existing curriculum and sparks new curriculum because of the interesting topics, relevant issues, and historical time periods that pique students' interest. And literature cultivates wonder in our teaching as it invites and encourages us to slow down, to ponder characters and plots, to present ways to think about the world we live in, and to inspire strategies for sharing this work with students (see Figure 7.5).

A *Book of Coupons*, by Susie Morgenstern. Illus. Serge Bloch. New York: Viking, 2001.

The Dot, by Peter H. Reynolds. New York: Walker, 2004.

Hooray for Diffendoofer Day, by Dr. Seuss and Jack Prelutsky. Illus. Lane Smith. New York: Random House, 1998.

The Magic School Bus and the Science Fair Expedition, by Joanna Cole. Illus. Bruce Degen. New York: Scholastic, 2006.

Miss Malarkey Leaves No Reader Behind, by Judy Finchler. Illus. Kevin O'Malley. New York: Walker, 2006.

Miss Nelson Is Missing, by Harry Allard. Illus. James Marshall. Boston: Houghton Mifflin, 1977.

Sister Anne's Hands, by Marybeth Lorbiecki. Illus. K. Wendy Popp. New York: Dial, 1998.

Thank You Mr. Falker, by Patricia Polacco. New York: Philomel, 1998.

A View from Saturday, by E. L. Konigsburg. New York: Atheneum, 1996.

The Year of Miss Agnes, by Kirkpatrick Hill. New York: Margaret K. McElderry, 2000.

FIG 7.5 *Books Featuring Fictional Teachers Who Teach with Wonder*

Cultivating wonder by reading aloud

We return one final time to the role of the read-aloud in the classroom. One of the many reasons the teachers we have featured in this book read aloud is because they believe stories will invoke wonder. Marianne explained, "[There are] many, many days that are not wonder filled for me or the students. But I also know that wonder happens in small moments—when the reluctant writer writes, the halting reader finds a book he loves, the conversations move from simplistic to inspired, and when silence is broken by flying pens following the last spoken word from the read-aloud." Marianne reads aloud to her seventh graders every day because it "binds [her] students to [her] in a way that [she] can't replicate through any other method. It is the shared experience of 'being the book' that allows each of us to express our feelings and emotions honestly." The read-aloud creates a sense of trust and a spirit of accomplishment that permeates the day and the curriculum. Because of the shared experience, students are not afraid to voice their opinions and wonderings that are based on a story they have heard.

Before beginning to read aloud a picture book or novel, teachers examine the cover illustration with their students. They read the title of the book and the names of the author and illustrator. Students' attention is drawn to characteristics of the cover such as the diamond-shaped cutout design featured on *Show Way*, by Jacqueline Woodson (2005), or the book title on the back cover of *Martin's Big Words*, by Doreen Rappaport (2001), that doesn't interfere with Bryan

Collier's stunning portrait of Dr. Martin Luther King Jr. on the front. They might question the significance of the running feet pictured on Jerry Spinelli's *Maniac Magee* (1990) or the beady eyes on the hardcover version of Carl Hiaasen's *Hoot* (2002). Sometimes removing the book jacket will reveal a hidden treasure such as the word *bag* on Gary Paulsen's *Nightjohn* (1993b) or a coffee cup and moon depicted against the backdrop of a city skyline on the burgundy cover of Cynthia Rylant's *An Angel for Solomon Singer* (1991). While examining a book cover, teachers may inquire what students think the story is about, but the purpose for their unhurried observation is not solely to make a prediction.

Once a book is opened, students' attention gravitates to the endpapers. These might reveal a pattern or detailed illustration or offer a solid-colored background, typical in chapter books. Children are more visually aware than adults, especially when they're invited to take notice of visual elements. They'll remember the striped endpapers in Barbara Kerley's picture book biography *The Dinosaurs of Waterhouse Hawkins* (2001) or discover how the pale blue beginning is repeated throughout Eric Rohmann's fantasy about imaginary friends, *Clara and Asha* (2005). After turning to the dedication page, students may wonder why Mark Teague dedicated *Detective LaRue: Letters from the Investigation* (2004) to Lillias and Ava or want to know the meaning behind the dedication in Kirby Larson's *Hattie Big Sky* (2006), which reads, "For Neil, who has never doubted." By now, fans of the Pigeon books know that Mo Willems' dedication "For Trixie at Bedtime" in *Don't Let the Pigeon Stay Up Late!* (2006) refers to his beloved daughter.

Reading the author's note about the inspiration or historical background for a book broadens readers' understanding about text. In *Counting on Grace*, Elizabeth Winthrop (2006) provides information in her author's note about Lewis Hine as well as the photograph of the young girl that inspired the story. Jeanette Winter's spare but powerful picture book *September Roses* (2004) begins with a note stating the story is based on two South African sisters who were stranded in New York City in the aftermath of September 11. In addition to the author's note, we are always grateful when an illustrator includes a note or the publisher provides information on the back of the title page about the media in which the illustrations have been rendered. After reading that Peter McCarty used pencil on watercolor paper to create the illustrations in *Moon Plane* (2006), students revisit the book and pore over the exquisite art. They want to know how Denise Fleming makes the paper she used for the pictures in *Lunch* (1992) and *Buster* (2003), and then they eagerly consult her website to learn how they can make their own paper. Children pay attention to illustrations and often ask questions, prompting teachers to learn more about artistic media and styles. Professional resources such as Molly Bang's *Picture This: How Pictures Work* (2000) and Julie

Cummins' *Children's Book Illustration and Design II* (1997) provide interesting and useful information to share with students.

Teachers often choose picture books for reading aloud to primary and intermediate students. This format poses its own challenge. Sometimes teachers hold a picture book facing them to read the text, then turn it briefly to show children the illustrations. This practice can limit the time children have to view the art. We've observed what we call the NASCAR approach to picture book reading, where the book zooms by with barely enough time to glimpse the illustrations. It is the slowing down of the read-aloud that impacts children's ability to notice, comprehend, and interpret story and art. Teachers need to determine how much time they will linger over a page before continuing the story. Sometimes children have so many comments and questions that the story line gets lost. Keeping sticky notes close by enables the teacher to mark a page with a unique illustration or an intriguing word, or that presents a critical point that can be revisited after the conclusion of the initial reading of the book. As we mark these pages, we also demonstrate the active thinking that readers do.

One of the rewards of reading aloud is that it forces both reader and listener to slow down and pay attention to the language, rhythm, and flow of the story. It offers an incredible opportunity to listen to children's comments, questions, and connections and to engage in interesting, thought-provoking, or humorous discussions. There's always that light bulb moment when a child (or the teacher) realizes that not everyone thinks or feels about a book in the same way. Through reading aloud, teachers discover insights into students' lives, determine topics of interest, and, in turn, evoke wonder.

Cultivating wonder through student response

In addition to the read-aloud, there are numerous ways to cultivate wonder, particularly through strategies in which students respond to literature. Kate's use of literary letters, leading in to chapters in this book, provides her with an understanding of the choices students make for independent reading and affords her some insight into students' thoughts and ideas associated with their books. This ongoing written dialogue also illuminates questions about and connections to characters, events, and other stories. Kate often marvels at what her students respond to as well as their willingness to share those thoughts; she often reads these letters to Nancy during her weekly classroom visits.

Literature circles also provide possibilities for developing wonder in our teaching. These small-group discussions allow children time to savor books while paying attention to story and craft. The pace is slowed and books aren't gulped down. When we participate in a literature circle with students, we realize that their connections to the story or art are often different from our own. Students respect our opinions just as they do each other's. Extension projects culminate the literature circle experience, further delighting us when students create images that depict events in the story, pay attention to color choice to indicate mood or tone, and carefully consider how to portray personal connections. Students consistently impress us with their talents displayed through both written and oral responses. Literature circles and other response strategies such as those shared in Chapter 3 invite wonder into the classroom because they open a world of possibilities for students to reveal themselves as learners and as individuals.

We cultivate wonder by slowing down, by expecting to be amazed, by noticing with awe what children read, what they say, and what they write. The way we nourish wonder in our teaching and learning stems from both the literature and students. We just have to be open to it. Megan has stated many times that we should never underestimate children. We believe the same is true about teachers and learning.

How Do Authors and Illustrators Partner with Us to Nurture Wonder?

Children's book authors and illustrators invest their lives in a world of imagination and disseminate that through the literature they create. Books that elicit response not only expect readers who wonder but fuel their imaginations in myriad ways. The fictional characters and fantastical situations in J. K. Rowling's Harry Potter series take readers of all ages along on the journey. Sandra Markle's lively nonfiction and Russell Freedman's biographies compel us to raise questions and kindle our curiosity. Eloise Greenfield's poetry pleases our ears, while Jack Prelutsky's poems tickle our funny bones. Jerry Pinkney's illustrations need to be touched and Mo Willems' pigeons beg to be copied. The act of creation requires a stance of "What if?" and a belief and trust that something important resides inside that wonder.

When authors and illustrators present readers with unpredictable plots, characters, and formats, they invite participation. David Wiesner's *Flotsam* (2006) and Barbara Lehman's *The Red Book* (2004) tell stories through images. They trust their reader to discover, uncover, and imagine a story through several readings. By rereading and reviewing we can't help but refine, retell, and re-create the layers of story these illustrations inspire. The opening pages of *The Invention of Hugo Cabret* (2007), Brian Selznick's 533-page "novel," defies our expectations. Where's the text? What's happening here? Who is this character?

Where's he going? Like the black-and-white soundless films that Selznick researched for this story, his book echoes a cinematic experience, revealing an engaging mystery with elements of the picture book, graphic novel, and film. As Selznick states about this inventive text: "The reader is in control of the story . . . what matters most is the reader turning the page" (2007). How can we not be curious when authors and illustrators present us with such wondrous creations and when they trust us to participate? (See Figure 7.6 for a list of books that inspire curiosity and wonder.)

Within more traditional forms of literature, some authors and illustrators address issues of wonder through their plots and characters. As Nancy reads aloud the opening chapters to Lois Lowry's *Gossamer* (2006) in her children's literature class, her students wonder about the character of Littlest One, noticing how realistic she seems, even though they can't yet figure out what kind of creature she is. And neither can Littlest. She overflows with questions, many about her identity. She can't stand still. She twirls and touches, ponders and wonders, all with the hope of figuring things out. But Fastidious, her teacher, finds this curiosity exasperating.

"I asked if we are a kind of dog."

"Whatever makes you ask such a thing? The other learners never ask questions like that."

"That's because they don't take time to think about things. I'm a thinker. Right now I'm thinking about whether I am a kind of dog." (2)

Imagine, by Norman Messenger. Cambridge, MA: Candlewick, 2005.

Imagine a Night, by Rob Gonsalves. New York: Atheneum, 2003.

Museum Trip, by Barbara Lehman. Boston: Houghton Mifflin, 2006.

The Mysteries of Harris Burdick, by Chris Van Allsburg. Boston: Houghton Mifflin, 1984.

Nothing to Do, by Douglas Wood. Illus. Wendy Anderson Halperin. New York: Dutton, 2006.

Once Upon a Banana, by Jennifer Armstrong. Illus. David Small. New York: Paula Wiseman/Simon and Schuster, 2006.

The Room of Wonders, by Sergio Ruzzier. New York: Farrar, Straus and Giroux, 2006.

Sector 7, by David Wiesner. New York: Clarion, 1999.

The Shape Game, by Anthony Browne. New York: Farrar, Straus and Giroux, 2003.

The Way Things Work, by David Macaulay. Boston: Houghton Mifflin, 1988.

FIG 7.6 *Literature That Fuels the Imagination*

Littlest One continues to think about things, to ask questions, to wonder not only about herself but also about others. Because Lowry reveals the plot bit by bit, readers wonder along with Littlest, and it's not until a few chapters later when we discover that Littlest is a dream-giver. But this only makes readers wonder more.

E. B. White also creates characters who are curious and who take the time to observe. Like Fastidious, the mother in *Charlotte's Web* (1952) worries about her daughter's overactive imagination, believing Fern is inventing wild tales when she retells some of the stories she's heard Charlotte tell. Seeking advice for her concern, Mrs. Arable pays a call to the family doctor, hoping his experience and wisdom will help her understand her daughter's desire to spend so much time at the Zuckerman farm. But Dr. Dorian finds Fern's behavior enchanting as he points out the miracles to be found in a spider's web. Mrs. Arable is not reassured . . . at least not right away.

> "I don't understand it, and I don't like what I can't understand."
>
> "None of us do," said Dr. Dorian, sighing. "I'm a doctor. Doctors are supposed to understand everything. But I don't understand everything, and I don't intend to let it worry me."
>
> Mrs. Arable fidgeted. "Fern says the animals talk to each other. Dr. Dorian, do you believe animals talk?"
>
> "I never heard one say anything," he replied. . . . "It is quite possible that an animal has spoken civilly to me and that I didn't catch the remark because I wasn't paying attention. Children pay better attention than grownups." (110)

Like the good doctor in *Charlotte's Web*, authors and illustrators respect children's wonder as healthy and worthy of their time and attention.

As we've suggested in previous chapters, we can also glean insight about the authors and illustrators whose presence we invite into our classrooms through their websites, through their published speeches, and in their biographic videos and publishers' materials. Viewing *Eric Carle: Picture Writer* (1993), we observe a beloved artist-storyteller at work in his studio, learning not only about his childhood inspiration and the adults who believed in him but also about how he prepares his colorful tissue papers and creates his brilliant collage. In this video-portrait, Carle tells the story of winding up his uncle's thinking machine when he was a child in order to be rewarded with his uncle's stories. This early apprenticeship under the tutelage of an imaginative storyteller, accompanied by opportunities and encouragement to paint to his heart's content, has given us a masterful "picture writer." As Carle gleefully spatters paint onto large sheets of paper, we can't help but want to join him. He gloats, "Look at me, a grown man. I'm like a child. I'm having fun!"

In Lois Ehlert's 2006 Boston Globe–Horn Book Award acceptance speech for *Leaf Man*, she remarked, "I think of my books as little love notes, records of things I care about. The words and pictures move from page to page, hand in hand. I hope to convey to young readers the same sense of excitement, wonder, and surprise I still have about the world around me" (2007, 20). Ehlert's illustrations in *Leaf Man* (2005) and *Pie in the Sky* (2004) may seem simple upon initial viewing, but closer inspection reveals that she has used ordinary objects such as leaves, fabric, feathers, and buttons in extraordinary ways. It is obvious Ehlert finds joy in the beauty and uniqueness in the world around her with wonder as a key element in collecting, envisioning, and constructing her art.

Ehlert is by no means the only author or illustrator whose writing and illustrations reveal keen imagination and reverence for children. Perhaps there's a thick layer of wonder living and breathing under the skin of the adults who create books for children. Perhaps curiosity courses through their veins. Perhaps, like Eric Carle claims, they've only lost a small percentage of their imagination as they've become adults. Or perhaps the child within is still very much alive, allowed to spring forth in the literature they create. It's certainly evident in the characters they conceive and in the places and situations they allow us to imagine. Time and again we're reminded of this kinship to childhood through the works and words of children's book writers and illustrators, and we're grateful they accompany us into our classrooms.

Professional Literature Cited

Bang, Molly. 2000. *Picture This: How Pictures Work*. New York: SeaStar.

Cummins, Julie, ed. 1997. *Children's Book Illustration and Design II*. New York: PBC International.

Elhert, Lois. 2007. "Picture Book Award Winner." *Horn Book* (Jan./Feb.): 20.

Graves, Donald. 2001. *The Energy to Teach*. Portsmouth, NH: Heinemann.

Selznick, Brian. 2007. American Library Association Midwinter Conference. January, Seattle, WA.

Spandel, Vicki. 2006. Association for the Advancement of International Education Conference. July, Seattle, WA.

Conversation with . . .
Author-illustrator David Wiesner

David Wiesner's unique style of visual storytelling grabs readers' attention and captures their imaginations. In this conversation, Wiesner provides some insight regarding a few of his wordless picture books, including **Hurricane** and **June 29, 1999**, as well as his three Caldecott Medal winners, **Tuesday**, **The Three Pigs**, and **Flotsam**.

Even though your stories would be considered fantasy, are any of them based in reality?

Hurricane is autobiographical and resulted from actual events, but is presented as fiction. This story is about a hurricane with an emotional twist to it—on the one hand there is a terrifying storm outside, which is intense and scary, while on the flip side there is the family inside the house calmly playing games. One morning, my brother, George, and I discovered an elm tree that had fallen in our yard that became an incredible plaything—a jungle, a pirate ship, a space ship—which later inspired the story. *June 29, 1999* also stems from when my brother and I were growing up. We would create UFOs by taking a thin plastic dry-cleaning bag, patching up the holes, making a loop in the bottom with a wire hanger, and then placing a wad of burning fabric inside the bag that would smolder and fill the bag with hot air. As the UFO drifted away, we would chase it. These UFOs were the impetus for that book.

What role does that sense of reality play in your other books?

I've always been fascinated with the idea of leaving one reality for another. This idea was the premise for *Tuesday*. If you were to look quick enough or peek around the corner in time, you just might see frogs flying and other stuff happening. It's this unseen reality and either you're paying attention or you're not. If things shifted a little bit, you might find it. I suppose it could be a scary prospect, but to me there is something very appealing about it. It appears there is an in-between place and you can get from

one place to another. That's where science fiction or time travel comes in with black holes that you go through and pop out someplace else.

Is that what happens in The Three Pigs***?***

The Three Pigs resulted partly from reading science fiction and also from enjoying comics as a kid. When I was seven or eight years old, I was watching a Bugs Bunny cartoon. Elmer Fudd was chasing Bugs Bunny through the forest for the hundredth time. Around and around they run, going through the usual routine of chasing each other through hollow logs, down rabbit holes, and up trees when all of a sudden, something different happens. Bugs and Elmer run right out of the frame of film. We see the sprockets at the edge of the filmstrip as other frames are running by, until the characters are left standing in the middle of a blank white space. They look around momentarily, then run back into the frame of film, and the chase continues.

What type of research did you need to do for this book?

In *The Three Pigs*, I always knew there would be three different breeds of pigs—Duroc, Hampshire, and Yorkshire—so that each one had a different look. And the colors would help tell them apart. I read books about pigs and made clay models of pigs and bought little plastic play pigs. I had to understand the pig's anatomy so that I could come as close to what the animal could actually do and stay as true as possible to its skeletal structure. Because pigs have bulges and bumps and things, I needed

to pick up the models to see how they would look from underneath and at a three-quarter angle. As I began painting the pigs, each took on its own personality. I played up the aspect that the straw pig is clumsy and knocks everything down and trips over things. And the brick pig is the brains of the group. He built the brick house and is a take-charge kind of guy. That is a case where painting them made me go back and play around with the elements.

Was The Three Pigs *intended to be a takeoff of the traditional tale?*

The text in *The Three Pigs* is there primarily as a prop or as part of the background rather than to tell the story. It really could have been any story. It could have been the three bears. It could have been Hansel and Gretel. I had to be clear that the pigs wanted out of the story. That's why there is very little text and most of it is contained within speech balloons. I discussed with my editor, Dinah Stevenson, how it was critical on the beginning pages that the reader understands what was happening. I couldn't be subtle. Visually, I needed to show the pig painted in a different way so that he is clearly coming out of the story, but I also had to state, "Hey, I'm coming out of the story." As the pigs got out, it naturally led them to finding other storybook characters in similar circumstances and then coming back and re-creating a world for themselves. It was very proactive—they were looking for a house. They wanted a home where they would be safe and find a new family. That was the emotional focus of the story.

What influenced the creation of Flotsam, *your third book to receive a Caldecott Medal?*

This book continues in the same line as the "it's more than meets the eye" books and the idea that this is what happens at night when you're not looking. The story stems from a kid going to the Jersey Shore, but it relates to when I was four or five years old and a puffer fish washed up on the beach. My response at that time was both "eeuw" and "cool." I realized that thing was right in the water where I swim! But it made me wonder, "What *else* is out there?" That idea was fed by science books and weird deep sea pictures of all kinds of fish and sea animals. So, I combined the image of the flotsam that washes up on the beach with mental flotsam—the ideas that float around in your head that wash up in your consciousness. *Flotsam* is a way to connect kids across time and space. Initially I had all these ideas and lots of text, but then I had to ask, "What kind of story can I wrap around these ideas?" The camera became the perfect way to show the "what else is out there" stuff.

How do you think your illustrations cultivate wonder in readers?

I'm really not thinking about that consciously. What I love is to get lost in the work and what I hope for from my readers is they'll respond with "Ooohh coool!" The best reaction is when they look at the pictures and the stories and their imaginations are excited—when they wonder about the ordinary, when they notice what's strange, and when they take pleasure in that world for a little while.

Flotsam, by David Wiesner. New York: Clarion, 2006.

Hurricane, by David Wiesner. New York: Clarion, 1990.

June 29, 1999, by David Wiesner. New York: Clarion, 1992.

The Three Pigs, by David Wiesner. New York: Clarion, 2001

Tuesday, by David Wiesner. New York: Clarion, 1991.

Side by Side by Side
Literature/Teacher/Learner: Fierce Wonderings

Book

Fletcher, Ralph. 1996. *A Writer's Notebook: Unlocking the Writer Within You*. New York: Avon.

> Chapter 2 in Fletcher's book for young writers, titled "Fierce Wonderings," suggests that writing about the things that haunt you takes honesty and courage. It's the kind of writing where you ask big questions that may not have tidy answers. These could be questions about identity and deep feelings. Maybe they're wonderings that keep you awake at night or linger in your subconscious for months or years. They might be scary questions or playful ones. In this short chapter, Fletcher reveals a few of his own big questions, along with some wonderings written by fourth and fifth graders: What does the world have in store for my eighty-year-old grandmother? What would I do at school if I had no friends? Is growing up as wonderful as adults say? What are crows really saying when they talk to each other?

Related literature

Do Princesses Really Kiss Frogs? by Carmela LaVigna Coyle. Illus. Mike Gordon. Flagstaff, AZ: Rising Moon, 2005.

Fireflies, by Julie Brinckloe. New York: Aladdin, 1986.

I Wonder Why, by Lois Rock. Illus. Christopher Corr. San Francisco: Chronicle, 2001.

I Wonder Why Mice Are Musical: And Other Questions About Music, by Josephine Parker. Boston: Kingfisher/Houghton Mifflin, 2007.

The Other Way to Listen, by Byrd Baylor. Illus. Peter Parnall. New York: Scribner's, 1978.

Where Is Grandpa? by T. A. Barron. Illus. Chris Soentpiet. New York: Philomel, 2000.

Teaching Response

It's early in the school year, the time that Kate dedicates her focus lessons to establishing purpose and sparking writing possibilities for students' writing notebooks. She's already read aloud sections of *A Writer's Notebook* and then followed the reading with opportunities for students to talk and then write from Fletcher's ideas by making connections to their own lives. Today's focus lesson invites her fifth graders to think about Fletcher's term *bottomless questions* as another way to generate writing. As she reads about fierce wonderings, including the chapter's many examples that provoke pondering, she pauses to give her students a chance to interject some of their own. Then, at the end of the chapter, she asks, "What is it about these questions that can lead to good writing?" After giving students a brief opportunity to think about this question with a partner, Kate repeats her question.

"They can't be answered easily," suggests Stuart.

"Or maybe they'll never be answered," Phelicia adds.

Jacqylyn notices, "What stood out to me is how some of the questions were really emotional, and some were not too serious."

Kate writes "Fierce Wonderings" on top of some chart paper, then adds ideas raised by the students:

- BIG questions
- not easy to answer
- some are serious, some are not
- "bottomless questions"
- questions that linger
- questions that keep you thinking, even if you don't want to

Following a few minutes of partner sharing to generate some fierce wonderings of their own, Kate sends them back to their desks to write for ten minutes, generating a list of their own fierce wonderings, or spending the full ten minutes writing about just one lingering question. Students then place these lists and writings in the front section of their writing notebooks for ready reference during writing workshop.

Student Response

Figures 7.7 and 7.8 show two students' fierce wonderings.

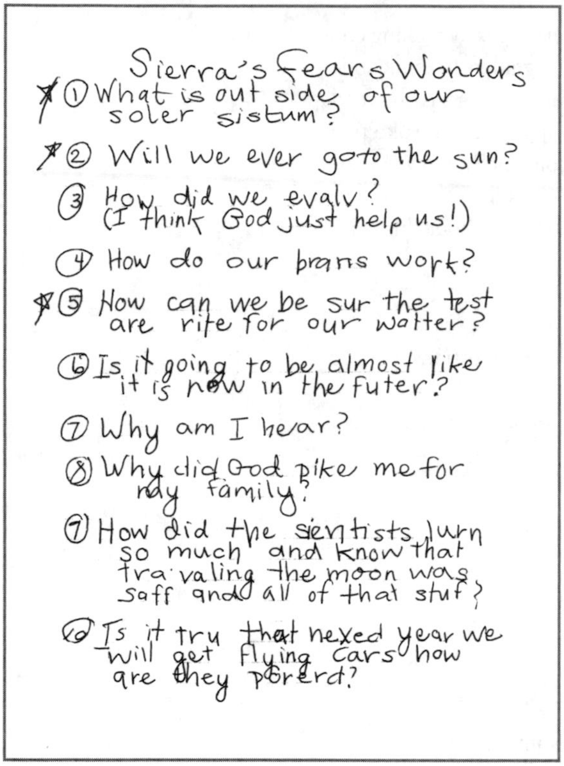

Sierra's Fears Wonders

✗① What is out side of our soler sistum?

✗② Will we ever go to the sun?

③ How did we evalv?
(I think God just help us!)

④ How do our brans work?

✗⑤ How can we be sur the test are rite for our walter?

⑥ Is it going to be almost like it is now in the futer?

⑦ Why am I hear?

⑧ Why did God pike me for my family?

⑨ How did the sientists lurn so much and know that travaling the moon was saff and all of that stuf?

⑩ Is it tru that nexed year we will get flying cars how are they porerd?

FIG 7.7 Sierra's Fierce Wonderings

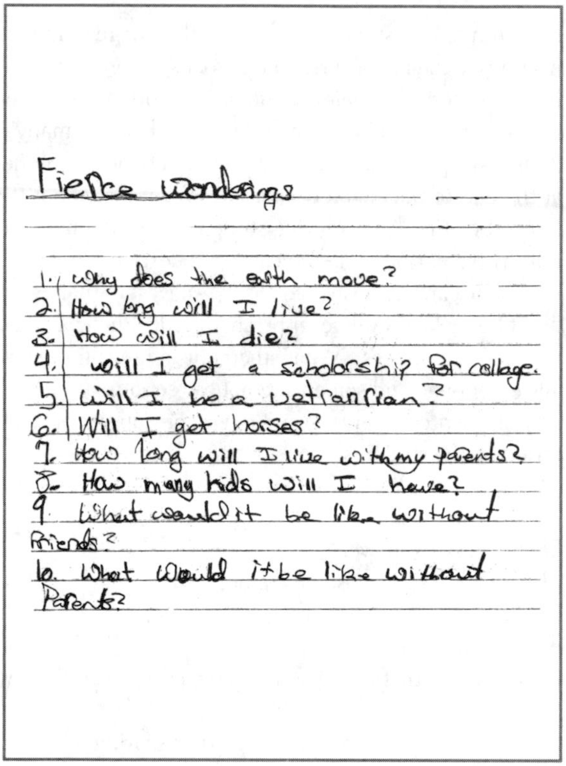

Fierce Wonderings

1. Why does the earth move?
2. How long will I live?
3. How will I die?
4. Will I get a scholorship for collage.
5. Will I be a vetranrian?
6. Will I get horses?
7. How long will I live with my parents?
8. How many kids will I have?
9. What would it be like without friends?
10. What would it be like without parents?

FIG 7.8 Alexis' Fierce Wonderings

Recommended Children's and Young Adult Literature

Adler, David. 1992. *A Picture Book of Harriet Tubman*. Illus. Samuel Byrd. New York: Holiday House.

Aldrin, Buzz. 2005. *Reaching for the Moon*. Illus. Wendell Minor. New York: HarperCollins.

Anderson, Laurie Halse. 1999. *Speak*. New York: Farrar, Straus and Giroux.

———. 2000. *Fever 1793*. New York: Simon and Schuster.

———. 2002. *Thank You, Sarah: The Woman Who Saved Thanksgiving*. Illus. Matt Faulkner. New York: Simon and Schuster.

Armstrong, Jennifer. 2000. *Shipwreck at the Bottom of the World: The Extraordinary True Story of Shackleton and the* Endurance. New York: Crown.

Avi. 1990. *The True Confessions of Charlotte Doyle*. New York: Scholastic.

———. 1999. *Poppy*. Illus. Brian Floca. New York: HarperCollins.

———. 2002. *Crispin: The Cross of Lead*. New York: Hyperion.

———. 2004. *The End of the Beginning: Being the Adventures of a Small Snail (and an Even Smaller Ant)*. San Diego: Harcourt.

———. 2006. *Crispin: At the Edge of the World*. New York: Hyperion.

Barry, Dave, and Ridley Pearson. 2006. *Peter and the Starcatchers*. New York: Disney.

Bauer, Marion Dane. 2007. *A Mama for Owen*. Illus. by John Butler. New York: Simon and Schuster.

Baylor, Byrd. 1974. *Everybody Needs a Rock*. Illus. Peter Parnall. New York: Atheneum.

———. 1978. *The Way to Start a Day*. Illus. Peter Parnall. New York: Atheneum.

Berg, Brook. 2003. *What Happened to Marion's Books?* Illus. Nathan Alberg. Fort Atkinson, WI: Highsmith/UpstartBooks.

Birney, Betty G. 2005. *The Seven Wonders of Sassafras Springs*. Illus. Matt Phelan. New York: Atheneum.

Bjork, Cristina. 1987. *Linnea in Monet's Garden*. Illus. Lena Anderson. New York: R and S.

Brown, Margaret Wise. 1949. *The Important Book*. Illus. Leonard Weisgard. New York: Harper and Brothers.

Bryant, Jen. 2004. *The Trial*. New York: Knopf.

Caputo, Philip. 2005. *10,000 Days of Thunder: A History of the Vietnam War*. New York: Atheneum.

Carle, Eric. 1993. *Today Is Monday*. New York: Philomel.

Carlson, Nancy. 1993. *How to Lose All Your Friends*. New York: Viking.

———. 1994. *Life Is Fun*. New York: Viking.

Catalanotto, Peter. 1989. *Dylan's Day Out*. New York: Orchard.

———. 1990. *Mr. Mumble*. New York: Orchard.

———. 2002. *Matthew A.B.C.* New York: Atheneum.

Christian, Peggy. 2000. *If You Find a Rock*. Photo. Barbara Hirsch Lember. San Diego: Harcourt.

Cisneros, Sandra. 1994. *The House on Mango Street*. New York: Knopf.

Cleary, Beverly. 1968. *Ramona the Pest*. Illus. Louis Darling. New York: Morrow.

———. 1988. *A Girl from Yamhill: A Memoir*. New York: Harper.

Clements, Andrew. 2002. *The Jacket*. New York: Simon and Schuster.

Cole, Joanna. 1990. *The Magic School Bus: Lost in the Solar System*. Illus. Bruce Degen. New York: Scholastic.

———. 2006. *The Magic School Bus and the Science Fair Expedition*. Illus. Bruce Degen. New York: Scholastic.

Coles, Robert. 1995. *The Story of Ruby Bridges*. Illus. George Ford. New York: Scholastic.

Colfer, Eoin. 2001. *Artemis Fowl*. New York: Miramax.

Collier, Bryan. 2000. *Uptown*. New York: Holt.

Collier, James Lincoln, and Christopher Collier. 1974. *My Brother Sam Is Dead*. New York: Simon and Schuster.

Conrad, Pam. 1991. *Pedro's Journal: A Voyage with Christopher Columbus August 3, 1492–February 14, 1493*. Illus. Peter Koeppen. Honesdale, PA: Boyds Mills.

Cooney, Nancy Evans. 1984. *The Blanket That Had to Go*. New York: Putnam.

Creech, Sharon. 1994. *Walk Two Moons*. New York: Joanna Cotter/ HarperCollins.

———. 1995. *Absolutely Normal Chaos*. New York: Joanna Cotter/ HarperCollins.

———. 2001a. *A Fine, Fine School*. Illus. Harry Bliss. New York: Joanna Cotler/HarperCollins.

———. 2001b. *Love That Dog*. New York: Joanna Cotler/HarperCollins.

———. 2002. *Ruby Holler*. New York: Joanna Cotler/HarperCollins.

Cronin, Doreen. 2000. *Click, Clack, Moo: Cows That Type*. Illus. Betsy Lewin. New York: Simon and Schuster.

———. 2003. *Diary of a Worm*. Illus. Harry Bliss. New York: Joanna Cotler/ HarperCollins.

———. 2005. *Diary of a Spider*. Illus. Harry Bliss. New York: Joanna Cotler/ HarperCollins.

———. 2006. *Dooby Dooby Moo*. Illus. Betsy Lewin. New York: Atheneum.

———. 2007. *Diary of a Fly*. Illus. Harry Bliss. New York: Joanna Cotler/ HarperCollins.

Curtis, Christopher Paul. 1999. *Bud, Not Buddy*. New York: Delacorte.

Cushman, Karen. 1994. *Catherine,Called Birdy*. New York: Clarion.

———. 1995. *The Midwife's Apprentice*. New York: Clarion.

Dahl, Roald. 1982. *The BFG*. Illus. Quentin Blake. New York: Farrar, Straus and Giroux.

———. 1983. *The Witches*. Illus. Quentin Blake. New York: Farrar, Straus and Giroux.

———. 1984. *Boy: Tales of Childhood*. New York: Farrar, Straus and Giroux.

———. 1988. *Matilda*. Illus. Quentin Blake. New York: Viking.

———. 1996. *James and the Giant Peach*. Illus. Quentin Blake. New York: Knopf.

———. 2002a. *George's Marvelous Medicine*. New York: Knopf.

———. 2002b. *The Twits*. Illus. Quentin Blake. New York: Knopf.

Davis, Katherine Gibbs. 2004. *Wackiest White House Pets*. Illus. David A. Johnson. New York: Scholastic.

Deedy, Carmen Agra. 1994. *The Library Dragon*. Illus. Michael P. White. Atlanta: Peachtree.

DiCamillo, Kate. 2000. *Because of Winn-Dixie*. Cambridge, MA: Candlewick.

———. 2003. *The Tale of Despereaux: Being the Story of a Mouse, a Princess, Some Soup, and a Spool of Thread*. Illus. Timothy B. Ering. Cambridge, MA: Candlewick.

Dotlich, Rebecca Kai. 2001. *When Riddles Come Rumbling: Poems to Ponder*. Illus. Karen Dugan. Honesdale, PA: Wordsmith/Boyds Mills.

Drake, Ernest. 2003. *Dragonology: The Complete Book of Dragons*. Illus. Dugald Steer. Cambridge, MA: Candlewick.

Draper, Judith. 2005. *My First Horse and Pony Book*. Photo. Matthew Roberts. Boston: Kingfisher/Houghton Mifflin.

Duvoisin, Roger. 1950. *Petunia*. New York: Knopf.

Ehlert, Lois. 1988. *Planting a Rainbow*. San Diego: Harcourt.

———. 2004. *Pie in the Sky*. San Diego: Harcourt.

———. 2005. *Leaf Man*. San Diego: Harcourt.

Ellis, Deborah. 2001. *The Breadwinner*. Toronto, ON: Groundwood.

Eric Carle: Picture Writer. 1993. Videocassette. New York: Philomel.

Elephants in the Bathtub and Other Silly Riddles. 2006. New York: Cartwheel/Scholastic.

Ewalt, Wendy. 2002. *The Best Part of Me: Children Talk About Their Bodies in Pictures and Words*. Boston: Little, Brown.

Ewing, Lynne. 1998. *Party Girl*. New York: Knopf.

Finchler, Judy. 2006. *Miss Malarkey Leaves No Reader Behind*. Illus. Kevin O'Malley. New York: Walker.

Fitzgerald, F. Scott. 1996. *The Great Gatsby*. Reprint. New York: Scribner.

Flake, Sharon. 2000. *The Skin I'm In*. New York: Jump at the Sun/Hyperion.

Fleischman, Paul. 1988. *Joyful Noise: Poems for Two Voices*. Illus. Eric Beddows. New York: Harper and Row.

Fleming, Denise. 1992. *Lunch*. New York: Holt.

———. 1993. *In the Small, Small Pond*. New York: Holt.

———. 1994. *Barnyard Banter*. New York: Holt.

———. 1996. *Where Once There Was a Wood*. New York: Holt.

———. 2003. *Buster*. New York: Holt.

Fletcher, Ralph. 1997. *Ordinary Things: Poems from a Walk in Early Spring*. Illus. Walter Lyon Krudop. New York: Atheneum.

———. 2002. *Poetry Matters: Writing a Poem from the Inside Out*. New York: Avon.

———. 2003. *A Writer's Notebook: Unlocking the Writer Within You*. New York: HarperTrophy.

———. 2005. *A Writing Kind of Day: Poems for Young Poets*. Illus. April Ward. Honesdale, PA: Boyds Mills.

Florian, Douglas. 2003. *Autumnblings*. New York: Greenwillow.

———. 2006. *Handsprings*. New York: Greenwillow.

Fox, Mem. 1985. *Wilfrid Gordon McDonald Partridge*. Illus. Julie Vivas. New York: Kane/Miller.

———. 2005. *Hunwick's Egg*. Illus. Pamela Lofts. San Diego: Harcourt.

Frank, Anne. 1947/1993. *Anne Frank: The Diary of a Young Girl*. New York: Bantam.

Freedman, Russell. 2006. *The Adventures of Marco Polo*. Illus. Bagram Ibatoulline. New York: Arthur A. Levine/Scholastic.

Funke, Cornelia. 2003. *Inkheart*. New York: Chicken House/Scholastic.

———. 2005. *Pirate Girl*. Illus. Kerstin Meyer. New York: Chicken House/Scholastic.

George, Jean Craighead. 1988. *My Side of the Mountain*. Reissue. New York: Dutton.

George, Kristine O'Connell. 2004. *Hummingbird Nest: A Journal in Poems*. Illus. Barry Moser. San Diego: Harcourt.

Gerstein, Mordicai. 2003. *The Man Who Walked Between the Towers*. New Milford, CT: Roaring Brook.

Giff, Patricia Reilly. 2002. *Pictures of Hollis Woods*. New York: Wendy Lamb/Random House.

Greenfield, Eloise. 1978. *Honey, I Love and Other Love Poems*. Illus. Leo Dillon and Diane Dillon. New York: HarperCollins.

Guarino, Deborah. 1989. *Is Your Mama a Llama?* Illus. Steven Kellogg. New York: Scholastic.

Hampton, Wilborn. 1997. *Kennedy Assassinated! The World Mourns: A Reporter's Story*. Cambridge, MA: Candlewick.

Hatkoff, Craig. 2006. *Owen and Mzee: The Story of a Remarkable Friendship*. Illus. Peter Geste. New York: Scholastic.

Hatkoff, Isabella, Craig Hatkoff, and Paula Kahumba. 2007. *Owen and Mzee: The Language of Friendship*. New York: Scholastic.

Hazen, Barbara Shook. 1979. *Tight Times*. Illus. Trina Schart Hyman. New York: Viking.

Henkes, Kevin. 1990. *Julius, Baby of the World*. New York: Greenwillow.

———. 1991. *Chrysanthemum*. New York: Greenwillow.

———. 1993. *Owen*. New York: Greenwillow.

———. 2000. *Wemberly Worried*. New York: Greenwillow.

Hesse, Karen. 1992. *Letters from Rifka*. New York: Holt.

———. 1994. *Phoenix Rising*. New York: Holt.

———. 1995. *A Time of Angels*. New York: Hyperion.

———. 1997. *Out of the Dust*. New York: Scholastic.

———. 1998. *Just Juice*. Illus. Robert Andre Parker. New York: Scholastic.

———. 1999. *Come On, Rain!* Illus. Jon J. Muth. New York: Scholastic.

———. 2001. *Witness*. New York: Scholastic.

Hiaasen, Carl. 2002. *Hoot*. New York: Knopf.

Hoffman, Mary. 1991. *Amazing Grace*. Illus. Carolyn Binch. New York: Dial.

Holt, Kimberly Willis. 1999. *When Zachary Beaver Came to Town*. New York: Holt.

Hopkins, Lee Bennett, ed. 1990. *Good Books, Good Times.* Illus. Harvey Stevenson. New York: Harper.

Hopkinson, Deborah. 1999. *Maria's Comet.* Illus. Deborah Lanino. New York: Anne Schwartz/Atheneum.

Hunter, Erin. 2004. *Warriors: Fire and Ice.* New York: Avon.

Janeczko, Paul B. 1990. *The Place My Words Are Looking For.* New York: Bradbury/Macmillan.

———. 2002. *Seeing the Blue Between: Advice and Inspiration for Young Poets.* Cambridge, MA: Candlewick.

Jenkins, Steve. 2005. *Prehistoric Actual Size.* Boston: Houghton Mifflin.

Jimenez, Francisco. 1999. *The Circuit: Stories from the Life of a Migrant Child.* Boston: Houghton Mifflin.

Johnson, Angela. 1993. *Toning the Sweep.* New York: Orchard.

Johnston, Tony. 1994. *Amber on the Mountain.* Illus. Robert Duncan. New York: Dial.

Joyce, Susan. 2001. *ABC School Riddles.* Illus. Freddie Levin. Columbus, NC: Peel Productions.

Kerley, Barbara. 2001. *The Dinosaurs of Waterhouse Hawkins.* Illus. Brian Selznick. New York: Scholastic.

Klise, Kate. 2007. *Imagine Harry.* Illus. M. Sarah Klise. San Diego: Harcourt.

Korman, Gordon. 2002. *No More Dead Dogs.* New York: Hyperion.

Kramer, Sydelle. 2004. *Who Was Ferdinand Magellan?* Illus. Elizabeth Wolf. New York: Grosset and Dunlap.

Kurtz, Jane. 2001. *I'm Sorry, Almira Ann.* Illus. Susan Havice. New York: Scholastic.

LaMarche, Jim. 2000. *The Raft.* New York: HarperCollins.

Larson, Kirby. 2006. *Hattie Big Sky.* New York: Delacorte.

Lasky, Kathryn. 1983. *Beyond the Divide.* New York: Simon and Schuster.

Lehman, Barbara. 2004. *The Red Book.* Boston: Houghton Mifflin.

Lewis, J. Patrick. 2001. *A Burst of Firsts: Doers, Shakers, and Record Breakers.* Illus. Brian Adjar. New York: Dial.

————. 2005. *Please Bury Me in the Library*. Illus. Kyle M. Stone. San Diego: Gulliver/Harcourt.

Little, Jean. 1986. *Hey World, Here I Am!* Illus. Sue Truesdell. New York: HarperCollins.

Long, Melina. 2003. *How I Became a Pirate*. Illus. David Shannon. San Diego: Harcourt.

Lowry, Lois. 1989. *Number the Stars*. Boston: Houghton Mifflin.

————. 1993. *The Giver*. Boston: Houghton Mifflin.

————. 2006. *Gossamer*. Boston: Houghton Mifflin.

Lyon, George Ella. 1999. *Book*. Illus. Peter Catalanotto. New York: DK Children.

MacLachlan, Patricia. 1994. *All the Places to Love*. Illus. Mike Wimmer. New York: Joanna Cotler/HarperCollins.

Maestro, Betsy. 1994. *Why Do Leaves Change Color?* Let's Read-and-Find-Out Science, Stage 2. Illus. Loretta Krupinski. New York: HarperCollins.

Martin, Ann. 2002. *A Corner of the Universe*. New York: Scholastic.

Martin, Bill Jr. 1992. *Brown Bear, Brown Bear, What Do You See?* Illus. Eric Carle. New York: Holt.

————. 1999. *A Beasty Story*. Illus. Steven Kellogg. San Diego: Silver Whistle/Harcourt.

Matthews, John. 2006. *Pirates*. New York: Atheneum.

McCarty, Peter. 2006. *Moon Plane*. New York: Holt.

McCaughrean, Geraldine. 2006. *Peter Pan in Scarlet*. New York: Margaret K. McElderry.

Meddaugh, Susan. 1992. *Martha Speaks*. Boston: Walter Lorraine/Houghton Mifflin.

Minor, Wendell. 2006. *Yankee Doodle America: The Spirit of 1776 from A to Z*. New York: Putnam.

Mochizuki, Ken. 1993. *Baseball Saved Us*. Illus. Dom Lee. New York: Lee and Low.

Mora, Pat. 2006. *¡Marimba!: Animales from A to Z*. Illus. Doug Cushman. New York: Clarion.

Morgenstern, Susie. 2001. *A Book of Coupons*. Illus. Serge Block. New York: Viking.

Morrison, Lillian. 2006. *Guess Again: Riddle Poems*. Atlanta: August House.

Moss, Marissa. 2001. *Rose's Journal: The Story of a Girl in the Great Depression*. San Diego: Silver Whistle/Harcourt.

Munson, Derek. 2000. *Enemy Pie*. Illus. Tara Calahan King. San Francisco: Chronicle.

Myers, Walter Dean. 1992. *Somewhere in the Darkness*. New York: Scholastic.

Napoli, Donna Jo. 2001. *Albert*. Illus. Jim LaMarche. San Diego: Silver Whistle/ Harcourt.

Naylor, Phyllis Reynolds. 1997. *Saving Shiloh*. New York: Atheneum.

Neubecker, Robert. 2007. *Wow! School!* New York: Hyperion.

Nichols, Catherine. 2002. *Harriet Tubman*. New York: Scholastic.

Nolen, Jerdine. 2002. *Plantzilla*. Illus. David Catrow. San Diego: Silver Whistle/ Harcourt.

Numeroff, Laura. 2004. *Beatrice Doesn't Want To*. Illus. Lynn Munsinger. Cambridge, MA: Candlewick.

O'Brien, Robert C. 1971. *Mrs. Frisby and the Rats of NIMH*. Illus. Zena Bernstein. New York: Atheneum.

O'Neill, Alexis. 2002. *The Recess Queen*. Illus. Laura Huliska-Beith. New York: Scholastic.

Osborne, Mary Pope. 1998. *Vacation Under the Volcano*. Magic Tree House 13. Illus. Sal Murdocca. New York: Random House.

———. 2006. *Blizzard of the Blue Moon*. Magic Tree House 36. Illus. Sal Murdocca. New York: Random House.

Osborne, Mary Pope, and Natalie Pope Boyce. 2006. *Magic Tree House Research Guide: Ancient Rome and Pompeii*. New York: Random House.

Pak, Soyung. 1999. *Dear Juno*. Illus. Susan Kathleen Hartung. New York: Viking.

Park, Barbara. 1995. *Mick Harte Was Here*. New York: Knopf.

Park, Linda Sue. 2002. *When My Name Was Keoko*. New York: Clarion.

Parker, Steve. 1993. *Rocks and Minerals*. Eyewitness Explorers. New York: DK Children.

Parr, Todd. 2004. *The Peace Book*. Boston: Little, Brown.

Paterson, Katherine. 1977. *Bridge to Terabithia*. New York: HarperCollins.

Paulsen, Gary. 1993a. *Harris and Me: A Summer Remembered*. San Diego: Harcourt.

———. 1993b. *Nightjohn*. New York: Delacorte.

Peters, Lisa Westberg. 2003. *Earthshake: Poems from the Ground Up*. Illus. Cathie Felstead. New York: Greenwillow.

Peterson, Jeanne Whitehouse. 1977. *I Have a Sister, My Sister Is Deaf*. Illus. Deborah Kogan Ray. New York: Harper and Row.

Piper, Watty. [1930] 1978. *The Little Engine That Could*. Illus. George and Doris Hauman. New York: Grosset and Dunlap.

Polacco, Patricia. 1992. *Mrs. Katz and Tush*. New York: Dell.

———. 1994a. *Firetalking*. Photo. Lawrence Migdale. Katonah, NY: Richard C. Owen.

———. 1994b. *My Rotten Redheaded Older Brother*. New York: Simon and Schuster.

———. 1994c. *Pink and Say*. New York: Philomel.

———. 1995. *My Ol' Man*. New York: Philomel.

———. 1998. *Thank You, Mr. Falker*. New York: Philomel.

———. 2001. *Mr. Lincoln's Way*. New York: Philomel.

———. 2004. *An Orange for Frankie*. New York: Philomel.

Prap, Lila. 2005. *Why?* LaJolla, CA: Kane/Miller.

Prelutsky, Jack. 1996. *A Pizza the Size of the Sun*. Illus. James Stevenson. New York: Greenwillow.

———. 2002. *Scranimals*. Illus. Peter Sís. New York: Greenwillow.

———. 2005. *Read a Rhyme, Write a Rhyme*. Illus. Meilo So. New York: Knopf.

Rappaport, Doreen. 2001. *Martin's Big Words*. Illus. Bryan Collier. New York: Hyperion.

———. 2004. *John's Secret Dreams*. Illus. Bryan Collier. New York: Hyperion.

Rathmann, Peggy. 1994. *Good Night, Gorilla*. New York: Putnam.

———. 1995. *Officer Buckle and Gloria*. New York: Putnam.

Reiss, Johanna. 1972. *The Upstairs Room*. New York: HarperCollins.

Rinaldi, Ann. 1992. *A Break with Charity: A Story About the Salem Witch Trials*. San Diego: Gulliver/Harcourt.

Ringgold, Faith. 1992. *Aunt Harriet's Underground Railroad in the Sky*. New York: Crown.

Rockwell, Thomas L. 1973. *How to Eat Fried Worms*. New York: Franklin Watts.

Rohmann, Eric. 2005. *Clara and Asha*. New Milford, CT: Roaring Brook.

Rosenthal, Amy Krouse. 2006. *Cookies: Bite-Size Life Lessons*. Illus. Jane Dyer. New York: HarperCollins.

Rotner, Shelley. 2001. *Parts*. New York: Walker.

———. 2003. *Lots of Feelings*.Brookfield, CT: Millbrook.

Rowling, J. K. 2007. *Harry Potter and the Deathly Hallows*. New York: Arthur A. Levine/Scholastic.

Ryan, Pam Muñoz. 1989. *Riding Freedom*. Illus. Brian Selznick. New York: Scholastic.

———. 1999. *Amelia and Eleanor Go for a Ride*. Illus. Brian Selznick. New York: Scholastic.

———. 2000. *Esperanza Rising*. New York: Scholastic.

———. 2002. *When Marian Sang*. Illus. Brian Selznick. New York: Scholastic.

———. 2004. *Becoming Naomi Leon*. New York: Scholastic.

Rylant, Cynthia. 1985. *The Relatives Came*. Illus. Stephen Gammell. New York: Atheneum.

———. 1991. *An Angel for Solomon Singer*. Illus. Peter Catalanotto. New York: Orchard.

———. 2002. *The Heavenly Village*. New York: Scholastic.

Sabuda, Robert, and Matthew Reinhart. 2005. *Encyclopedia Prehistorica Dinosaurs: The Definitive Pop-Up*. Cambridge, MA: Candlewick.

Schachner, Judy. 2003. *Skippyjon Jones*. New York. Dutton.

———. 2005. *Skippyjon Jones in the Doghouse*. New York: Dutton.

Schaefer, Carole Lexa. 2007. *Dragon Dancing*. Illus. Pierr Morgan. New York: Viking.

Schroeder, Alan. 1996. *Minty: A Story of Young Harriet Tubman*. Illus. Jerry Pinkney. New York: Dial.

Scieszka, Jon. 1991. *The Time Warp Trio: Knights of the Kitchen Table*. Illus. Lane Smith. New York: Viking.

Selznick, Brian. 2007. *The Invention of Hugo Cabret*. New York: Scholastic.

Sendak, Maurice. 1963. *Where the Wild Things Are*. New York: Harper and Row.

Sender, Ruth Minsky. 1986. *The Cage*. New York: Simon and Schuster.

Shannon, David. 1998a. *A Bad Case of Stripes*. New York: Blue Sky/Scholastic.

———. 1998b. *No, David!* New York: Blue Sky/Scholastic.

Sidman, Joyce. 2006. *Butterfly Eyes and Other Secrets of the Meadow*. Illus. Beth Krommes. Boston: Houghton Mifflin.

Sierra, Judy. 2004. *Wild About Books*. Illus. Marc Brown. New York: Knopf.

Sís, Peter. 1991. *Follow the Dream: The Story of Christopher Columbus*. New York: Knopf.

———. 1996. *Starry Messenger*. New York: Frances Foster/Farrar, Straus and Giroux.

Smith, Robert Kimmell. 1984. *The War with Grandpa*. New York: Delacorte.

Smith, Roland. 1999. *The Captain's Dog: My Journey with the Lewis and Clark Tribe*. San Diego: Gulliver/Harcourt.

Spinelli, Jerry. 1990. *Maniac Magee*. Boston: Little, Brown.

———. 1996. *Crash*. New York: Knopf.

St. George, Judith. 2000. *So You Want to Be President?* Illus. David Small. New York: Philomel.

Staples, Suzanne Fisher. 1989. *Shabanu: Daughter of the Wind*. New York: Knopf.

Stewart, Sarah. 1995. *The Library*. Illus. David Small. New York: Farrar, Straus and Giroux.

Stine, R. L. 1992. *Monster Blood*. Goosebumps series. New York: Scholastic.

Takabayashi, Mari. 2004. *I Live in Tokyo*. Boston: Houghton Mifflin.

Taylor, Theodore. 1987. *The Cay*. New York: Delacorte.

Teague, Mark. 2004. *Detective LaRue: Letters from the Investigation*. New York: Scholastic.

Thimmesh, Catherine. 2000. *Girls Think of Everything: Stories of Ingenious Inventions by Women*. Illus. Melissa Sweet. Boston: Houghton Mifflin.

Turner, Ann. 1987. *Nettie's Trip South*. Illus. Ronald Himler. New York: Simon and Schuster.

———. 1997. *Mississippi Mud: Three Prairie Journals*. Illus. Robert J. Blake. New York: HarperCollins.

Turner, Glennette Tilley. 2006. *An Apple for Harriet Tubman*. Illus. Susan Keeter. Morton Grove, IL: Albert Whitman.

Vail, Rachel. 2002. *Sometimes I'm Bombaloo*. Illus. Yumi Heo. New York: Scholastic.

Van Laan, Nancy. 1990. *Possum Come A-Knockin'*. New York: Knopf.

van Straaten, Harmen. 2007. *Duck's Tale*. New York: North-South.

Vaugelade, Anais. 2001. *The War*. Minneapolis: Carolrhoda.

Viorst, Judith. 1973. *Alexander and the Terrible, Horrible, No Good, Very Bad Day*. Illus. Ray Cruz. New York: Atheneum.

Walsh, Ellen Stoll. 1994. *Pip's Magic*. San Diego: Harcourt.

Weatherford, Carole Boston. 2006. *Moses: When Harriet Tubman Led Her People to Freedom*. Illus. Kadir Nelson. New York: Jump at the Sun/Hyperion.

Weeks, Sarah. 2004. *So B. It*. New York: Laura Geringer/HarperCollins.

What Pets Teach Us: Life's Lessons Learned from Our Best Friends. 2004. Minocqua, WI: Willow Creek.

White, E. B. 1945. *Stuart Little*. Illus. Garth Williams. New York: HarperCollins.

———. 1952. *Charlotte's Web*. Illus. Garth Williams. New York: Harper and Row.

Wiesner, David. 2001. *The Three Pigs*. New York: Clarion.

———. 2006. *Flotsam*. New York: Clarion.

Wiles, Deborah, 2001. *Love, Ruby Lavender*. San Diego: Gulliver/Harcourt.

———. 2005. *Each Little Bird That Sings*. San Diego: Gulliver/Harcourt.

———. 2007. *The Aurora County All-Stars*. San Diego: Harcourt.

Willems, Mo. 2003. *Don't Let the Pigeon Drive the Bus*. New York: Hyperion.

———. 2006. *Don't Let the Pigeon Stay Up Late!* New York: Hyperion.

Winter, Jeanette. 1998. *My Name Is Georgia*. San Diego: Silver Whistle/Harcourt.

———. 2004. *September Roses*. New York: Farrar Straus and Giroux.

———. 2005. *The Librarian of Basra: A True Story from Iraq*. San Diego: Harcourt.

———. 2006. *Mama: A True Story, in Which a Baby Hippo Loses His Mama During a Tsunami, but Finds a New Home, and a New Mama*. San Diego: Harcourt.

Winter, Jonah. 2002. *Frida*. Illus. Ana Juan. New York: Arthur A. Levine/Scholastic.

Winthrop, Elizabeth. 2006. *Counting on Grace*. New York: Wendy Lamb/Random House.

Wise, William. 2006. *Zany Zoo*. Illus. Lynne Munsinger. Boston: Walter Lorraine/Houghton Mifflin.

Wong, Janet. 2002. *You Have to Write*. Illus. Teresa Flavin. New York: Margaret K. McElderry/Simon and Schuster.

Woodson, Jacqueline. 2005. *Show Way*. Illus. Hudson Talbott. New York: Putnam.

Worth, Valerie. 1994. *All the Small Poems and Fourteen More*. Illus. Natalie Babbitt. New York: Farrar, Straus and Giroux.

Yolen, Jane. 1987. *Owl Moon*. Illus. John Schoenherr. New York: Philomel.

———. 1988. *The Devil's Arithmetic*. New York: Viking.

———. 1992a. *Encounter*. Illus. David Shannon. San Diego: Harcourt.

———. 1992b. *A Letter from Phoenix Farm*. Photo. Jason Stemple. Katonah, NY: Richard C. Owen.

———. 2000. *Color Me a Rhyme: Nature Poems for Young People*. Illus. Jason Stemple. Honesdale, PA: Boyds Mills.

Index